AF522645

Tourism
Promotional Perspectives and Issues

Tourism

Promotional Perspectives and Issues

Edited by
G Radha Krishna

2010

Icfai Books
The Icfai University Press

TOURISM: PROMOTIONAL PERSPECTIVES AND ISSUES

Editor: G Radha Krishna

First Edition: 2010
Printed in India

Published by

The Icfai University Press
52, Nagarjuna Hills, Punjagutta
Hyderabad, India – 500 082
Phone: (+91) (040) 23430–368, 369, 370, 372, 373, 374
Fax: (+91) (040) 23352521, 23435386
E-mail: info@icfaibooks.com, icfaibooks@icfai.org, ssd@icfai.org

ISBN: 9788131408124

Editorial Team: Bala Krishna A V and Madhavi R
Quality Support: M Monorama and Battu Yugandhar

Contents

Overview

The book takes the readers through the promotional landscapes of Indian tourism. This book is divided into three sections: Section I: **Emergence of Indian Tourism – Promotional perspective,** Section II: **Advertising Strategy, Role and Issues** and Section III: **Cases and Applications.**

Section I: Emergence of Indian Tourism – Promotional perspective

The first section provides an overview of the book by emphasizing how Indian tourism acquired prominence over the decades and reached the present position. The role of advertising in promoting Indian tourism and how advertising strategies impacted its growth have been discussed.

The first article titled "**Indian Tourism: Long Way to the Top?**" written by *Bhisham Mansukhani*, provides an overview of Indian Tourism Industry. It discusses hype surrounding India's emergence as a major tourist destination and captures the true picture, when compared to China, its neighbor and upcoming tourist attraction. It captures tourist arrivals in the last few years and compares with other neighboring countries' statistics, mainly with that of China. The article further highlights the shortcomings in such areas as plan layout and infrastructure development. It also provides state wise analysis within the country with respect to new tourist arrivals. The article showcases projections for the coming decade.

The second article titled "**Indian Tourism Industry Over the Decades**" written by *R Arun Shenoy*, discusses how India is suffering from the lack of competitiveness as a major tourist attraction, despite being very rich in variety of tourist spots. The article further highlights Indian Government's lack of proper attention to tourism industry. It emphasizes that insufficient budget allocation to the tourism sector, lack of development of proper infrastructure, rigid administration, lackluster promotions for tourism sector, giving least priority when compared with other sectors and, above all, its incohesive policies and hostile environments were the shortcomings. The article also discusses the potential of the tourism industry in generating employment and its correlation with GDP. The article compares Indian Tourism Industry with other tourism industries especially that of Asian countries.

The third article titled "**Promoting Indian Tourism: An Advertising Perspective**" written by *G Radhakrishna*, gives a background of marketing of Indian tourism. India became a spotlight for world travelers not only because of its rich cultural heritage and possession of diversified tourist spots but also, because of its emergence as an upcoming economy in the world map with software, hospitality and services sector occupying the prime focus. The article discusses some aspects of marketing mix for Indian tourism. Indian tourism marketing is not only depending on just on marketing aspects but also on how tourism would be integrated with other related support sectors, such as transport, hospitality etc. The article further discusses the role of promotional mix and its relative importance in marketing Indian tourism. Finally, the article highlights the role of advertising in promoting Indian tourism with some illustrations.

Section II: Advertising Strategy, Role and Issues

The second section discusses strategies undertaken by different Indian States to attract tourists to their respective states and how different tourism products, such as religious tourism, ecotourism, sports tourism, health tourism have been successfully used to attract tourists. Issues surrounding eco-friendly tourism and the role of information technology in the development of tourism have been captured. How different Government departments, such as Indian Railways and Ministry of Tourism have initiated new ventures to promote tourism have also been captured.

The fourth article titled "**Tourism Marketing in India: Inviting the Domestic Traveler**" written by *Anil Gupta* and *Anupam Ghosh*, highlights the advertising strategies employed by various states to attract domestic as well as international travelers. The article emphasizes that the recent campaign undertaken by India, such as "Incredible India" has projected a positive image in the minds of in-bound international travelers. However, the article emphasizes that India, has yet to explore the true potential of domestic tourism and yet to tap the segments of leisure travelers. The article further discusses the positioning strategies employed by various state governments and highlights their brand building exercises such as celebrity endorsements. It also discusses how films and television media are being used to promote various tourist destinations.

The fifth article titled "**Ecotourism Policy: A Framework for India**" written by *Seema Purushothaman, Jojo T D* and *Sheethal P*, stresses that ecotourism in the Indian context has significant implications for nature, cultural conservation, rural livelihood and conservation education. The article highlights that experiences from within the country and outside the country necessitate an appropriate institutional mechanism to streamline ecotourism policy. Against this backdrop, the authors propose setting up of ecotourism directorates under the ministry of tourism both at the national and state levels. The authors envision that national directorate will be instrumental in providing a clear definition and strategic direction and can engage stakeholder groups in dialogue related to multilateral agreements and local self-governance in the context of ecotourism. Regarding the role of state directorates, the authors view that they can play a more regulatory and facilitating role. The article also briefly discusses the constitution and mandate of these agencies. The article further demonstrates the process of assessment and monitoring of ecotourism ventures and suggests ways of linking them to incentives.

The sixth article titled "**Religious Tourism: An Overview**" written by *V Partha Sarathy* emphasizes that religious tourism has a huge potential in generating revenue. It captures various pilgrimage attractions of India with respect to Hindus, Sikhs, Buddhists, Christians and Jains. Different tourist destinations attract huge crowds on different occasions such as festivals, melas and birthday celebrations. Religious tourism acquires new prominence both nationally and internationally on various occasions. The article on the above perspectives captures various issues related to religious tourism.

The seventh article titled "**Medical Tourism: Positive Publicity is the Need of the Hour**" written by *Saji Salam*, discusses the measures needed to gear up for the challenges likely to be posed in the expected increase of medical tourists' traffic flow to India. The article discusses the shortcomings in the area of healthcare specialists, legal and infrastructure areas. It discusses the brand building exercises needed to alter the perceived image of India amongst the developed countries' patients. It highlights the Government's expected role to make the change of image. It also compares India's competitive position vis-à-vis other countries, such as South American Countries, South Africa, Middle East Countries and other South East Asian Countries.

The eighth article titled "**Sports Tourism Flags Off in India**" written by *Bhavika Jhaveri* explores how sports tourism in India has evolved and delves on its trends, opportunities and challenges. World trends indicate that sports tourism accounts for 32% of the total tourism market. Some travel agents in India are promoting specific sports events such as Formula 1 race. Reputed travel agents such as

Thomas Cook and SOTC are promoting sports events such as FIFA World Cup and 2007 Cricket World Cup as part of their promotional campaigns. The article compares the trends of Indian Sports tourism with those of World Sports Tourism.

The ninth article titled "**Message in Tourism Advertising: An Indian Perspective**," written by *Srividya Raghavan,* focuses on "tourism advertising," and the relevance of "ad message." in this context. The article describes the case of how Oasis, an advertising agency, based in New York, has helped design a campaign for improving Indian Tourism among North Americans. The article by making use of this case as illustration, discusses the process of idea generation, importance of research, message design and format etc.

The tenth article titled "**Nowhere in the Picture**" written by *Reema Sisodiya* discusses the potential role of Indian Cinema in projecting tourist destinations to the outside world. Many National Tourist offices (NTOs) of foreign countries approached Indian Film Makers and offered attractive tourist packages, discounts and concessions to woo them. India, despite being rich in variety of tourist spots, lacks effective promotional policy to woo these filmmakers. The article discusses the existing bottlenecks and bureaucratic hurdles in this regard. The article highlights some exceptional promotional policies offered by some State Governments, such as U.P., Punjab and Haryana. The article also suggests a few steps to attract filmmakers.

The eleventh article titled "**Application of Information Technology in Tourism Advertising Strategies**" written by *Venkatesh Tamlurkar*, is a summary of the white paper titled "White Paper on Advertising Strategy and Information Technology in Tourism" written by Ulrike Gretzel, Yulan Yuan and Daniel R Fesenmaier. This article explores how the application of information technology helps to build up advertising strategies, particularly in the field of tourism, which has been growing exponentially for the past few decades. Information technology plays an important role in the development of tourism for the countries all over the world. Its application in the advertising strategy proved very useful for the Destination Marketing Organizations (DMOs) which achieved the desired results by coordinating it with their organizations' mission/goal. The Worldwide Web was formed as a new advertising medium offering extranets for the suppliers, intranet for the employees, along with a variety of sales and service links for customers. The article further looks at the importance of information technology in advertising strategies related to tourism, the assistance provided by information technology to the destination marketing organizations to promote tourism and the organizational barriers that impact the implementation and use of Web-based advertising and their implications to the organization.

The twelfth article titled "**Advertising: The Wings of Tourism Industry**" written by *T Kalai Selvi*, looks at the growing attractiveness and potential of Indian Tourism Industry and delves into how it is lacking an appropriate advertising strategy to catch up with the rest of the world. It highlights that Indian advertising industry's misplaced focus on selling as against marketing, seasonal as against continuous effort, a few segments as against the full potential and lack of cohesion among tourism and allied services is causing its lagging behind the world trends. The article concludes by highlighting that, within the background of ever rising incomes, changing social status amongst Indians, the advertising industry has become very attractive for MNCs and advertising industry has to gear up for these changes to realize its full potential.

The thirteenth article titled "**On the Right Track: Joyful Travel**" written by *Samita Bhatia*, highlights the efforts of Indian Railways in wooing the visiting tourists by modernizing their efforts. Indian Railways identifying the needs of the tourists to visit ancient historical sites as well as enjoy modern comforts started some special trains such as Palace on Wheels, The Royal Orient, The Fairy Queen and Deccan Odyssey. Apart from Heritage trains, which make a tour to the wealth of historical places, Indian Railways are also using toy trains to show the attractive hilly areas. The article further showcases the travel experiences of a few prominent personalities – Shahnaz Husain, a well-known beautician of India and Shruthi Seth – a VJ.

The fourteenth article titled "**Athithi Devo Bhava – Indian CRM Way**" written by *A V Bala Krishna*, discusses in detail how Ministry of Tourism, Government of India, has picked up "Athithi Devo Bhava," a well-known Sanskrit slogan in its new drive to initiate a nationwide campaign, that aimed at sensitizing key stakeholders towards in-bound foreign tourists through a process of training and orientation. The article highlights the necessity of introducing the concept. It is seen as a complement to the "Incredible India Campaign," undertaken by Ministry of Tourism, Government of India. It is a capacity building program for tourist service providers and all the stakeholders of the Indian tourism industry such as taxi drivers, immigration officials, tourist police, travel agents etc. Athithi Devo Bhava program is a training and induction program for all the stakeholders of tourism industry. The program involves sensitization, screening, induction, training and orientation, certification and feedback. The article looks at the implementat ional issues in different parts of the country. The initiative was proposed to be implemented in two phases. The article also looks at issues related to the Athithi Devo Bhava Program and its future perspectives.

Section III: Cases and Applications

The third section deals with case studies. It touches upon success stories of initiatives undertaken by different State Governments and Governmental institutions.

The fifteenth article titled "**Luxury on Wheels**" written by *Achal Dhruva*, is a case study. It captures the traveling experiences in India's new luxury train, 'Deccan Odyssey'. This initiative taken by Maharashtra State Government is on the lines of the initiative "Palace on Wheels," taken by Rajasthan State Government. Deccan Odyssey, with 21 coaches has a luxurious look both from within and from outside. The train starting from Mumbai, takes the passengers on a weeklong trip through Goa, to Pune to Nashik and finally back to Mumbai. The case study also looks into fare and service patterns aboard the train for the passengers.

The sixteenth article titled "**A Success Story**" written by *R Krishna Kumar*, is a case study. It captures the innovative strategies employed by Kerala State Government in promoting tourism without degrading the environment. Increased private participation coupled with promotion of the tourism to up-market segment as against mass market segment yielded good results. The strategy of developing tourism infrastructure and a simultaneous implementation of promotional strategies simultaneously by hiring the services of Santosh Sivan, a noted film personality achieved it a unique honor from WTTC the 'partner' status. Kerala's natural bounty coupled with promotion of innovative tourism products such as medical tourism, culinary holidays etc., achieved the present status of the most attractive tourist destination of the country. Against this backdrop, the article also highlights the shortfalls in such areas as infrastructure to promote sustainable tourism.

The seventeenth article titled "**Marketing of Buddhist Destinations in Orissa: A Development Perspective for Tourism Services**" written by *Rajnandan Patnaik* is a case study that discusses the strengths of Orissa to market the Buddhist destinations to the in-bound tourists. The recent excavations have pointed out the rich abundance of Orissa in Buddhist 'chaityas' and 'viharas.' This abundance acts as the strength to market Orissa as the Buddhist pilgrimage destination to Buddhist pilgrims. Lalitagiri, Ratnagiri and Udayagiri are three prominent places of Buddhist culture, which could become attractive spots for visiting tourists. Against this backdrop, the article explores the issues related to the development of an integrated marketing strategy to market Orissa as an attractive Buddhist circuit.

The eighteenth article titled "**Medical Tourism: India's Competitive Advantage**" written by *Dakshi Mohanty* and *T Phani Madhav* is a case study that captures the rising potential of India as a destination for medical tourists.

Rising costs of medication in developed countries and long waiting periods and poor medical facilities in underdeveloped countries leads to this scenario. India, even though a developing country economically, has a well-developed private health sector and is equally competitive with developed countries in the technology area as well as in the provision of facilities, which act as a boost to medical tourism in India. Indian government, in collaboration with different state governments, took measures to promote India as a destination for medical tourists. In this background, the case study also discusses the efforts made by Indian Hospital Chains like Apollo Group and Hinduja Group to attract foreign medical tourists to India. The case study further captures the challenges ahead.

The nineteenth article titled "**Health Tourism in Kerala :The Ayurvedic Way**" written by *Priyaa Ravikanth* looks at the potential of Ayurvedic tourism in the Indian State of Kerala. Kerala, for generations is well-known as the land of Ayurveda. Kerala's Unique Selling Proposition (USP) with respect to tourism is Ayurveda, Backwaters and Culture. The article further looks at how Kerala State is promoted as a medical tourist destination.

The twentieth article titled "**Apollo Hospitals: Leading the Way to Healthcare Tourism**" written by *Sarosh Thadamalla, Ruchi Mankad, Amy Sonpal Patel, Seema Agrawal, Anandan Pillai* and *Himani Yadav*, is a case study. It traces the origin and the growth of healthcare tourism in the world and how Asian countries could attract more number of foreign patients than their counterparts in other parts of the world and their potential for future. Even though health tourism in India is a comparatively new concept, it picked up within no time and India became one of the leaders in this line because of its technological and infrastructural strengths in the medicinal field. The case study discusses India's competitive position in health tourism and highlights that unlike its competitors, India lacks coordination among various nodal agencies and allied services. The major players in India in the field of medical tourism and the relative position of Apollo Hospitals Group among them are captured. The successful march of Apollo Hospitals Group since its inception in 1983 in Madras and how the group became an attractive destination for healthcare tourists is captured in detail. Apollo Hospitals Group geared itself to serve healthcare tourists and achieved its present status with a continuous effort. The case study also looks at the experiences shared by a few healthcare tourists who were treated at Apollo Hospitals. The case study concludes by highlighting the future prospects for Apollo Group in the healthcare tourism area.

The twenty-first article titled "**Community Initiatives in Ecotourism: A Case Study from Sikkim, India**" from *Regional Community Forestry Center for Asia and Pacific, RECOFTC* is a case study. The scope of ecotourism in both protecting the rich cultural heritage and improving the living conditions of local community presents a huge scope for marketing Sikkim to promote on the platform of Ecotourism to achieve the twin objectives. Sikkim, blessed with rich natural and cultural resources, possesses huge potential for ecotourism. The Sikkim Biodiversity and Ecotourism Project (SBEP) which is a collaborative effort of different organizations aimed to increase the revenues, contributes to the policies and increases general awareness regarding resource conservation. In this background, the case study captures how the SBEP project is implemented.

The twenty-second article titled "**Lullaby @ Varkala's Awakening**" is a case study that discusses a social awakening project implemented by Kerala Travels Interserve Ltd (KTIL). It was targeted at empowering anganwadis in the area of Varkala block and simultaneously promoting tourism by creating social awareness of the need for ecologically sustainable tourism. The project was a successful initiative and its first phase of implementation yielded good results in the provision of basic facilities to them. The second phase was targeted at promoting environmentally sustainable tourism and involving local communities in the development of tourism, apart from initiating further steps of empowering these anganwadis. The project aimed at benefiting the local community through the provision of revenues of tourism also targeted at developing tourism related activities by bringing together the local communities and the visiting tourists. The bottom-line of the book is to take the readers through a journey with advertising as a binocular to watch the tourism industry market and give them different perspectives regarding promotion of tourism.

Section I

Emergence of Indian Tourism – Promotional Perspective

1

Indian Tourism: Long Way to the Top?

Bhisham Mansukhani

Contrary to popular belief (both within and outside the country), of India being one of the fastest emerging destinations around the world, the ground reality is far different from the overtly hyped bracket designated to us. A study of the available statistics revealed that the Indian inbound segment continues to languish at Number 46 at the expense of its own immense potential. Bhisham Mansukhani explores.

The subject is so beaten, it almost seems politically incorrect to broach Indian inbound segment in a negative vein. Yet, the parallel and consistently growing outbound segment unintentionally shows inbound tourism in poor light. While the problems are visibly apparent to everyone including the wildlife which is becoming as scant a sight as international tourists, India's precise position in comparison to its peers is interesting in as much as it underlines the urgency of expunging these problems. The contemporary issue of infrastructure however has assumed a pre-eminence in the minds of international tourists which is unfortunately lost on India's powers-that-be but not on its competition.

Source: www.expresstravelworld.com © Indian Express Newspapers (Mumbai) Limited. Reprinted with permission.

Driving Economies

Tourism is the world's largest industry, with an annual revenue of almost $500 billion. And it is growing fast, with airline arrivals expected to double by 2010. Leisure is estimated to account for 75 percent of all international travel. Domestic tourism is generally thought to be up to five times that of international arrivals. The WTO puts global revenue from tourism in 2003 at US$ 514.4 billion. Globally, tourism accounts for roughly 35 percent of exports of services. The World Travel and Tourism Council (WTTC) predicts that the ten new accession countries which joined the EU in 2004 will generate up to 54.6 billion US$ of travel and tourism GDP, and create an extra three million jobs.

In 2004, the top 10 tourism destinations accounted jointly for more than 363 million international tourist arrivals or almost half of the 760 million arrivals reported worldwide. According to the preliminary data by WTO, an estimated 460 million international tourist arrivals were recorded worldwide in the first seven months of 2005. This represents an increase of some 25 million arrivals compared with the respective period of 2004, or a 5.9 percent growth. It means that international tourism is not only on track to consolidate the bumper year it had in 2004 (+10.7 percent), but it will also exceed the forecast long-term average growth of 4 percent.

Year 2004 Country Rankings for India within World Countries List

India	2004			2014		
	Absolute Size	Relative Size	Growth1	Absolute Size	Relative Size	Growth2
Personal Travel & Tourism	19	134	28	14	127	7
Business Travel	28	—	9	25	—	5
Government Expenditures	30	166	73	30	166	24
Capital Investment	15	149	32	14	142	6
Visitor Exports	37	118	98	35	141	8
Other Exports	41	108	22	27	90	2
Travel & Tourism Demand	21	—	50	17	—	2
T&T Industry GDP	16	136	98	14	136	10
T&T Economy GDP	19	161	88	16	159	6
T&T Industry Employment	2	103	151	2	114	147
T&T Economy Employment	2	146	143	2	146	135

Where is India?

Top 10 States' Share in Domestic Tourist Visits During 2004	
States	**% share**
UP	24.4
Andhra Pradesh	24.4
Tamil Nadu	11.5
Karnataka	7.4
Rajasthan	4.4
Maharashtra	3.6
West Bengal	3.4
Uttaranchal	3.2
Madhya Pradesh	2.3
Bihar	2.2
Others	13.2
Total	**100**

According to WTTC, India will rank sixth worldwide in terms of real growth of international tourist spend in the forthcoming decade (2006 to 2015) and Indian tourism is expect to grow at an impressive 8.6 percent for the same period. The 'Incredible India campaign' was awarded the 'PATA Gold Award' and India was appointed chairperson of the WTO Task Force to draw up a strategy for rehabilitation of tourism in the tsunami affected areas. Add to this the fact that international tourist arrivals was up by 23.5 percent over 2003.

Now, this would be a good time to abjure any of the celebratory pre-emptions made so far regarding the Indian market because even the most casual analysis puts the optimist on very thin ice. Presently, the over-hyped comparison doing the global rounds is that of India and 'friendly' neighbour China. It is quite surprising to note that in every comparison, which involves emerging destinations, China and India feature glaringly. But on closer inspection, the facts are further than skin deep. China beats India from the onset and the gap only widens. It would just be preposterous to even have a notion of such a comparison when concrete fact stares you in the face. According to the 2005 WTTC tourism report, on account of visitor exports in 2005, which includes expenditures by international visitors on goods and services within the resident economy, India stood at a lowly 46th position generating US$3.7 billion, while China is seventh, generating US$27.3 billion. Perhaps, the futility of rank comes across most evidently in the future forecast wherein, in 2015, China will remain seventh but will generate US$59.8 billion while India will climb up to number 36 and yet generate a relatively average US$10.5 billion.

In 2005, travel and tourism in India is expected to generate US$44.7 billion of economic activity and will be at 22nd, while for China it will generate US$265 billion. In 2015, India will climb the ladder to sixteenth and generate about

US$121.3 billion while China will have an incredible ascent to the number two slot with US$875.1 billion. According to the travel and tourism economy, an indicator of the direct and indirect gross domestic product, China is currently 6th in terms of revenue generation (US$217.8 billion), while India is way down in 20th position generating a mere US$35.2 billion. In 2015, China is expected to climb up to the second position generating US$675.1 billion and India will only trudge up to 14th generating a modestly better US$81.5 billion.

As for personal travel and tourism, which includes all personal spending by an economy's residents on services and goods, India is 19th with US$ 22 billion. Comparatively, China is in 8th position with US$89.8 billion. In 2015, India will only climb up to 13th position with US$56.4 billion, while China will be 3rd with 306.4 billion.

As for government expenditure, China is predictably in the top ten (9), generating US$8.2 billion, while India is number 31 spending under a billion (US$857.4 million). Even Singapore spends more on tourism development (US$1,219.5 million). By 2015, India would have only spent US$1.8 billion while China would have spent US$17.6 billion.

Top 10 Internatonal Markets for India During 2004

Country	No. of Arrivals	% share
USA	520531	15.5
UK	499997	14.8
Sri Lanka	129401	3.8
France	133445	4
Canada	134902	4
Germany	102112	3
Japan	98446	2.9
Malaysia	83963	2.5
Australia	80315	2.4
Italy	66197	2
Others	1518664	45.1
Total	**3367980**	**100**

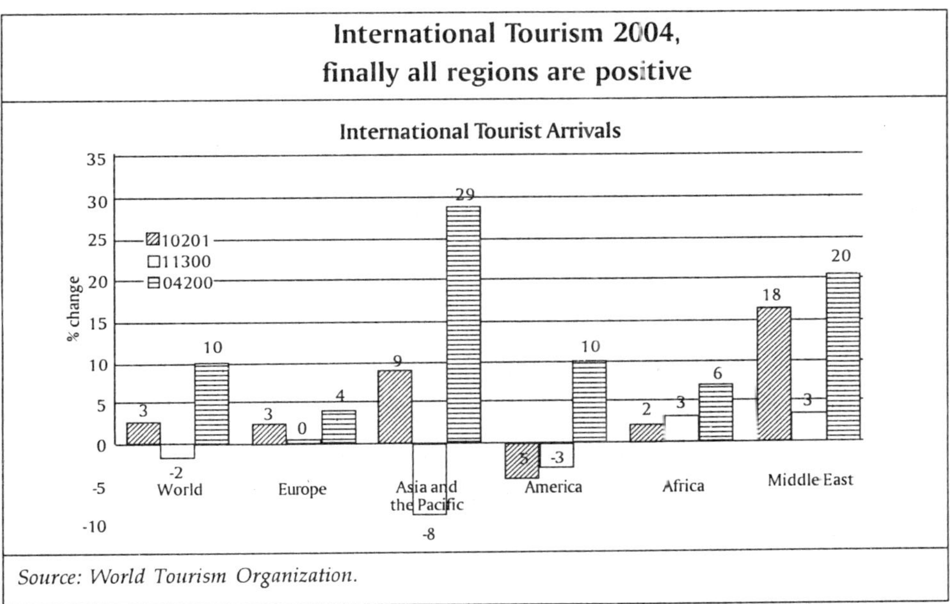

Source: World Tourism Organization.

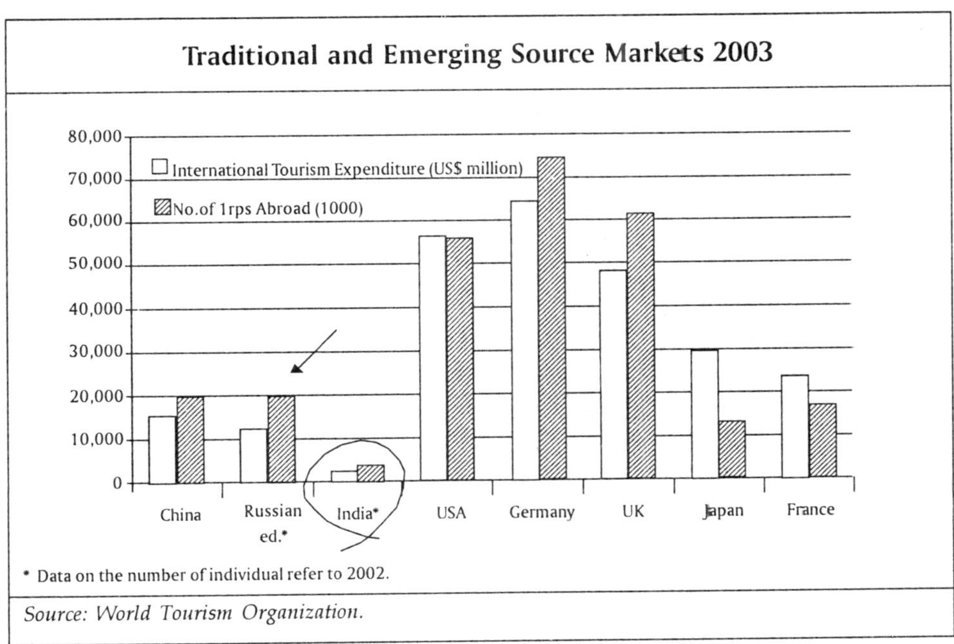

Source: World Tourism Organization.

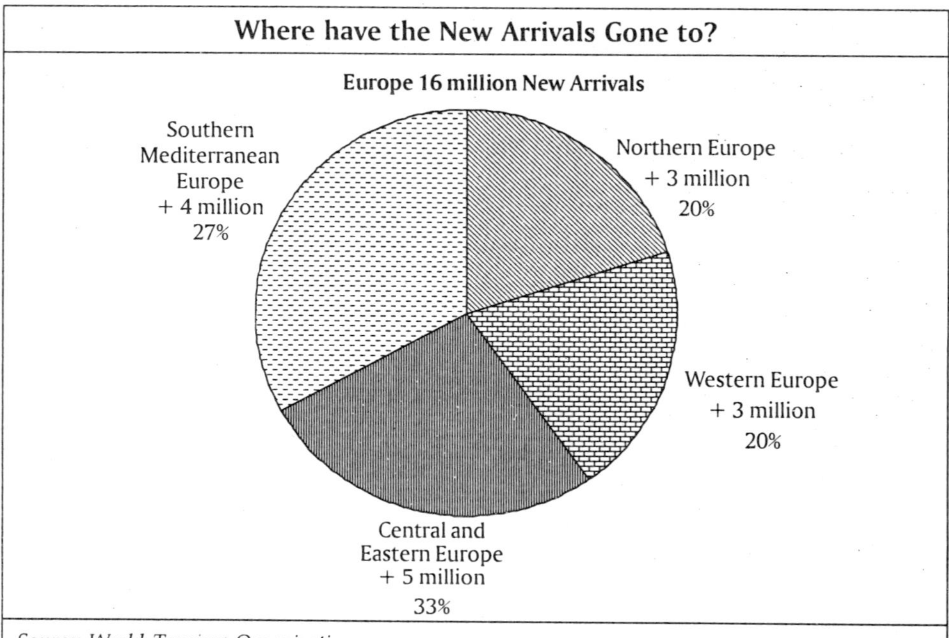

Source: World Tourism Organization.

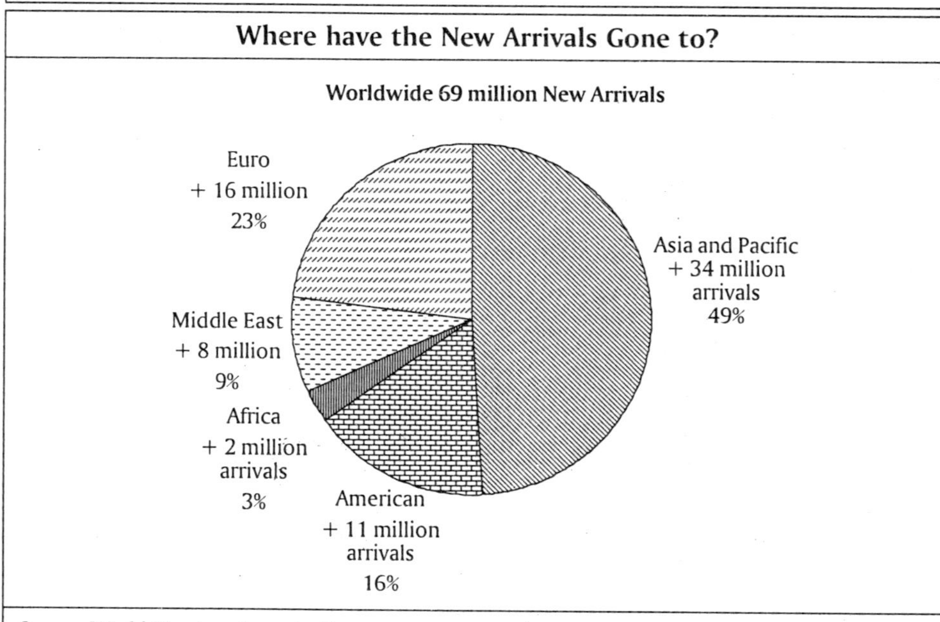

Source: World Tourism Organization.

The Short-Haul Factor

India's inherent habit of ignoring a golden opportunity has not surprised many. So when other countries, and much smaller ones are riding heavily on the short-haul element of travel, India is looking at the finger instead of the moon. Though worldwide, long haul travel is expected to grow faster, at 5.4 percent per year over the period 1995-2020, than intra-regional travel, at 3.8 percent, the difference is huge. The ratio between intra-regional and long-haul travel will shift from around 82:18 in 1995 to close to 76:24 in 2020, which again does not take much from those destinations who focus on short-haul travel. Again, India's old 'competitior' China receives more than 80 percent of its tourists from short-haul markets. By comparison, United Kingdom and the United States alone account for close to 55 percent of its inbound traffic.

Singapore's instance further drives home the point. For example, Singapore received 703,901 visitors in September 2005. Now it is crucial to note that this number largely comprised tourists coming in from short-haul destinations. Indonesia (1,36,000), China (67,000), Australia (61,000), Japan (57,000) and Malaysia (44,000) were Singapore's top five visitor-generating markets in September 2005. These markets accounted for 52 percent of total visitor arrivals for the month. Perhaps this myopic approach is at the root of India's parsimonious share of world tourism (0.44 percent). Looking at the sheer numbers, India definitely needs to take the cue.

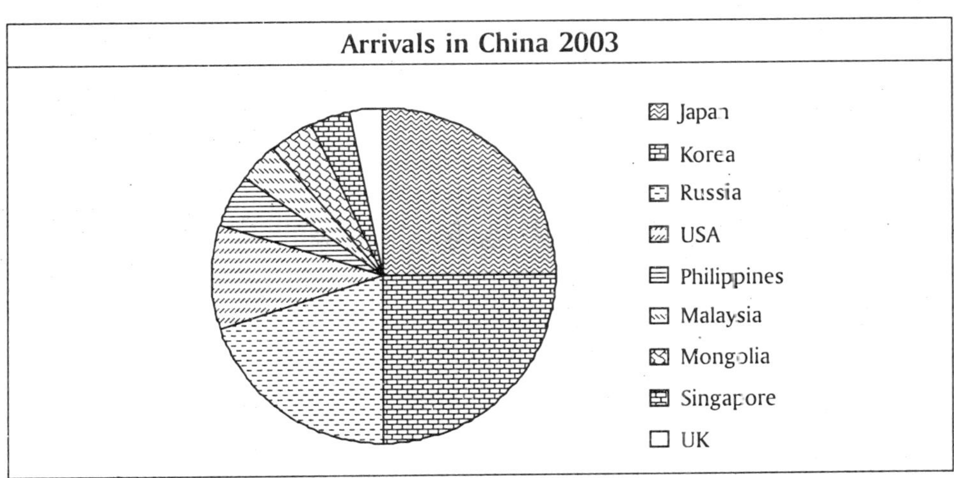

Arrivals in China 2003

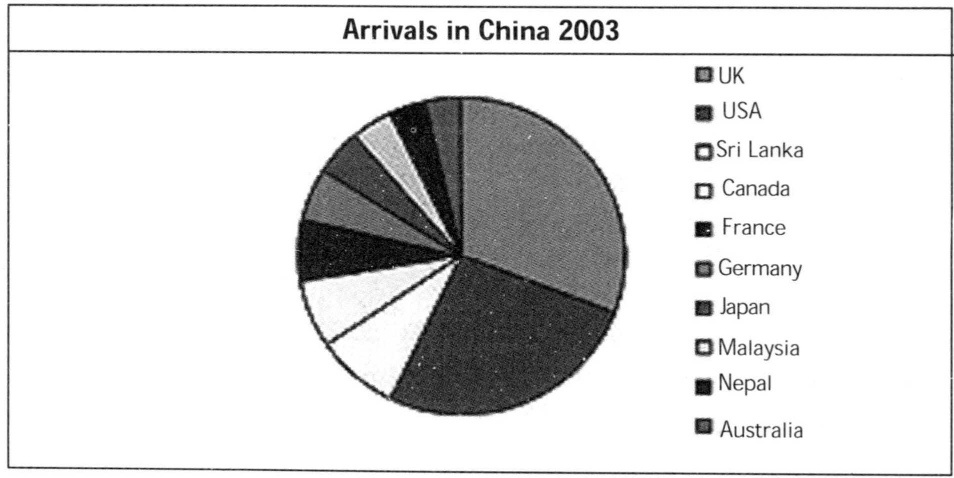

Ground Reality

So where is India, really? Is it actually poised to become as prominent a tourism player as WTTC has kindly forecast it to be or must we again apply context? In truth, India is way below its justified position, considering its size, population and resource. And any criticism, of the dismal state of India's infrastructure and modest spending towards improving it, abysmal room inventories when juxtaposed with those of other South and South East Asian destinations and a local ignorance of tourism's socio-economic significance, hasn't even been delved into herein, not only because it is already too visible but also overstates the gloom.

Foreign Tourist Arrivals in India

Year	Arrival (in million)
2001	2.54
2002	2.38
2003	2.73
2004	3.37
2005	2.97
(Till October)	

The optimism however dwells not just in the forecasts. An attentive 10th five-year plan, which concedes all of these problems and charts out a roadmap for the future, a domestic aviation sector growing by more than 24 percent that is increasing its footprint and making air travel more affordable and a bounty of hotels across premium and mid segments are laying the pitch to sustain the present resurgence in numbers. That in itself is refreshing because the story until recently was always about turning things around before they went awry again.

While the cold statistics continue to embarrass India in the face of its potential, she is finally walking, if not cantering in the right direction as tourist numbers haven't looked south since 2002, touching 3.37 million in 2004. 'Keep walking', the famous kicker for one of India's famous whisky imports is now however outmoded in her case. Time to run, as it's still a long way to the top.

2

Indian Tourism Industry Over the Decades

R Arun Shenoy

This article discusses how despite its huge potential both in generating revenue and employment Indian Tourism Industry could not occupy its designated place in the Indian plans because of policy lapses.

How different other factors such as poor development of infrastructure, over-priced services and impediments in the visa processing also caused the poor performance of Indian tourism industry is also captured. While other tiny Asian countries such as Singapore, Thailand and Malaysia could successfully gain from the new opportunities generated by the World tourism because of their new emphasis on destination marketing, India failed to capture its due share because of its inappropriate policies and negligence of the tourism sector. The article also captures how the Indian Government's new initiatives try to tap the tourism sector's true potential.

"The one land that all men desire to see and having seen once, by even a glimpse would not give the glimpse for all the shows of rest of the globe combined."[1]

– Mark Twain[2] on India.

"A masterful evocation of the country's spiritual heritage combined with sensuous images, creates a kind of Nirvana that can be surpassed only by a journey to India itself."[3]

– Conde Nast Traveler[4].

India, an Asian country with a population of more than a billion[5] (2000) and an area of 32,87,263 sq km[6], is known for its beautiful beaches, deserts, forests, mountains and backwaters. The country is also known for its traditional and spiritual richness. It has a rich culture which is more than 5000 years old.[7] All this makes India a tourism goldmine. However, ever since its independence from Britain in the late 1940s, due to policy lapses and constant governmental indifference, Indian Tourism Industry failed to tap its potential. Comparatively much smaller countries like Singapore, Thailand and Malaysia could outsmart India as global tourist destinations even though India had a competitive edge over them in terms of its sheer capacity to showcase variety. France, a country much smaller than India, topped the top global tourist destination[8] list in 2001 due to its focused government policies. After many years of step-motherly treatment to the tourism industry, by the turn of the 21st century, there had been a noticeable change in the mindset of the government of India that was expected to accelerate the growth engine of the Indian Tourism Industry.

A Brief History

Since it's independence in 1947, Indian policy-makers had traditionally neglected the tourism industry as they considered it to be a luxury segment, benefiting only a few. As Indian economy depended a lot on agriculture, the governmental policies had always aimed to develop agriculture and other allied areas. Tourism was always viewed as an industry serving the elite instead of being accepted as a means to provide employment with highest 'multiplier effect'.[9] In 1955, the first Planning Commission of India[10] had placed tourism industry 269th[11] in its priority list. As a result, in 1950s, the number of international tourists visiting India was just around 15,000.[12] The Indian policy-makers treated tourism as an easy way to correct the foreign exchange shortage. Consequently, hotel rooms, food, beverages, handicrafts and many other items in most of the tourist destinations in India had traditionally been overpriced. So the foreign tourists in

India ended up paying more than the real economic value prevalent in these products and services. Apart from these policy indifferences, whenever the industry showed any signs of revival, certain events such as the National Emergency[13] and introduction of a stringent 'Foreign Exchange Regulation Act',[14] hampered its recovery.

Missed Opportunities

Although in 2000, Global tourism industry represented one of the largest industries in the world with revenue of $595 billion[15] and the number of tourist arrivals globally as high as 698 million,[16] India's share in global tourism remained low (Exhibit 1).

Exhibit 1: Global Vs Indian Tourism for the Year 2000

	World	India	Percentage Share of India
International Arrivals	698 million	2.64 million	0.38%
Tourism Receipts	$ 595 billion	$ 3.2 billion	0.69%
Domestic Tourism Worldwide	6980 million	210 million	4.6%

Source: "Tenth Five-Year Plan (2002-07), Government of India", http://planningcommission.nic.in

The Indian tourism and travel economy[17] contributed 5.3% to its GDP and India's global ranking in this aspect was 140[18] (Exhibit 2). In comparison, tourism sector's contribution to the GDP of New Zealand, Malaysia, and Singapore was 8.9%[19], 7%[20] and 10%[21] respectively. It was estimated that if India could raise the contribution of its tourism and travel economy to 10% of its GDP, it could create 12 million[22] more jobs.

Exhibit 2

	World Average (%) (2000)	India (%) (2000)	World Rank (2000)
Contribution of travel and tourism economy to GDP	10.7	5.3	140
Contribution of travel and tourism industry* to GDP	4.2	2.5	124
Contribution of travel and tourism economy to employment	8	5.6	140
Contribution of travel and tourism industry to employment	3.1	2.9	111

* Contribution of travel and tourism industry refers to only direct impact of tourism industry.

Source: "Tenth Five-Year Plan (2002-07), Government of India", http://planningcommission.nic.in

It was also ›pined that an average investment of Rupees[23] 10 lakh in tourism would create 89 jobs[24] in the tourism industry alone. This investment in tourism would also inlirectly create 12.6[25] jobs in the manufacturing sector and 44.7[26] jobs in the agicultural sector. The same amount of investment in agriculture and manufacturin; sector could create only 45 and 13 jobs respectively.[27]

While th Indian Government constantly neglected Indian tourism, other South East sian countries were busy developing their infrastructure for world class and hig-end tourism experiences. Singapore, for example, concentrated on building a ate-of-the-art airport.[28] While many international tourists were prepared to ay higher for a trip to Singapore because of its top class infrastructure, India had tbe satisfied only with the "backpackers".[29] In 2000, a mere 6.4% of India's GD went as capital investment to the tourism industry against a world average of 1.8%.[30] The budgetary allocation to the tourism industry averaged 0.16% of e total plan outlay from the third to 'Ninth Five Year Plan'.[31] In the tenth plan2002-07), the Indian government allocated 0.72% of the outlay[32] for touris Still, it was very low when compared to countries like Malaysia (5.1%), Nal (5%), Indonesia (8.4%), Maldives (15.7%), and China (3.8%)[33] with the 6bal average at 6.8%.[34] This kind of miniscule spending resulted in deplorabload and airport facilities, poor rail infrastructure, inadequate aviation seating cacity, and insufficient hotel accommodation. Further, the Indian Tourism dustry also lacked basic competitiveness (Exhibit 3) and private investors re not willing to make sufficient investments in the industry due to adverse grnment policies (Exhibit 4).

Exit 3: Factors Affecting India's Competitiveness in Tourism
• Lof concern for competitiveness • (plex Visa Procedures • equate facilitation services • of quality infrastructure • of emphasis on product quality • of training at the 'cutting edge' • of hygiene • utilisation of modern marketing and publicity tools.
Source: th Five-Year Plan (2002-07), Government of India", http://planningcommission.nic.in

Exhibit 4: Governmental Barriers Discouraging Private Investments in Indian Tourism

- Absence of legislative support
- Lack of policy integration and co-ordination
- Lack of long-term investor friendly policies
- Heavy and multiple taxes
- Restrictive aviation and land policies

Source: "Tenth Five-Year Plan (2002-07), Government of India". http://planningcomission.nic.in

Archaic civil aviation policies had long been detrimental to th growth of international tourism in India. Aviation infrastructure in India was ano er concern. When compared with airports in Singapore, Indian airports laggedfar behind. Rajasthan, a North Indian State with great tourist potential did't have an international airport. According to Mr. Ravi Bhoothalingam, head ofie tourism committee at Confederation of Indian Industries, "Our airports areursting at the seams. We not only need more airports, but also better roads. T Cochin[35] airport is a fine example of private enterprise. Privatisation is the onlyiswer and we have to move towards open skies. The Government must accept tt aviation is no longer a luxury—it is the basic need of a growing economy[6] Besides infrastructural problems, passenger carrying capacity was another constnt. India could offer only 5.3 million seats in the international segment agains demand of 10 million seats. In the domestic segment, only 9.79 million dostic seats were available against a demand of 19 million seats.[37] Indian aviationctor was also plagued by the high cost of aviation fuel in India. Premium was irged on the aviation fuel to make up for the subsidy that the government bore fcerosene, which was considered as an essential commodity for the Indian pic. As a result, by the late 1990s, domestic travel became expensive to the Inds than a journey to the neighboring countries and many upwardly mobile Inns were traveling abroad instead of domestic travel. Moreover, lesser tax on toun in the neighbouring countries made tour packages cheaper and more attrac to the Indian tourists. Amitabh Kant, Joint Secretary in the Ministry of Toun, said, "We create similar attractive options within the country, a lot of Indi would chose to explore India. Today, Thailand attracts 9 million tourists anly and of this, 4 million are Indians. Malaysia attracts 10.5 million tourists,which

4.5 million tourists are from India."[38] Singapore attracted 3,75,000 Indian tourists in 2002.[39] All this created a big gap between outbound tourists[40] and inbound tourists.[41] In 2003, the outbound tourist figures were 4.5 million[42] as against the inbound tourist figures of 2.8 million[43] .

To add to the woes of the Indian tourism industry was the country's visa facilitation process. Visa eligibility requirements and procedures in India were stringent and troublesome and created a lot of discomfort for international tourists. The biggest impediment was the "reciprocity" policy of the Indian government under which, visas were permitted only to nationals of those countries, which gave visas to Indian citizens. On the other hand, Bhutan, Nepal, Singapore, Seychelles, Maldives, Thailand, Turkey, Taiwan and Indonesia offered 'visa on arrival' to the international tourists with or without reciprocation. For example, Thailand had 'visa on arrival' policy without "reciprocity" for 140 countries.[44] Indian government cited security reasons to support its reciprocity policy. Mr. Bhoothalingam opined, "We should abolish visa requirements for main source markets such as the USA, European Union and Japan. For other countries it should be 'visa on arrival'. Finally we could have a third list of countries, which could qualify for strict visa requirements."[45] Indian tourism industry also lacked the backing of a developed hospitality business. In spite of the presence of big hotel chains, Indian hotel industry still could not meet the growing demand for rooms. For example, in 2000, 60000 rooms were available against a demand of 130000.[46] The archaic Indian land laws made land acquisition tough, thereby crippling the development of hotel industry in India. India's taxation policy also handicapped the hotel industry with an average expenditure tax of 30%-40% against 4% to 6%[47] in most other Southeast Asian countries while China had no taxes at all. Multiple point taxation was also another problem. Luxury tax was imposed on food items (as a result, food items accounted for one third of a tourist's expenditure) apart from the normal sales tax levied on them.

India also lagged behind other Asian countries in marketing itself as a hot tourist destination through effective 'destination branding'.[48] In 2000, while the "Amazing Thailand" campaign fetched Thailand 10 million tourists, Malaysia attracted 8.5 million and Singapore, 7 million tourists[49] through the "Malaysia Truly Asia" and the "Live it up Singapore" campaigns respectively. Meanwhile,

India's tourist arrivals were stagnated at 2.6 million.[50] Lack of promotional activities was hitting India's image as a tourist destination. According to a survey by the Malaysian Tourism Board, tourists viewed Singapore as "clean, modern and safe". China's main attraction was its culture. Malaysia was regarded to be "multicultural" whereas Thailand had a strong brand identity of "exotic, fun and friendly people".[51] Despite being a country filled with varieties of experience, India failed to showcase its diversity. After being left behind in the 'destination branding' for long, the Government of India in 2002 launched its global "Incredible India" campaign through well-known television channels and also through the print media. 'Ogilvy and Mather', India's leading advertising agency, handled the campaign.

Though the Indian tourism ministry was responsible for tourism in India, it had administrative limitations. Its role was mainly related to marketing its destination and guiding the tourism industry, while other ministries decided upon the core issues, which affected the tourism industry. The Ministry of Civil Aviation handled the aviation policy and airport management, Indian visa was directly under the control of the Ministry of Home Affairs/External Affairs, and the Ministry of Finance decided the budgetary allocations to the tourism industry and the taxation on the tourism sector. The lack of coherence between these ministries reduced the focus of the policies and also complicated the web of bureaucracy, which adversely affected the progress of the tourism industry.

The Growth Binge

After decades of political indifference, the Indian government started focusing on the tourism industry towards the end of 2002. The Tenth Five Year Plan acknowledged the potential of the Indian tourism industry as a huge employment generator and foreign exchange earner for the nation and proposed definite initiatives to give a boost to the tourism industry (Exhibit 5).

Atal Bihari Vajpayee, the former Prime Minister of India (2003), observed, that "Tourism is a major engine of economic growth in most parts of the world. Several countries have transformed their economies using the tourism potential the fullest... Tourism has great capacity to create large scale employment of diverse kind – from the most specialised to the unskilled and all of us know that generation of massive productive employment opportunities is what India need the most."[52]

Exhibit 5: Focus on Tourism in the Tenth Five-Year Plan
• To develop a national consensus on the role of tourism in the development agenda of the nation through the National Development Council. • To enhance the effectiveness of public sector investment through the inter-sectoral convergence and prioritisation of tourism-related infrastructure programmes in other sector like special tourism trains, and aviation links, rural roads etc. • To remove the barriers to growth to leverage private sector investment. • To mobilise the support of primary players. viz., the State Governments in tourism development. • To mobilise public support by creating awareness of the socio-economic benefits of tourism for the host country. • To provide legislative and regulatory support to protect the tourism industry, the consumer and the environment. • To involve the rural sector in tourism and start mobile training units for service providers in rural areas identified for development of tourism. • To augment training facilities in hotel management and food craft and build the capacity of service providers at cutting edge. • To create world-class circuits and destinations.
Source: "Tenth Five-Year Plan (2002-07), Government of India", http://planningcommission.nic.in

Since 2002, the Indian government took lot of initiatives to boost the tourism industry (Exhibit 6&7). The 2003-2004 Union Budget granted the tourism industry the much-needed "Infrastructure-Status". It was believed that the Infrastructure status would enable the Indian tourism industry to avail long-term funds at cheaper rates. The budget allocated Rs.225 crore[53] to the industry and also withdrew the expenditure tax. Further, the union finance ministry advised the various state governments in India to abolish the luxury tax on food and

Exhibit 6: Inter-Sectoral Support to Boost Indian Tourism Industry
• Railways to run tourist trains on nominated sectors with Government/private enterprise. • Competition introduced in telecom service segments, improving communication links. • Work on the 'Golden Quadrilateral' highway project and North-South and East-West corridors in progress. • Delhi, Mumbai, Chennai and Kolkata airports to be modernised. • New airports proposed to be set up in Bangalore, Hyderabad and Goa. • Integrated development of mega cities and small and medium towns underway. • 'Pradhan Mantri Gram Sadak Yojana' (PMGSY) to provide connectivity to rural areas.
Source: "Tenth Five-Year Plan (2002-07), Government of India", http://planningcommission.nic.in

Exhibit 7: Issues Taken up by the Department of Tourism with the Ministry of Finance

- Reduction of expenditure tax.
- Rationalisation of service tax.
- Incentives under the Income Tax Act for the Tourism Industry.
- Reduction of levies on Aviation Turbine Fuel (ATF)
- Waiver of inland air travel tax.
- Rural tourism to get the same benefits agriculture.
- Part refund of excise duty for luxury buses.

Source: "Tenth Five-Year Plan (2002-07), Government of India", http://planningcommission.nic.in

lodging. Apart from tax reforms, the aviation policy was also liberalised. The government started allowing daily flights from Southeast Asian Countries and permitted additional flights from France (Lufthansa), Singapore (Singapore Airlines), and Malaysia (Malaysia Airlines). "The prime minister has taken a bold decision that will lead to better air connectivity and will increase tourist inflows",[54] said Amitabh Kant. To enhance the standards of the international airports in India to global standards, the Indian government, in its tenth plan, proposed the modernisation of the airports at the four-mega cities in India–Delhi, Mumbai, Chennai and Kolkata.

The 'Incredible India' campaign that was launched in December 2002 at a cost of $5 million[55] also paid off. Lavanya Anirudh, an accounts director at Ogilvy and Mather said, "Before (this campaign) India was being promoted differently in different countries, if at all. There weren't two or three distinct images. This campaign changed that."[56] The campaign didn't try to window dress the real picture of India. Amitabh Kant said, "Our aim was to develop India in to a global brand, with world wide brand recognition and strong brand equity. Thus was born the 'Incredible India' branding process, which aimed to create a unique identity for India as a tourist destination and differentiate it from competition. The strategy is to reposition India as a premium destination for upscale tourists with all communication sharply focused to attract the up market clientele, that is, the early adopters who lead the way to the rest of the markets. Markets are deferential and responsive to the views and requirements of upscale tourists, which in turn have a positive impact on the nature of development itself."[57]

By 2003, Indian Tourism had seen few positive changes. Many tourists started visiting many other locations in India, breaking away from the earlier trend of seeing only the golden triangle of Delhi-Agra-Jaipur. SARS[58] didn't adversely affect the Indian tourism. Between January and September 2003, while tourist inflows in countries like, Malaysia, Thailand, and China declined by 28.5%, 12.75% and 23.5% respectively[59] and Singapore saw a decline of 23.45% for the period January-October 2003.[60] India witnessed an increase in its tourist inflows by 15.3%.[61] In turn, India's foreign exchange earnings in 2003 also increased by 20%[62] over the previous year.

Arjun Sharma, owner of the 'Heritage Village Club'[63] in Goa, opined, "India is in the limelight in every sense of the word. Confidence about everything Indian is pretty high. There are Indians at the top of their professions all over Europe and in the United States and the great Indian economic story is becoming known all over the world."[64] 'Annual Readers Travel Awards 2003'[65] of *Conde Nast Traveler* placed India among top ten tourist destinations in the world. One more fact that came out through the magazine's survey was that the readers found India as a better destination[66] when compared to countries like Singapore, Malaysia, and even Greece and Switzerland. While the World Travel and Tourism Council estimated a 4.5%[67] annual increase in global tourism related economic activity between 2002 and 2012, it was estimated that India could be the fastest tourism growth centre after Turkey with an expected annual growth rate of 9.7%[68] over the next ten years.

However, with roads and airports still below global standards, infrastructure remained a big hurdle for the tourism development in India and skepticism ran high regarding the sustenance of the newly found growth in India's tourism industry. Mr Uttam Dave of 'PKF[69]', a travel outlook consultancy, said, "You can throw around millions of dollars but the product has to be consistently up to the scratch. The airports and roads in this country are still pathetic and tourism has to be seen as a matter of national pride. (Tourism Minister) Jagmohan is on the right track, but one can't improve things selectively. We need more and better infrastructure."[70]

(R Arun Shenoy is associated with Icfai Business School Case Development Centre, Hyderabad.)

Endnotes

1 Kant, Amitabh, "The Branding of India", Advertising Express, January 2004.

2 A nineteenth-century American literary personality.

3 op.cit "The Branding of India".

4 *Conde Nast Traveler* is a premier magazine, which focuses on travel, leisure, tourism and adventure. It features breath-taking locations, stunning photography and independent travel articles.

5 "India Facts – General", *www.india-tourism.com*

6 *www.india-tourism.com*

7 *www.meadev.nic.in*

8 *www.infoplease.com*

9 Multiplier Effect refers to the ratio of total change in income (resulting from successive rounds of spending) to an initial autonomous change in expenditure.

10 The planning commission was set up by a resolution of the Government of India in 1950. The Planning Commission was charged with the responsibility of making assessment of all resources of the country, augmenting deficient resources, formulating plans for the most effective and balanced utilisation of resources and determining priorities. The First Five Year Plan was launched in the year 1951.

11 "Tenth Five Year Plan, 2002-07, Chapter 7.5, Tourism, Government of India", *http:planningcommission.nic.in*

12 ibid.

13 The national emergency was declared by Late Mrs. Indira Gandhi on June 26, 1975. In June 1975, the High Court of Allahabad found her guilty of using illegal practices during the previous election campaign, and ordered her to vacate her seat. There were demands for her resignation. In response to these demands, Mrs. Indira Gandhi declared emergency which involved mass political arrests, strict press censorship and freezing of fundamental rights of Indian citizens.

14 A stringent act passed in 1973, which regulated the foreign exchange transactions in India and affected the foreign investment in the country.

15 op.cit "Tenth Five Year Plan, 2002-07, Chapter 7.5, Tourism, Government of India".

16 ibid.

17 Contribution of travel and tourism economy accounts the direct as well as indirect impact of tourism. In other words it considers all indirect benefits arising through tourism's impact on allied sectors.

18 op.cit "Tenth Five Year Plan, 2002-07, Chapter 7.5, Tourism, Government of India".

19 Tourism Satellite Account (1999-1997).

20 "SARS Affects Growth Projections in Asia", April 25th 2003, *The Hindu.*

21 ibid.

22 "Tourism Industry Sets in Buoyant Zone", *www.krchoksey.com*

23 Indian currency.

24 Kakkar, Ashwini, "Section 2: Industry Review, BSE Annual Market Review '03".

25 Bhardwaj, Brij. "Budget should focus on tourism", *www.dayafterindia.com*

26 ibid.

27 op.cit "Section 2: Industry Review, BSE Annual Market Review '03".

28 Changi Airport with a total area of 1,300 hectares was situated in the eastern tip of Singapore. Changi airport was designed to resemble a complete city with all necessary amenities like hotels, gym, flower shops, prayer rooms, science museums etc. It was officially inaugurated on December 29th 1981.

29 Backpackers refer to low-end travelers. Literally they refer to travelers carrying clothes, food, and camping equipment in packs on their backs.

30 Agarwal, Alok, "Tourism in India – another case of missed opportunities?", *www.domain-b.com* September 13th 2000.

31 Third Five Year Plan: 1961-62 to 1965-66, Ninth Five Year Plan: 1997-98 to 2001-02

32 Tenth Five Year Plan, 2002-07, Chapter 7.5, Tourism, Government of India *http:planningcommission.nic.in*

33 ibid.

34 op.cit "Tourism in India – another case of missed opportunities?".

35 Cochin is a city in the tourist state of Kerala in South India.

36 op.cit "Tourism in India – another case of missed opportunities?".

37 ibid.

38 "Lower Airfares Boost Domestic Tourism", *The Economic Times,* January 10th 2004 39 *www.kinexlog.demon.co.uk*

40 Indian tourists traveling outside India.

41 International tourists coming to India.

42 op.cit "Lower Airfares Boost Domestic Tourism".

43 ibid.

44 op.cit "Tourism in India – another case of missed opportunities?".

45 ibid.

46 ibid.

47 Bhardwaj, Brij. "Budget should focus on tourism", *www.dayafterindia.com*

48 Destination branding refers to using marketing and branding tools to position a country as an ideal tourist destination.

49 Kant, Amitabh, "The Branding of India", *Advertising Express*, January 2004.

50 ibid.

51 ibid.

52 Excerpt from Prime Minister's address at Conference of Chief Ministers & States Tourism Ministers on October 30th 2001.

53 Kakkar, Ashwini, Section 2: Industry Review, BSE Annual Market Review '03.

54 Neelakantan, Shailaja, "India Reaps Rich Rewards", *www.feer.com,* January 22nd 2004.

55 op.cit "India Reaps Rich Rewards".

56 ibid.

57 op.cit "The Branding of India".

58 Severe Acute Respiratory Syndrome is a deadly respiratory disease that originated in China in 2003. Its symptoms include fever, cough, breathing disorders. This had a great impact on Asian Economies.

59 op.cit "India Reaps Rich Rewards" 60,61,62 ibid

63 It is a three star comprehensive resort in Goa (an Indian Tourist State).

64 op.cit "India Reaps Rich Rewards".

65 op.cit "The Branding of India".

66 The survey ratings were determined by an 'index of satisfaction with travel facilities and service', maximum score being 100. Readers were asked to rate countries based on various criteria such as culture, food/restaurants, environmental friendliness, scenery, people/hospitality, safety, service and value for money.

67 op.cit "Tenth Five Year Plan, 2002-07, Chapter 7.5, Tourism, Government of India".

68 ibid.

69 PKF is a UK based travel, hotel and leisure consultants who had done extensive assignments in Europe, Middle-East Asia and Africa.

70 op.cit "India Reaps Rich Rewards".

3

Promoting Indian Tourism: An Advertising Perspective

G Radha Krishna

This article focuses the promotional perspective of Indian tourism. It gives the brief introduction growth of tourism development in India. Then it takes the readers through the various perspectives of marketing mix perspective with reference to promoting Indian tourism. The core of the article details the strategy of advertising the tourism as segments of the market and targeting through right media mix, message mix. This article illustrates the above promotional strategy using caselets of Kerala tourism, Maharashtra etc. This article introduces a concept of multiple USP for tourism and gives some generalized suggestions for promotional strategy for the same.

I. Introduction

The history of Indian tourism is replete with odysseys undertaken by historians like Megasthenes and Tsi-chang wherein they described the entire gamut from nature's beauty to hidden dimensions of socio-cultural fabric of India. Lately, the following aspects made Indian tourism emerge as a new economy entity and Indian tourism acquiring a significant prominence.

- Tourism as an industry is emerging as a major economy built with meagre contribution to GDP of the nation since India's tourism is in still a fledgling state. Because it has hidden sights, cultural exuberance, diversity of terrain and a miscellany of attraction has made India a spotlight for the 21st century economy of the world.
- Tourism is an economy cascade trigger for various other industries like taxis, food and beverages, theatres, hotels, employment, guides and a vast variety of other things across contributing to their growth.
- Indian software expertise – on world map paved the path for world travelers to destination India not only as Mecca of software skills, but also renowned skills of silk weaving to pottery making and historical monuments with rich heritage.
- Emerging growth of complementary sectors such as hospital services, hospitality services and travel services makes tourism a prospective industry.

With the above backdrop, it can be seen that marketing Indian tourism cannot be done in isolation, but the marketing and promotions strategies should be integrated to other related support sectors such as transportation, hospitality etc., which forms a blueprint for promotion and marketing of Indian tourism. This article commences the following sections, which discuss different dimensions of promoting Indian tourism in detail. Section II deals with marketing perspectives to promote Indian tourism and section III highlights importance of promotional mix elements as Personal selling, Sales promotion, Public Relations and Advertising. Section IV depicts the role of advertising in tourism with respect to selected promotional campaigns in Indian tourism and finally section V concludes the discussion.

II. Promoting Indian Tourism Services: A Marketing Perspective

The promotion, planning and strategy of tourism can be well executed, if promotional managers have a perspective of tourism as a service in the form of basic marketing tools of McCarthy's Marketing Mix mentioned briefly below:

- **Product:** The product with respect to tourism is the tourists' place. The most important issue in the service product is to understand what benefits and satisfaction the customer seeks from the service. The promotion of services will be successful only if there is a match between the service product from the customer's viewpoint and the supplier's viewpoint. To find this match, as a manager one would have to analyze the tourist service at the following four levels. The customer benefit concept (places coverage and the stay), the service concept (convenience, support with information), the service offer (stay + transport) and the service delivery system (Cross functional from the place management, operators of transport). Based on the above factors content in the advertising is designed.

- **Pricing:** Generally tourist services use differential pricing or flexible pricing/ bundling depending upon number of persons and places of choice.
- **People:** People constitute an important dimension in services both as performers of service and as customers. People as performers of service are important because, "A customer sees a company through its employees. The employees represent the first line of contact with the customer. They must, therefore, be well informed and provide the kind of service that wins customer's approval. The firm must recognize that each employee is a salesman for the company's service" (E M Johnson, "An introduction to the problems of service marketing management"). People's performance in tourist services is equal to satisfaction of the customers. The importance of customers in services stems from the fact that most of the services imply active and involved customer-organization interface. Customers are important because they are also a source of influencing other customers. Based on this, the theme of "Athithi Devo bhava"emerged in Indian tourism recently.
- **Physical Evidence:** There may be two kinds of physical evidence – Peripheral Evidence and Essential Evidence. Information, Brochures and the place itself are examples of peripheral evidence. In detail it can be the facilities of transportation and hospitality services, which provide basic amenities.
- **Customer Contact:** Integrative approaches help to deliver better. In case of tourist services, the customer can come into contact with a particular tourist place, but the encounter should be able to provide all information across other places.

III. The Role of Promotional Mix and its Relative Importance in Marketing Indian Tourism Services

Promotional mix takes care of tools available for marketer such as personal selling, sales, promotion, public relation and advertising. Each of these tools is having its own pros and cons, depending on the type of product or service, for example, consultancy service requires personal selling as it requires one-to-one interaction with the client and the customization required do very high, but is also supported by other tools of promotional mix such as advertising and PR. Likewise, a promotional manager of tourism services should understand the characteristics of promotional mix element so that promotional design can be done effectively. The following paragraphs briefly depict the relative importance of promotional mix elements.

- *Personal Selling* is a form of communication that takes place face-to-face amongst tourist operators and travel agents, guides and telemarketing. Relative importance is given when high involvement and need to cultivate relationship is required.
- *Sales Promotion:* American Marketing Association (AMA) defines it as "the media and non-media marketing pressure applied for a pre-determined period, limited period of time at the level of consumer retailer, or wholesaler in order to stimulate trial (encourage consumers to try the product or service) increase consumer demand or improve product availability". This technique is generally used by all service sectors where some or few can be illustrated here. Off-season discounts for tourist places like rainy season in the North Eastern States, winter season in Himachal Pradesh and Kodaikanal. This tool is to be used when initiation for sales is to be done or to maintain off-season crowd.
- *Public Relations:* According to Public Relations Society of America as "PR helps an organisation and its public adapt mutually to each other." One element of PR is stimulating demand for a product or an awareness of an organisation by obtaining favorable commentary about it on radio, TV, or some other medium not paid for by the sponsor. This is a more powerful tool for services marketer to create an image of credibility for the branding purposes. Any of the service provider will not miss, given an opportunity to create a platform to talk about the services in the public forums/press meets, travel magazines and travel channels.

- *Advertising:* According to AMA Advertising is the "placement of announcements and persuasive messages in time or space purchased in any of the mass media by business firms, non-profit organization, government agencies and individuals who seek to inform and/or persuade members of a particular target market or audience about their products, services, organization or ideas." It's a much better tool for marketer to support, substantiate, supplement and complement other promotional mix tools. Its versatility of amplification and depiction of service benefit in aesthetic way makes the advertising a strategic tool for service marketer to use it in an effective way.

IV. The Role of Advertising in Tourism: A Study of Selected Promotional Campaigns in Indian Tourism

If you think seeing is believing, a company should believe that the advertising plays a major role in promoting tourism as it can create mass awareness, dramatize the idea and emotions can be communicated effectively to the target customers i.e., tourists. The role of an advertisement is to position the service proposition in the consumer's mind which is relative with competitor regarding the benefit, offer, price, quality, features, package, attributes of service. This helps a service organisation to build the brand too. But incase of Indian tourism it's the value proposition positioning with benefits of tourist place as a platform rather than any competitive entity. These benefits include medical tourism, religious, scenic and adventurous etc. They form a base for advertising to project the required information based on the target group.

A. Conceptual-Operational Perspective

The sub-sections i-vi below gives a template for a manager of tourism who wants to prepare an advertising campaign.

i. The author looks at the various queries asked by a marketing manager who is promoting tourism services in order to form a blueprint for advertising campaign.

The queries may be:

- What type of tourists you are targeting?
- What is their need profile?
- What expectations?
- What he expects? (value/satisfaction? By tourism service offers and its execution.)
- Is he/she ready to pay (price/premium) for the same?
- What choices of tourist services are available? (Distribution, Assortment of services, areas of coverage)
- How conveniently he gets and uses pertinent information about tourism services and tourists places? (promotion)
- Who does the delivery (Related sector internal customers) of tourist operators, taxis, food and beverages, theatres, hotels employment, guides? (People)
- How does delivery occur for marketing a tourism product? (Process)
- What tangible part of tourist services does a customer look for? (Physical infrastructure).
- Combination of answers to above queries can be used in a specific manner to arrive at the promotion of strategy for tourism.

The above queries establish the need profile of customer which gives direction to advertising decisions as message decision, media decision and budgeting decisions.

ii. *Advertising campaign sketch* is given to execute the strategies for the marketing manager promoting tourism services. The advertising objectives for tourism differ from place to place and can have the following outline.

   - To create awareness and attention regarding a place such as sanctuary, pilgrimage etc.
   - To create functional message interest about the place of visit.
   - To kindle or generate or desire regarding the tourist place (Emotional message).

– To make the customers to take action i.e., buying a ticket for tourist place or it can be done by attaching a coupon or direct mail or advertising.

Decide the target customer segments suggested as below:

- Executive Traveler-Business
- Adventure Travelers
- Spiritual Travelers
- Historical Travelers
- Traveling is Leisure/Pleasure
- Traveling as an Expedition.

iii. Understand and develop each of the above segments's AIO profile (Activities Interest and Opinions). The need of the segments decides execution of message style. It also makes the media mix decision i.e., which media vehicle to choose press or TV or media selection. The need of the segments decides message selection and execution of message. It also makes the media mix decision i.e., which media vehicle to press or TV or media selection, number of insertions of advertisements in print and channel timing in electronic media

iv. Message Decisions: Message structure – sequencing/presentation of advertisements, message content what information it should have including headlines slogans and copy. Message execution styles relate to the choice of running the advertisements.

v. Media Mix: It will decide choice of print or electronic media or both.

vi. Choice of USPs: Once you know the profile of target segments you can pitch in the Multiple USPs for same places.

B. Selected Promotional Campaigns

i. **Caselet of Kerala Tourism:** It has used "Multiple USPs" in various execution styles like: Shot of a Mohiniaattam danseuse gazing through a 'window'. Super – 'National Geographic Traveler...' – can be for tarveller leisure, Shots of the calm blue waters of Thekkady, dotted with tiny islands. Super – ...has chosen Pleasure traveler and sports etc.,Wild elephants cavort joyfully in the cool waters. Super – '...Kerala, India...' leisure and pleasure Shot of the Vazhachal waterfalls. Super – '...as one of the nature lovers profile.

Shot of local physicians administering traditional ayurvedic formulations – medical tourism perspective – patient travelers, Shots of several snake boats plowing through the backwaters...sports lovers Cut to a display of the ancient martial art kalaripayattu by warriors... historical travelers A colourful Kathakali dancer... and Mohiniaattam performance... and the Thrissur pooram. For leisure and historical travelers.

ii. **Caselet of Maharastra Tourism:** Its television advertisements basically aimed at a couple whose busy life schedule makes them to look for leisure and pleasure. The message execution style used is slice of life, fantasy and mood together.

iii. **Incredible India Campaign:** We have seen various campaigns, but the Exhibit 3 is aimed at creating awareness about monumental preservation using celebrities like Shahrukh Khan explaining the concept of cleanliness. The target group is monument travelers and the execution style used is slice of life and Personality symbol can be used to drive the message across.

iv. **Learning Proposition from Campaigns:** Pitching different positioning perspectives from same place of tourism using predominantly message execution styles slice of life for sports and dance, moods for nature's picturesque scenes photographed for Kerala. For Maharashtra campaign fantasy, moods and slice of life is used. For the incredible campaign the USP is taken off as the cleanliness of surroundings using credible source as personality symbol. Advertisement campaigns of different states like Karnataka, Tamilnadu pitched as religious tourism, Goa as pleasure and leisure, north eastern with basic platform of nature sanctuaries for nature lovers with factual messages. Andhra Pradesh is focusing on various places of historical and religious importance as a platform to talk on their campaigns.

v. Summary of the Advertising Campaigns Strategies Outline is given in Figure 1 and Table 1.

Figure 1 depicts the range of options available from rational to emotional message execution styles. The message's impact of an advertisement depends not

Figure 1: Advertising Strategy Spectrum

Advertising Strategy Spectrum

Generic	Rational Approach
Pre-Emptive	Relies on persuasive power of features, attributes and rational benefits
USP	
Positioning	
Brand-Image	
Resonance	Relies on persuasive power of emotions, feelings and associations
Affective	Emotional Approach

only on what is said, but also often more important, on how it said. Some ads aim for rational positioning and others for emotional positioning.

Any message can be presented in a number of execution styles as mentioned below:

- Straight sell or factual message
- Slice of Life
- Lifestyle
- Fantasy
- Mood or Image
- Musical
- Personality Symbol

- Technical Expertise
- Scientific Evidence
- Testimonial
- Demonstration
- Comparison
- Animation
- Dramatization
- Humor
- Combinations of any of the above.

The table 1 below gives the types of traveler's customer segment with suggested Message Execution styles and Media choice for advertising tourism services.

Table 1

S.No.	Traveler Type	Message	Media
1.	Executive/Business	Factual	Business traveler, business magazines, media TV business channels
2.	Adventurous	Demonstration	Sports Magazines
3.	Spiritual	Mood/Image	Electronic: TV, print brochures at tourists booking offices
4.	Historical	Music/Mood	Magazines like India Today, channels like Discovery, National Geographic
5.	Leisure/Pleasure	Mood/Lifestyle	Travelers magazine, channel of travel

The particular mode of preference of promotions of tourism in toto depends upon the Objective of Communication (creates awareness, generate interest, creating demand, creating desire, action. favorability etc,) regarding the tourist place. Service one wants to offer from the tourist place and the status of customers' being innovators, adapter's or late majority as tourists and state's resources (small/ medium/large)

V. Coda

The advertising strategies for services and in particular tourism depends on the type of consumers, tourists you are targeting, the tourists' place and the proposition you are marketing, the message strategy you want to include and the media decisions you have taken. The Message execution styles can form a sound advertising strategy which is based further on tourism promotion, as tourism is a high involvement and rational buying involved with emotions. The messages have entire gamut of covering Slice of Life, Lifestyle, Fantasy Mood or Image Musical all of which are all involve more of a tone of emotional element in advertising spectrum of strategy as used by various Indian tourism campaigns. In promoting tourism emotional element,/degree of involvement which drives the consumer to take a decision regarding choice of place forms the base for choice of message and media. To conclude, advertising became an important and inevitable tool in promotional program. The latest happenings across the country make India as emerging, as a new promising economy in new Global economy and tourism contributing substantially to the GDP. It is important to sustain and maintain tourist traffic and promotion of tourism places is a must.

(G Radha Krishna, Faculty Member, the Icfai Business School, Hyderabad.)

References

1. Berry, Leonard. 1995. "Relationship Marketing of Services – Growing Interest,
2. Emerging Perspectives". *Journal of Academy of Marketing Science, Vol. 23:236-254.*
3. George E Belch and Michael A Belch "Advertising and Promotion", 5th Edition TATA Mcgraw Hill Keaveney.
4. Susan M. 1995. "Customer Switching Behavior in Service Industries: An Exploratory Study". *Journal of Marketing 59* (April): 71-81.
5. Philip Kotler, "Marketing Management" 11th Edition Pearson Education.
6. Supranant, C F and Solomon, M R 1987. "Predictability and Personalization in the Service Encounter". *Journal of Marketing 51: 86-96.*
7. Thomas J Burns, "Effective Communication and Advertising for Financial Institutions" (ENGLEWOOD CLIFFS , N J: Prentice Hall 1986 pp. 133-134).
8. James A. O'Brien, "Management Information Systems: Managing Information".
9. "Technology in the Internet Worked Enterprise", Fourth Edition, 1999.
10. Dorsch, Michael, Scott Swanson, and Scott Kelley. 1998. "The Role of Relationship Quality in the Satisfaction of Vendors as Perceived by Customers". *Journal of the Academy of Marketing Science 26 (spring)*: 128-142.
11. Garner, Thesia I and Janet Wagner. 1991. "Economic Dimensions of Household Gift Giving". *Journal of Consumer Research 18* (December): 368-379.

Exhibit 1: Kerala Tourism	

Shot of a Mohiniaattam danseuse gazing through a 'window'. Super: 'National Geographic Traveler...'	Shots of the calm blue waters of Thekkady, dotted with tiny islands. Super: ...has chosen...'

Wild elephants cavort joyfully in the cool waters. Super: '...Kerala, India...'	Shot of the Vazhachal waterfalls. Super: '...as one of the...'
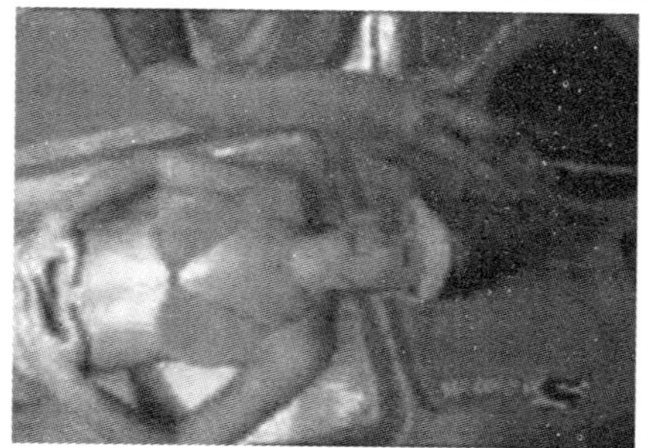	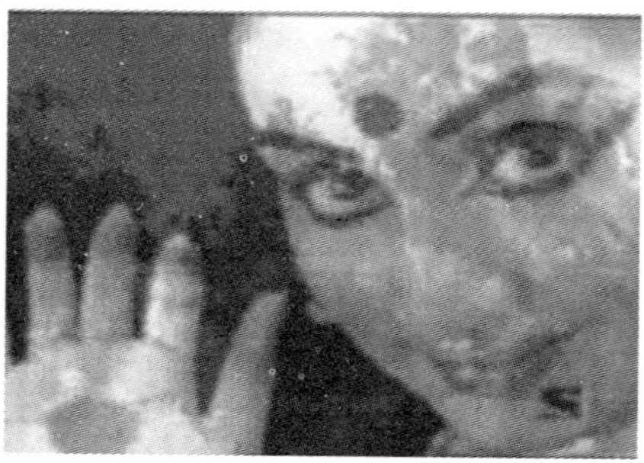
Shot of local physicians administering traditional ayurvedic formulations.	Super: '...50 greatest destinations of the world.'
	Contd...

Contd...	
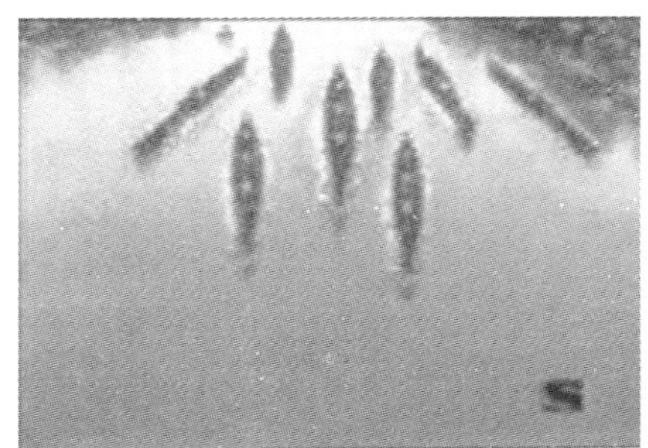	
Shots of several snake boats plowing through the backwaters...	Cut to a display of the ancient martial art kalaripayattu by warriors...

A colourful Kathakali dancer...	...and Mohiniaattam performance...

...and the Thrissur pooram.	Super: 'God's own country.'

<table>
<tr><th colspan="2">Exhibit 2: Maharashtra Tourism</th></tr>
<tr><td></td><td></td></tr>
<tr><td>With his sweetheart next to him a guy strolls along the beach.</td><td>As he looks into her eyes, the VO plays, "this is all I want. To...</td></tr>
<tr><td></td><td></td></tr>
<tr><td>...be with you. Let me take you away." The guy picks up a conch...</td><td>...and places it next to his ears. The next moment he finds himself...</td></tr>
<tr><td></td><td>
</td></tr>
<tr><td>...sitting in the office hearing a credit card offer on the phone when he realises that it was only...</td><td>...a dream. The ad ends with the voiceover: "Unlimited reasons to get lost." Super: "Maharashtra unlimited."</td></tr>
<tr><td colspan="2">Source: TVAdIndx.com</td></tr>
</table>

<table>
<tr><th colspan="2">Exhibit 3: Incredible India</th></tr>
<tr><td></td><td></td></tr>
<tr><td>In holiday mood a family of four visits the Taj Mahal. Soon they start littering...</td><td>...its lawn with food wrappers andother waste. Next comes Jaipur, where the...</td></tr>
<tr><td></td><td></td></tr>
<tr><td>...family does everything to make the pink city look dirty. They leave the city to go to the Gateway of India.</td><td>Posing for a photograph, the man in the family spits paan in front of the great historical monument.</td></tr>
<tr><td></td><td></td></tr>
<tr><td>Back in home the family gets the shock of their life as they see it in complete mess.</td><td>Cut to the shot of Shahrukh Khan advising, "jab bhi aap apna shehar ganda karte hain...</td></tr>
<tr><td colspan="2">*Contd...*</td></tr>
</table>

Contd...

...toh yoon hi samajhiye ki aap apna ghar

...shehar ko saaf rakhne ke liye kachra peti

Source: TVAdIndx.com

SECTION II

ADVERTISING STRATEGY, ROLE AND ISSUES

4

Tourism Marketing in India: Inviting the Domestic Traveler

Anil Gupta and Anupam Ghosh

...And you thought brand ambassadors are used only to promote products and services. Check out this, Amitabh Bachchan was signed in as a brand ambassador to promote the State of Uttar Pradesh in October 2003. And then in February 2004, the State of Karnataka followed up and signed in Rahul Dravid and singer Vasundra Das to promote their state to international as well as domestic tourists. Tourism marketing and advertising in India is entering a new phase with a majority of states looking to tap international as well as domestic tourism traffic to boost their respective economies.

Travel and tourism is the second highest foreign exchange earner for India. Though inbound tourism definitely is of high priority today the states also want to tap the potential of domestic tourism. According to estimates, domestic tourism is expected to generate revenue worth Rs.600 billion. Contrast this with the inbound tourism spending, which is estimated at approximately Rs.170 billion with approximately 2.2 million foreign tourists visiting India in 2002. However, experts in this industry still feel that Indian states are yet to tap the potential of

Source: Advertising Express, April 2004.

domestic tourism. According to international standards the ratio between domestic and international tourism is approximately 10:1 whereas, in India it is only approximately equal to 3:1.

Moreover, according to a study[1] by Pannell Kerr Forster Consultants, globally 50% of domestic travelers go out of home for holidays, whereas 35% of them move out to meet their friends and relatives. This study goes ahead to provide an estimate for Indian domestic tourism. According to their study, travel to meet friends and relatives dominates the domestic tourism scenario at approximately 31.5%, whereas leisure domestic tourism is still very low at 13.8%. As against the expectations only 6.9% of domestic tourism is related to spiritual or religious tourism whereas 10.4% of people travel for business purposes. India is yet to tap the potential of domestic leisure tourism.

India Incredible

Government of India's "India Incredible" campaign has definitely given a positive image to the global traveler. Today, India has become one of the hot destinations for foreign tourists. The campaign laid stress of the diversity of India and its potential to offer various kinds of tourism adventure, history, medical, spiritual, beach and religious tourism. Can India sell itself to Indians?

Though India is yet to sell India to Indians, there is a changing trend, which has been observed. With the changing socio-economic profiles of Indian consumers and emergence of nuclear families, domestic leisure tourism is expected to increase. Indians are looking forward to explore the diverse landscape and beauty across various parts of India. Fortunately every Indian state has unique characteristics in terms of architecture, art and craft, food, festivals, monuments, landscape, and weather. This rich history and heritage provides an opportunity for domestic travelers to explore their own country. Growing tourism infrastructure like emergence of world-class hospitality facilities is also expected to facilitate the growing domestic tourism. However, to tap this enormous potential, creating awareness is critical. Today, many of the Indian states have taken tourism as a serious business and are in the process of restructuring their tourism boards. Tourism advertising is entering a new phase in India. Just look at Table 1 that mentions the positioning statements of various states in India.

---

1 *http://www.tourismofindia.com/misc/time.htm*

Table 1

State	Positioning
Kerala	God's Own Country
Karnataka	Theatre of Inspiration
Andhra Pradesh	Kohinoor of India
Tamil Nadu	Enchanting Tamil Nadu
Pondicherry	Peaceful Pondicherry—Give Time a Break
Goa	Go Goa, 365 days on a holiday
Gujarat	Vibrant Gujarat
Uttar Pradesh	Many Faiths, Many Journeys
Uttaranchal	Experience the Divine
Jammu and Kashmir	Welcome to Paradise
Punjab	Passionate Punjab
Rajasthan	Hospitality Amidst Royal Ambience
Maharashtra	Maharashtra Unlimited
Madhya Pradesh	Magical Mystical Madhya Pradesh—the very heart of India
Orissa	The Soul of India
West Bengal	The land of exotic charms
North East	Unexplored Paradise

Source: www.tamilnadutourism.org

Let us see how some of the Indian states promote tourism with an objective to woo the domestic traveler.

God's Own Country: Kerala

Kerala has taken a lead in promoting tourism and is now a Super Brand in Indian tourism industry. It has always laid stress on tourism and sees tourism as a key industry. For the financial year 2003–04 the state has an outlay of Rs.74.25 cr. Positioning itself as the "Green Gateway of India" and "God's Own Country" Kerala has been advertising to woo the international and domestic travelers.

Kerala has been blessed with beautiful beaches like Kovalam, Chowara, Shanghumugham, Varkala Papanasam, Bekal, and Quilon beach. The state government has taken various initiatives to develop all these beaches as major tourist attractions. Another attraction of Kerala has been the backwaters and lagoons that stretch over 1900 km. Kerala has also taken the lead in promoting Ayurveda all across the world and with penetration of "Kerala Ayurveda Centers" all across the country, the domestic tourist is also getting attracted to this special advantage of visiting Kerala. Today, apart from the state's inherent attractions like long beaches, backwaters, hill stations, ayurveda, Kerala is promoting village tourism as a new product. This state has been focusing on sustainable tourism since all the tourism products are natural. An innovative project called "Canal Walk Project" is also underway in the state. This project is on the lines of the River Walk Project in San Antonio in the United States. The walk way is to be constructed along Veli and Akkulam lakes.

The state has also taken various other initiatives like conducting road shows, organizing events like Kerala travel mart, national boat show, and Kerala gold fest to promote tourism in the state. In fact, the state has been winning a host of awards given by the Ministry of Tourism, Government of India for the "Best Tourism Performing State" for more than four years in a row. The state has also won awards for Most Innovative Use of Information Technology and for the Best Tourism Film in 2002. It has also taken initiatives by entering into MoUs with Indian Railways, Indian Airlines and IBP to boost domestic tourism. In 2004 the state won the PATA gold award for its Thenmala Eco Tourism Project and for promoting Ayurveda. In fact, the state created a CD titled "Ayurveda: The Mantra of Nirmaya". This initiative has been a step ahead in supporting its sustainable tourism model. Kerala has emerged as a "Power Brand" in the tourism business.

Theatre of Inspiration: Karnataka

Karnataka has followed the strategy of Uttar Pradesh and has recently signed up Rahul Dravid and Vasundra Das to promote Karnataka as a favorite tourism destination. Rahul Dravid is expected to promote the state to international tourists whenever he visits any country. Especially he is expected to promote the state in Pakistan.

Karnataka is promoting the two World Heritage sites – Hampi and Pattadakal to woo those who are interested in history and heritage. For those who are interested in natural beauty, Karnataka is promoting its dense forests and natural falls like Jog Falls, which is Asia's highest waterfall. With the advantage of having Bangalore, the state is also promoting business tourism for domestic corporate class. Bangalore provides an advantage of having world-class facilities for meetings, conventions, trade shows, and exhibitions. It has also been promoted as a destination among the youth and professionals. A dream destination to relocate the state is capitalizing on inviting the youth to visit the state once. Karnataka is also being positioned as shoppers' paradise. The state has taken initiatives to promote Mysore silk, Sandalwood carvings, Rosewood carvings, Metalware, Mysore paintings, Bijapur sarees and Gokak toys.

The Dusshera festival of Mysore is also very famous across India. The state has taken initiatives to promote the fairs and festivals like Dusshera of Mysore, Vijaya Utsav or Hampi festival, Vairamudi Festival and the Kambalathe popular buffalo race. In addition, it is also promoting its exquisite cuisines especially the Udipi cuisine, famous across the country.

365 Days on a Holiday: Goa

No doubt Goa has been a hot favorite among the domestic tourists when it comes to leisure travel. And the punch line of Goa tourism makes it a destination to be visited at any time of the year. The state has positioned itself as a land of dreams and romance. It promotes Goa as a land of sun, sand and sea and a land of monuments and historical sites. Goa also boasts of having some of the most romantic beaches in the world. The destination has also been marketed as one of the places where people can come and relax, a place where the traveler will be greeted with warmth and love. Goa enjoys strong brand equity in the minds of the domestic traveler. And with some marketing efforts, Goa can take away a major chunk of leisure travel in times to come.

Kohinoor of India: Andhra Pradesh

This state does not want to remain a laggard. After matching Bangalore in IT and taking lead in pharma, the state is all ahead in promoting tourism to the domestic traveler. Positioned as "Kohinoor of India" the state is positioning itself as the ultimate tourist destination. Andhra Pradesh is promoting the state across a variety of themes like beaches, Buddhist centers, caves, eco-tourism, hills and valleys, monuments, museums, pilgrim centers and wildlife. One of the most popular pilgrim centers, Tirupati, is in the state of Andhra Pradesh. The state is taking a lot of initiatives in promoting domestic tourism. It is also building appropriate infrastructure to support the brand building campaign. In fact, Hyderabad won a National Award for the best growing city and the Golconda Fort in the city also won the award for the best-maintained monument.

Enchanting Tamil Nadu

Tamil Nadu is promoting the destinations within the state with catchy captions like

"I am not behind: Other States Catching on."

Following all these states, the other states are catching on. States like Orissa, Uttaranchal, Uttar Pradesh, Chattisgarh, and Madhya Pradesh are also devising their marketing strategies and are finding their niche. Then there are states like Rajasthan, Punjab, Maharashtra and Gujarat, which are trying to rebuild their images by promoting tourism. Some of the popular tourist destinations like Himachal Pradesh have lost on account of marketing strategies. The state that has enormous tourism potential is yet to be seen in the media space creating awareness. States like J&K despite having enormous potential have lost on account of militancy and terrorism. However, at its own level it is trying to promote tourism by projecting normalcy in the state.

Table 2

Place	Some Attractions	Positioning
Chennai	Beach Resorts, Planetarium	The Gateway to the South
Chidambaram	The Church of Zion, The Gate, Masilamaninathar Temple	Seat of the Cosmic Dance
Coimbatore	Indira Gandhi Wildlife Sanctuary, Maruthamalai Temple	Manchester of the South
Kancheepuram	Vellore, Vedanthangal, Elagiri Hills	The City of a Thousand Temples and Silks
Kanyakumari	Suchindram, Nagercoil, Pechipara Dam, Udayagiri Fort	Where the three seas meet
Kodaikanal	Palani, Hill range	Princess of hill stations
Tirunelveli	Tiruchendur, Manappad, Thuthukudi, Panchalamkurichi, Ettaiyapuram, Kazhugumalai, Sankarankovil, Tenkasi, Courtallam, Krishnapuram	The Nine falls

Source: www.tamilnadutourism.org

North Eastern states have formed a consortium and have started a campaign wherein they are trying to promote the entire north as a single tourist destination. In order to boost the domestic traffic in the eight jewels of the North East, the Department of Tourism has undertaken a new ad campaign designed by Grey Worldwide. Positioned as "Unexplored Paradise" these eight states in the North-East plan to capture a major chunk of domestic tourism in times to come.

In-film Placements: Being Innovative

Tourism marketing and advertising is catching on in India. States are looking for innovative ideas to promote destinations among the domestic tourists. States like Chattisgarh are looking forward to promote the state using "in-film" or "in-serial" strategy. Placing the locations in the films or the serials makes it possible for the domestic tourist to get the feel of the locations and creates awareness as well. The popularity of "Khandala" increased after it was placed in the film "Ghulam". Other progressive states like Andhra Pradesh, Rajasthan, West Bengal and Maharashtra are also moving ahead to place their locations in films. Another popular medium to promote destinations is TV serials. Popular serials like *Kyunki*

Saas Bhi Kabhi Bahu Thi have enormous potential to promote destinations in the Indian households. And there are some speciality serials like "Yatra" that can be tapped to promote destinations. Coming years will see more competition and the media space will see more of tourism advertising. Keep watching!!

(Anil Gupta and Anupam Ghosh are working in the Icfai Institute for Management Teachers, Hyderabad.)

5

Ecotourism Policy: A Framework for India

Seema Purushotthaman, Jojo T D and Sheetal P

Ecotourism in the Indian context has significant implications for nature and culture conservation, rural livelihoods and conservation education. Experience from within the country and outside highlights the need for an appropriate institutional mechanism to streamline ecotourism policy. We propose setting up of ecotourism directorates under the Ministry of Tourism both at the national and state levels. National directorate will be instrumental in providing a clear definition and strategic direction and can engage stakeholder groups in dialogues related to multilateral agreements and local self-governance in the context of ecotourism. State directorates can play more regulatory and facilitating role. The constitution and mandate of these agencies are briefly discussed. We also demonstrate a process for assessment and monitoring of ecotourism ventures and suggest ways of linking them to incentives.

Introduction

The objective of a tourism policy is to provide tools for containing growth of tourism beyond viable, acceptable and sustainable natural, social and economic

Source: Ashoka Trust for Research in Ecology and the Environment(ATREE)©ATREE. Reprinted with permission.

thresholds. Tourism policy should also enable identification and mitigation of impacts. It should cater to all aspects of the tourism production function (Batta 2000) – primary inputs (resources), intermediate inputs (facilities and services) and the final output (experiences). While all environmental legislations apply to all tourism enterprises, general tourism policies are not congenial for ecotourism sub-sector because of potentially significant socio-ecological impacts. As of now, targeted legislations in ecotourism are rare. The objective of a policy in this context should be to prevent the now well-known 'resort cycle' (Butler, 1980) by avoiding the phase of rapid decline due to environmental degradation. Clear planning and control of the ecotourism sector is a globally identified need (Martin and Uysal, 1990). This paper intends to outline the policy needs of ecotourism sector in India, which is also targeted at the policy planners, makers and implementers concerned with the sector in other developing economies.

There seems to be only a thin line of difference between tourism and ecotourism (ET). Often, the difference is more in what you call it than in what you do. This ambiguity is dangerous as tourism in general and ET in particular involves rare and pristine landscapes. Being 'eco-friendly' is seen as a business opportunity and nature based activities are becoming increasingly popular. On the other hand, this could be an opportunity for policy-makers to take leverage of this perception on profits to achieve sustainable development on the ground. Viewing ecotourism merely as an exclusive profit earner and discount its value as a conservation and livelihoods tool will end up missing this route towards sustainability. But, outcomes of ecotourism depend on government's priorities – it could be conservation, poverty alleviation or generation of foreign exchange. These outcomes are governed by stated priorities which in turn determine who should be involved in policy-making, what are the guiding principles, why do we pursue ecotourism, where should it take place and what the expected outcomes are. The definitions adopted by the society at large and the government should have a shared vision and should reflect in integrated and cohesive ecotourism policies.

Broad acceptance of certain essential constituents of ecotourism facilitates clear answers to the above policy questions. A definition-based policy model of ET will also help in developing indicators for monitoring and a possible certification process. Hence, the concept of ecotourism is unveiled in the first section. Section II talks in general about the process of policy changes and section III draws lessons from ecotourism policies across countries. This is followed by a section (IV) that presents a review of existing guidelines and policies in India. Subsequent two sections (V and VI) narrate the recommendations that will be most suited for India's ecotourism sector and section VII elaborates a set of criteria and indicators to assess impact of the sector.

I. Characteristics of Ecotourism

The tragedy of mass tourist-spots digging their own graves and the emerging global market for ethnic and unique experience gave rise to enterprises under the banner of ecotourism in various parts of the world. In spite of its increasing importance as a business opportunity and its phenomenal growth within the tourism industry, the concept of EcoTourism (ET) is not well defined. Used as a tool to harvest consumer's surplus in the context of economic growth and environmental degradation, ET practices vary from wildlife and heritage to health and adventure. ET is generally perceived as 'high value low volume enterprise' depending on a few interested tourists with high willingness to pay. Developing countries are gradually realizing that ET can be a livelihood tool for rural communities and can also result in sustainable management of natural resources. The educational and cultural attributes attached to ecotourism add value to the business and also make us think that it may not be the quantity of tourists but the quality, which we need to address first. It is also known that in natural environments, tourist satisfaction is inversely related to the user intensity and well-known ecotourism destinations (e.g., Galapagos islands) face threat due to over visitation. The challenge lies in reconciling conservation, community benefits and business proposition and this calls for careful planning, implementation, monitoring and regulations.

Existing ET enterprises often highlight some conservation activities like energy saving gadgets or restricted use of plastics, but tend to ignore the overall impact on natural and cultural integrity of the destination. There are instances where this has either led to eventual degradation of the marketed tourism product itself or to social unrest. Distinguishing the components of ET enterprises can clarify the ambiguity in the concept and practice of ET in any country. In many countries, 'home grown' definitions are in vogue (Edward *et al* (1998)), groomed to meet specific needs of the context. Based on various definitions of ET (TIES 1991, Wood 2002, Jafari 1996, WWF 2001 and FAO 1997), we can distinguish ET for the developing country context by the following four essential characteristics.

1. Nature-based activities
2. Eco-cultural sustainability
3. Conservation Education (for tour operator and the tourist) as major component
4. Significant involvement of and benefits to local people.

Mainstream tourism is geared towards tourist satisfaction alone, while ET has conservation (of nature and culture) and livelihoods (economic and educational benefits) as essential constituents. While it is obvious that tourism should at least be harmless to nature and society at large, ET needs to be pro-active towards all the four components mentioned above. Mass tourism could be based on pleasure, relaxation, religion or carnivals. ET enterprises need to be focused on the natural environment. A resort near seashore or inside a protected forest could meet all the four characteristics of ET, while the regular mass visitation to a beach or to a forest temple can only be made eco-friendly. Last two components of ET do not prevail as dominant in mass tourism ventures located in the same destination. In fact it is often considered desirable to keep mass tourism away from local communities to retain the cultural uniqueness un-invaded.

While cultural nuances evolve in the natural uniqueness of any region, both these together need to be sustained for continued tourist attraction. Natural and cultural sovereignty is crucial in projecting the handicrafts and culinary traditions as vibrant economic products. It is also worth mentioning that tourism in developing economies emerged as an industry in the post-war era due to the adverse terms of trade in agricultural commodities. Major contribution of the sector was perceived as improving the balance of payments situation. Hence there has been a conventional focus on international tourists, in spite of the environmental costs in long distance travel, leakage of benefits from the destinations and greater uncertainty. In any case, the number of foreign tourists is not a large proportion of the total visitors (Figure 1). ET, led by objectives of nature and culture conservation, livelihoods and education, needs to be different.

Figure 1: Percentage of Foreign Tourist to Total

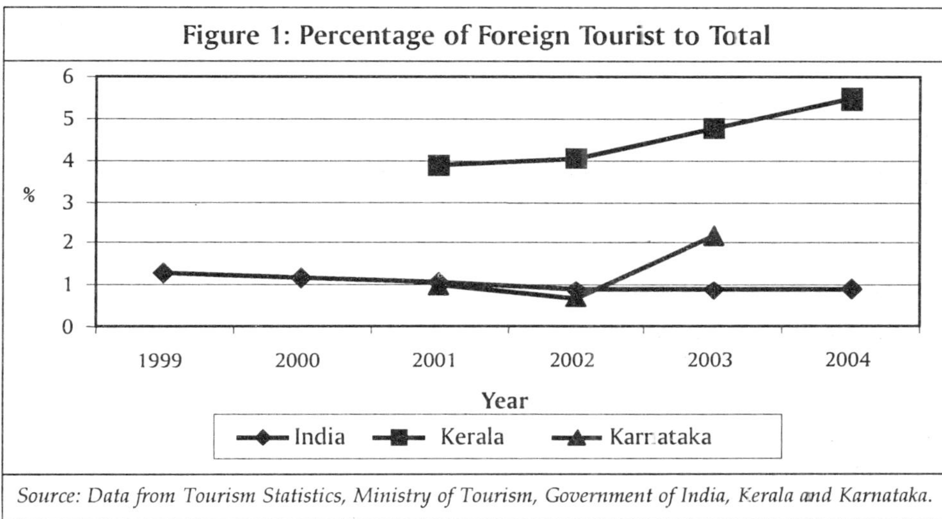

Source: Data from Tourism Statistics, Ministry of Tourism, Government of India, Kerala and Karnataka.

Role of participatory tourism initiatives is well laid out in George and Reid (2005). This is envisaged as the most important feature of ET, because it is only a sub-sector under the vast tourism arena, focusing on the willingness to pay for certain unique experiences with minimum eco-cultural footprint. Any tourism venture with a potentially large impact or dependence on local ecology and/or culture could be regarded as eco-tourism. It need not be confined to forests and could include home stays, houseboats, or beach tourism. This realization is based on the understanding that there is increasing willingness to pay for eco-tourism activities and the sector is expanding fast with increasing number and variety of players. Also there are increasing volume of visitors to natural reserves (Li and Han, 2001) that needs to be spread across a wide variety and number of locations.

II. The Process of Restructuring Policy

Policies are dynamic in nature reflecting the evolving understanding of the society. Policies may need periodic revisions based on emerging perspectives and techniques. Therefore policy formulation benefits from guidelines brought out at different times, at different governance levels and by different agencies. The policy framework being recommended here, also finds its origin in existing practices, policies and guidelines both within India and across other similar contexts. Nevertheless, it is realized that ecotourism is a vast business domain having wide repercussions on the socio-ecological fabric of an economy. Therefore, it is time now, to develop these broad guidelines into clearer regulations, strategies and action plans. While guidelines can be national, policies need to reflect state-specific needs and imperatives of ET. Hence the suggested framework provides space for regions and communities to innovate and to retain their ecological and cultural integrity. In terms of the process of policy formulation, there has to be dialogue, consensus, bottom-up approach, decentralized governance and redressal mechanisms. (The World Ecotourism Summit, 2002[1]). Following this process, we propose national and state level institutions and mechanisms to promote and sustain ET in India as a tool for conservation, livelihood and development.

This paper is the culmination of state level consultations and assessment of ET enterprises in four regions of India – two in the Western Ghats (Kerala and Karnataka) and two in the Eastern Himalayas (Darjeeling and Sikkim). The biodiversity hotspots of Western Ghats and Eastern Himalayas were chosen because of prevailing linkages between ET practices and sensitive ecosystems in these regions. Consultations involved formal and informal exchanges with identified stakeholders and review of literature.

III. ET as Practiced and Institutionalized in Different Countries

ET policies in selected countries are reviewed to draw insights for a suitable institutional structure, incentive mechanisms and monitoring process for India's socio-political context. Apart from the country-wide policies discussed below, comprehensive guidelines for planning and monitoring community based ET with case studies can be found in WWF, (2001). ET related policies in five countries and one region are briefly reviewed here.

Bhutan

With its mighty mountain ranges and relatively undisturbed ethnicity, Bhutan is a natural destination for ET. Bhutan's new long-term ET policy (previous ET policy was formulated in 2001) from Tourism Ministry continues its emphasis on 'high value low impact' tourism and tries to enhance community participation and conservation capacities. For a large functional democracy as India, high value low impact may not be an ideal slogan because of its trade-off with local economic and educational benefits. (Tandi, 2004)

Nepal

Ministry of Culture, Tourism and Civil Aviation (McCTCA) is responsible for policy, planning, licensing, regulations and overall monitoring of the tourism industry. Nepal Tourism Board (NTB) conducts planning, research and product development. Country's National Ecotourism strategy and marketing programme of 2004 emphasizes cross-sectoral cooperation at national planning level, more private participation, poverty alleviation through promotion of village tourism and a full-fledged marketing programme. Other government agencies in Nepal's ET sector include National Planning Commission and Department of National Parks and Wildlife Conservation. Nepal plans to set up a new body under NTB to coordinate ecotourism development, stressing on community participation in decision-making, planning and participatory techniques. (National strategy and marketing programme of Nepal[2], 2004)

Insights for India from Nepal's ET sector includes involvement of the departments of culture and civil aviation and the need for research and training support. A designated ET Board at the center as the hub of ET co-ordination and regulation may not be useful in the Indian context due to large-scale cultural and political diversity in India. But India could have a smaller cell at the center, as an umbrella for state level agencies, bringing out policy guidelines and providing inputs to international agreements.

Thailand

Thailand used open, well-marketed, mass tourism for economic recovery from the Asian crisis of the last century. This resulted in largescale interference with local ecology and Thai culture. Thus from 1995-96, Thailand started focusing on sustainability and in 1997 set up National Ecotourism Councils comprising of representatives of the public, academic, private, and NGO sectors. The purpose of these councils was to oversee the development of National Ecotourism Policy and Action Plan as well as to appoint sub-committees on various aspects of ecotourism management. National Ecotourism Action Plan is a five-year implementation plan for the period 2002 to 2006 with details of the projects needed to be implemented. Thrust areas include tourism resources and environment management, education and awareness building among the public, co-operation among local people, marketing promotion and tour guide, basic infrastructure, services development, investment support and promotion. (Ecotourism Policy and Plans[3], 2001)

The broad-base structure of ET councils may be suited to Indian context. This could help the state institutions of varied nature in timely revisions and could provide space for consultations on international agreements and other national policies impacting the sector. Among the new thrust areas of Thailand, public awareness to provide quality ecotourists and stress on co-operation among and within communities are India's concerns too. An implication to be drawn from this constitutional monarchy is the dependence on international tourists leaving behind conspicuous cultural footprints.

Sri Lanka

Heavy dependence on highly fluctuating flow of international tourists and the absence of national ecotourism policy leave the ET sector in Sri Lanka unable to grow beyond the occasional ecotours and eco-lodges organized by some tour operators. The Sri Lanka Ecotourism Foundation (SLEF) is planning to establish a 'National Secretariat" to guide ecotourism in Sri Lanka, broadly representing all stakeholders. Spice/plantation walks (agroforestry/ botanical tours) are emerging as popular eco-tourism activity and helps to save many indebted planters of this island economy.

Lessons for India from Sri Lankan experience include the scope of farm tourism and risks associated with putting too many eggs in an industry far too sensitive to insecurity and instability. Leakages in terms of proportion of receipts from tourism flowing out of the economy for Sri Lanka, leakages are around 27% (Batta, 2000) makes the over dependence on international tourists a not-so-viable proposition. Experience of Thailand and Sri Lanka implies that quality domestic tourists would be more valuable to ET because of low cultural impact, higher domestic educational value and more predictable demand. (Sri Lanka Ecotourism Foundation[4], 1998)

Australia

'Ecotourism Australia' (1991) is an incorporated not-for -profit association of lead industries with diverse members. It develops certification program along with Co-operative Research Center for Sustainable Tourism. Australian certification is accepted as 'International Eco-tourism Standards' in 2001. 'Green Globe 21' (a global Affiliation, Benchmarking and Certification program for sustainable travel and tourism) has exclusive license for the distribution and management of the International Ecotourism Standard. An important insight from Australian policy is the freedom for aborigines to choose the way they wanted to be involved: as employees, investors, or participants in preventing negative impacts. (Tsung-Wei Lai[5], 1995)

Africa

Wildlife tourism generates almost one third of Kenya's foreign exchange earnings. In South Africa, there has been spectacular increase in the number of visitors to game and nature reserves. The integrated policy on cultural or village tourism of the African region was formulated in the line of the regional policy on Community National Parks Management. This provides an example for the South Asian Region, with comparable context of culture and history. African policy recognizes that 'low-volume' need not be 'low-impact' if quality tourism is not ensured by regulations and awareness. African policy sets the precedence of participatory identification of criteria and indicators. Involving stakeholder communities, they have adopted a broad set of criteria and a complementary set of model-specific indicators from World Tourism Organisation.

Many developing nations including India have made commitments under the World Trade Organisation's General Agreement on Trade in Services (GATS). The scope of GATS extends to all member governments, which includes national and local governments. There is a realized need to strengthen discussions on revising Article VI of GATS (Working Party on Domestic Regulations), which has repercussions on ET and on government's ability to privilege certain issues in certain contexts. Regional associations for specific sectors like ET can strengthen these arguments in the GATS negotiations. The basic tenet of ET in considerable local stakes may be jeopardized by the commitments under GATS if rights and powers of local stakeholders (and local self governments) are not recognized. (Marshall[6] 2004)

IV. ET Institutions and Practices in India

The Ecotourism Policy and Guidelines (1998) brought out by Government of India, identifies key players in Ecotourism and prescribes operational guidelines for these key players at the national level. The National Ecotourism policy lays out cardinal principles suggesting the importance of involvement of local communities, minimizing conflicts between livelihoods and tourism, environmental and socio-cultural carrying capacities. This perceives that ET should be part of integrated development of the area. The policy emphasizes the role of careful planning in infrastructure development and a detailed benefit cost analysis prior to implementation. It talks about standards, continuous monitoring and codes of conduct for visitors. The policy is yet to come up with clear mechanisms to achieve these.

Some states have their own policies or regulations broadly catering to ecotourism, even though most of them do not have any institutional mechanism to manage ecotourism. We present a review of existing guidelines and policies in India in the backdrop of a diversity of institutions in the sector. Subsequently we arrive at recommendations that will be most suited for India's ecotourism sector.

Existing ET enterprises in India vary in their origin and scale of operation. They can be broadly categorized into the following – Government initiated and managed, Public sector corporate, Small-scale/individually owned, Self-Initiated and community managed, NGO initiated and community owned and Government supported and community managed. The policy needs for this variety of ventures in terms of regulations and incentives differ. Therefore we need policies and institutions, which can capture the diversity and take the sector through a sustainable path. Table 1 provides an overview of the strengths and weaknesses of existing policy documents related to ET in the country at national and state levels. It brings out the need for broad comparability of policies across states, even allowing for contexts to determine this to a great extent (mountains, coast, wildlife rich, etc). There is a clear picture of confusion that surrounds the states' definition of ET and their articulation of what they want to achieve—ET as a business proposition in MP, privileged access to public sector in Karnataka, to detailed institutional set up in HP and enabling decentralization in Kerala and Sikkim.

Table 1: Status of Existing Policy Initiatives in the Ecotourism Sector, India

Region	Policy Title	Objectives	Strengths	Weaknesses
India	Ecotourism in India: Policy and Guidelines 1998[7]	Same as general tourism; to be a unifying force and preserving natural and cultural heritage	Identify key players in ecotourism	No institutional set-up, fiscal incentives or community ownership.
Karnataka	Wilderness Tourism Policy 2003[8]	Opening up forest areas for ecotourism	A beginning	Public sector gets priority/monopolized access to forest areas
Kerala	Kerala Tourism Eco initiative 2004[9]	Eco-Certification Scheme to make each sub-sector within the tourism sector eco-friendly	One of the first standards issued by a state, intends to cover all sectors of tourism	Less stress on socio-cultural aspects including local employment, insufficient incentives for achieving the standards
	Conservation and Preservation of Areas Act 2005[10]	Avoid unsustainable tourism	Regulate unplanned growth of tourism	May conflict with the expected powers and rights of 'panchayathi raj' institutions
	Participatory Ecotourism programme by Forest Department 2005[11]	Promote participatory Ecotourism programme through EDC/VSS	Inter-departmental cooperation, financial assistance for establishing community ecotourism	Difficult procedural formalities involving many sanctioning authorities
Sikkim	Sikkim wildlife (Regulation of Trekking) Rules, 2005[12]	Regulate trekking activities in the state	Details penalties for offences and rewards for reporting offences	Confines only to trekking activities
	Singalila Ecotourism Promotion Zone, 2006	To promote sustainable community-based ecotourism with minimum negative impacts	Participatory enforcement of tourism regulations	Clear-cut monitoring methods need to emerge
Madhya Pradesh (MP)	Eco & Adventure Tourism Policy 2002[13]	Opening up forest areas for eco/adventure	A beginning	Stresses on adventure tourism and private sector. Lack of community involvement
Himachal Pradesh (HP)	Policy on Development of Ecotourism 2001[14]	Opening up forest areas for community-based ecotourism	Community involvement, well detailed institutional set up	Too much stress on trekking and less on other ecotourism activities

Policy Gaps in Ecotourism in India

From the policies compared here and from the on-going practices we analysed, the policy gaps in Indian ET sector can be identified as the following:

- *ET policies often conflict with policies of the Tourism sector*

  Tourism policies promote infrastructure development and recommend simplification of environmental regulations to attract large capital inflows. ET objective is to minimize new infrastructures and comply with all environmental regulations.

- *Role of Government and other institutions not specified*

  Except in Kerala, there has been no attempt to craft a nodal agency for ET, where the roles of different government departments are specified in any policy document.

- *Conservation – heavy and local benefits not emphasized*

  Due to the conceptual ambiguity in defining ET, most of the stakeholders, except forest department have not taken a proactive role. The result is an apparent conservation bias at the cost of local stakes.

- *Lack of community involvement*

  Even in cases where local community is projected as beneficiaries, benefits mostly confine to employment of a few locals as guides and cooks. Other forms of benefit sharing are nearly absent in the sector. Even the employment benefit could be higher if capacity building was considered as a prerequisite for assessing the eligibility of locals for different jobs.

- *Lack of clear and measurable indicators to monitor*

  Except for self-imposed regulations in specific activities (e.g., picking up waste thrown around while trekking, checking the number of plastic articles etc.) there are no clear guidelines for monitoring even the environmental impact. Impact on socio-cultural parameters remains unplanned and unmonitored so far.

- *Absence of links between monitoring and regulations/incentives*

  Wherever some regulations exist, they are not linked to continuous monitoring. Well-laid out incentives linked to regular monitoring and standards can streamline the connectivity between practices and policy.

Increasing commercial presence of ET in the country envisages evolving the existing broad guidelines into clearer regulations and institutions. The way to go ahead is to develop these guidelines into action plans, incorporating the missing components – institutional support, monitoring criteria, incentives and regulations. The identified gaps are interconnected and are the consequence of a lack of commonly accepted definition of ET. In the Indian context, policies cannot overlook the essential components of any ET venture in natural and cultural conservation, conservation education and rural livelihoods. National policies and guidelines should be drawn for this set of accepted goals of ET, within the purview of international environmental treaties and related Indian legislations, incorporating equity and fair trade principles. State wise regulatory institutions and regulations can be based on these guidelines, but should reflect grassroots ecological and cultural integrity. Extensive decision-making powers of local government institutions under schedule XI of Indian constitution could be made use of to ensure realization of the declared goals of ET. These constitutional rights need to be taken into account for negotiations under international agreements like GATS. These goals also envisage regular monitoring, facilitating regulations and implementing agencies.

V. Proposed Institutional Network

Figure 1 depicts the recommended framework of institutions and linkages for ET sector in India. State and national departments of tourism can host the nodal agencies to coordinate and regulate ET. These agencies should have deputed officials from related departments like Forests and Cultural affairs. Other departments should be invited in as and when needed by the nodal agency. For instance, to discuss a guideline for ET in a tribal belt, Ministry of Tribal Affairs should be involved; for waste management guidelines, Central Pollution Control Board and for incentive mechanisms, Ministry of Commerce/Finance should be represented.

National Ecotourism Directorate (NED)

The proposed nodal Agency at the center, National Ecotourism Directorate (NED), hosted by Ministry of Tourism can refine existing National Guidelines in the following lines:

- Remove ambiguity in the concept, definition and practice of ET. The NED can correct the imbalance across states by setting broad basic operational guidelines for all ET ventures.
- Groom ET as a successful industry, conservation driver and livelihood tool overcoming the self destructive tendencies evidenced by mass tourism.
- Help the industry leave minimum eco-cultural footprint and reap maximum socio-economic benefits.
- Mandate setting up of state level nodal institutions to facilitate and monitor ET sector.
- Suggest departments to be represented in the nodal ET institution at the center and the states.
- Suggest criteria to develop site specific indicators for monitoring.
- Suggest potential incentives linked to monitoring.
- Liaison with other departments for needed inputs and participation (e.g., upholding the rights of local self governments in matters of ET).
- Provide a platform for consultations on international agreements having implications on the sector.

Deliberating on the present situation wherein definition and practices of ET are nebulous, it is recognized that bringing all ecotourism initiatives on one platform is essential to keep a watch on their individual and collective impact. Thus the need for a formal operational channel in the state ET sector emerges. A nodal agency at the state can be the responsible government body to facilitate responsible tourism. The nodal agency at the state caould be State Ecotourism Directorate.

State Ecotourism Directorate (SED)

SED is supposed to clearly identify Ecotourism ventures falling under the purview of the definition elaborated in section I, which will be articulated in the guidelines from NED. It can legitimize through a process of registration, usage of the tag 'Ecotourism". SED can allow ratings/certification of enterprises based on well laid out criteria/indicators and encourage socio-ecologically responsible tourism by incentives linked to monitoring of natural and social impacts. It can adopt

Figure 2: Proposed Institutional Mechanisms and Linkages

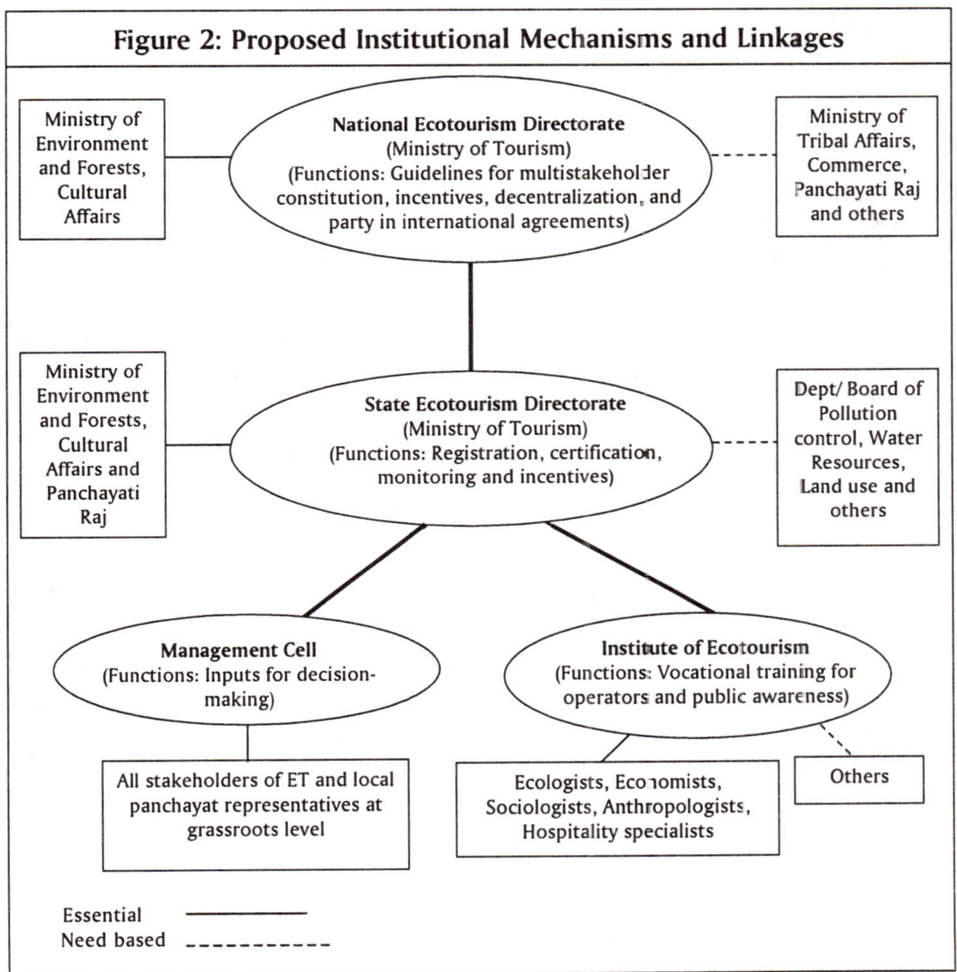

with needed improvements, existing guidelines (WWF, 2001) to assess feasibility of; and plan, develop and strengthen; community-based ventures. Potential Tasks of the SED include:

- A multi stakeholder agency, SED could be headed by an expert in managing social and natural resources.
- Set up ET management cell with representative natural and cultural resource managers and local institutions (*ex-officio:* agriculture, forests, rural development, culture, tribal, water, pollution control board, etc).

- The cell can assess and decide on proposals to be registered as ET enterprises based on relevant criteria and indicators, where consultations with local communities is mandatory.
- Prepare proposal format for ET, and associated procedures like when to mandate public hearing and consent from concerned local government agency.
- Develop (with guidance from the proposed Institute of Eco-Tourism) participatory monitoring processes based on indicators suggested by NED and link the performance/scores with ratings (certification) and incentives.
- Implement phased decentralization till district level, cognizant of constitutional and legal provisions for decentralized governance.
- Establish conflict resolution mechanisms so that participatory processes comes with efficiency, streamlined responsibilities, powers, constitution and regulations integrating essential components of ET.

Institute of Eco Tourism (IET) in the States

IET will be a vocational training and research agency to support SED in identifying capacity building needs of various models, prepare modules and conduct training/ courses and exposure visits. The institute could be a government or private or a joint effort with experienced trainers in all fields needed for ET practice. The purpose of IETs should be to

- Provide research and training support to the SED.
- Facilitate participatory monitoring and assessment of carrying capacity or 'Limits to Acceptable Change' in an ET destination. Basic indicators for the purpose are elicited in section VII.
- Suggest periodic revisions in regulations e.g., to prevent bio-piracy and cultural invasion in potential cases.
- Institute and analyze feed back mechanisms.
- Publish ET newsletter for dissemination of news and events.

Awareness campaigns on responsible travel (street plays, folk arts etc). IETs could spread mass awareness on responsible travel and tourism for sensitization of potential visitors so as to leave minimum impact in terms of ecology and culture. This could leverage on folk art forms and public media. Visitor's capacity as ecotourists can make them guardians of nature and culture and hence should be an important component in ET. IET can build capacity of the employees of ET sector. The identified capacity needs of the ET sector as follows:

- Feasibility assessment
- Writing ET proposals
- Environmental regulations
- Ecotourism policies and institutions
- Monitoring methods
- Marketing strategies
- Certification process
- Hospitality
- First aid
- Sanitation
- Naturalists/guides
- People to people contact (local content, reed rafts, folk music, rituals and cuisines)
- Waste Management Policies
- Guest profiling
- Visitor education.

VI. ET Co-Ordination and Enforcement in States

While NED can be largely a strategic and co-coordinating agency, SED needs to be pro-active and enforcing. SED will be responsible for streamlining processes involving registration, monitoring, certification and incentive mechanisms. The dichotomy between mass tourism and ET needs to be clarified by SED in distinctive terms taking the local natural and cultural thresholds.

Any one/society/company/foundation which wants to use the title eco-tourism should be registered under respective model (based on origin and scale, described in section IV) category with the SED. SED could be decentralized to help inclusive and speedy processing, in a phased manner till district level. Decisions (registration of a proposed ET venture, certification, incentives, monitoring etc.,) should be taken by a representative committee with officials from concerned departments in the proposed destination (e.g., pollution control board, water authority, revenue, land use, agriculture, horticulture) and concerned community representatives. The directorate would facilitate the realization of the concept of ET i.e., of nature and culture conservation, education and local ownership.

Certain areas with unique ecology or ethnicity could be declared by SED as 'ecotourism zones' to imply that all tourism activities in that locality shall confine to ecotourism. Initiative to declare eco-tourism zones can spearhead from the co-coordinating agency or any concerned agency/person and should be facilitated by the ET directorate in pursuing the processes involved.

Registration

Once SED receives a proposal for an ET venture, it needs to set up a decision-making committee for assessing the feasibility of the proposal, involving all concerned stakeholders. Therefore the first step envisaged in processing a proposal for ET registration is to identify the stakeholder groups. Later, in a time bound process, the proposal should be evaluated with necessary site visits, stakeholder consultations, and scientific assessment of potential ecological, socio-cultural and economic criteria under the guidance of the IET. A potential list of indicators under relevant criteria with methods of scoring is provided in section IV. A sub-set of these indicators with additions if found necessary, could be used for *ex-ante* assessment. Cut-off scores for certain indicators, based on location specific features and weightage have to be determined in a participatory manner by the management committee in consultation with IET. Based on the multi criteria assessment of any proposed ET enterprise, if the ecological and socio-cultural criteria score with respect to the cut-off limit, the proposal could be recommended by the decision making committee for registration to the ET director as an ecotourism enterprise. Registration fees could be differentially charged – nominal for community owned enterprises and highest for private corporate sector.

Regulations

1. Prior Informed Consent from the local governing bodies made mandatory for a proposal.
2. When deemed necessary as per the scale and impact of operation of the proposed model, the directorate shall conduct a public discussion on the social and environmental impact assessments and possible cultural fences.
3. Community owned ET models: Group of people applying for registration as ET enterprise should be registered in an appropriate category (society, trust, company etc.,) with the government. They also should have the approval of the local administration and should have well laid out bye-laws for equitable benefit sharing.
4. High-end tourism operators should be contributing a proportion of their profits to the local administration as a cess for using local ecosystem services. The quantum of conservation cess should be fixed by the SED in consultation with the management cell and IET. This cess should be ploughed back to conservation activities of the environment and local cultural traditions.

Monitoring

The approach to monitoring as in the case of assessment should be integrated and based on multiple criteria so as to cover the triple bottom line of eco-tourism. Multicriteria assessment/monitoring is needed for registration, certification or incentives. Enterprises can establish a monitoring procedure for self-evaluation. Indicators for which attaining a high score is practically difficult due to absence of systems or technology in place (e.g., solid waste management) should be taken up by the SED with concerned authorities for improving the system. SED will be responsible for monitoring the growth of the sector as a whole and to judge carrying capacity of the landscape along with the IET at regular intervals. SED should discuss the guidelines issued from time to time by the international Ecotourism society and NED and the rating criteria prescribed by various agencies to formulate needed indicators and regulations in the local context.

Certification

Certification allows inclusion of an enterprise as per request in a specific category of rating (e.g., five star or three or two stars) which should be linked to careful monitoring by the decision-making committee and IET, based on selected parameters and indicators. This is proposed in order to link ratings to price charged and incentives. Voluntary compliance based ratings already existing in the field may not fully achieve this. The categories can be identified with range of cut-off scores attached to each model in each of the three sets of criteria elaborated in the next section (ecological, socio-cultural and economic). Ratings should follow a process: application to SED, setting up a committee for site visits and valuation of the criteria. The committee will meet and discuss the scores under each of the three criteria and decide on granting certification with inputs from IET on cumulative rating under relevant criteria.

Incentives

1. Considering the societal benefit of ecotourism, these enterprises should be eligible for income tax relief. This incentive should be differentially distributed as minimum relief to the corporate and maximum to community owned initiatives. Incentives could be linked to the scores under social benefits especially to the indicators of employment and multiplier benefits. In essence, SED shall determine and utilize measures of direct and indirect societal benefits to provide differential fiscal incentives to models.

2. Part of investment cost in complying with selected input intensive parameters (e.g., rain water harvesting, non-conventional energy etc) could be extended as green loans under a subsidized lending rate. SED could recommend such lending schemes to the banking sector, based on the scores under economic criterion.

3. Operational eco-friendly inputs (like insecticides, fertilizers and water purifiers of organic origin or reviving endangered skills using local natural assets) should be considered for green subsidies to all registered ecotourism enterprises.

Capacity Building

The SED should facilitate capacity building through the IET for people involved in running the enterprises as also in sensitization of public on responsible travel and visits. SED and IET can guide advertising agencies to contextualize ET destinations in the light of the complete concept of ET. Support from IET in different aspects of Ecotourism helps in scientific monitoring as well as periodic assessment of policy needs.

VII. Criteria and Indicators for Assessment and Monitoring

The process of linking incentives to right practices in ecotourism has been discussed in the context of monitoring in the previous section. Now, the mechanism of selecting indicators for the relevant criteria for right practices is to be elicited. Indicators of the triple bottom-line of ecological sustainability, social sustainability and economic viability are used here based on our experience in different models of ET and a review of existing literature on the topic. The objective of the exercise is to see how can the ET practices comply with the accepted characteristics of ET. The indicators chosen here can only be indicative of a complete set of indicators for any model for the purpose of initial assessment of ET proposal, monitoring and certification of an on-going project, or in laying out targeted incentives and regulations. The methodology of monitoring spelt out here can be replicated by concerned stakeholders for any ET venture. For community ET enterprises like home-stays, as it is a supplementary livelihood and not an exclusive source of income/profit, the performance in economic indicators should not be the basis of decision-making. Profits are an essential but not at all a sufficient criterion for any model of ET.

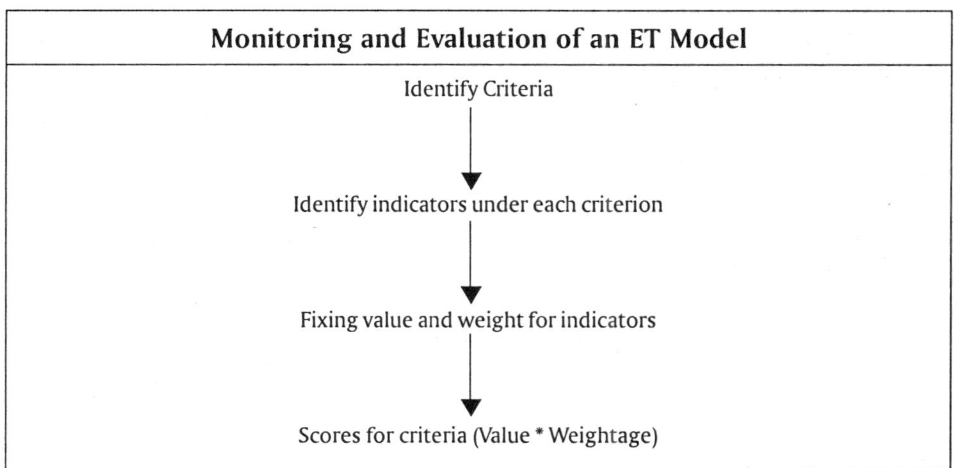

Value: is the measure of impact of the enterprise on various parameters based on observations and calculations. The value here is taken as ranging from -3 to 3. These values can be given appropriate weightage as their importance varies depending on the characteristics of immediate environment and operational conditions.

Weightage: is site specific; models compared here belong to different sites and hence are not weighted. But weightage is crucial when any one impact can have severe consequence e.g.: water pollution from houseboats can be weighed more than the use of imported material in boat construction.

Ranges of values for an indicator taken in the score tables below are as follows:

+3 = major positive impact

+2 = improvement

+1 = potential improvement

0 = no change/status quo

-1 = major negative impact

-2 = negative change

-3 = potential negative change

Monitoring the socio-ecological indicators is important for the sector not only in terms of assessing the impact but also for financial sustainability, as in many cases, the demand is related to ecological aspects like biodiversity (Naidoo and Adamowicz, 2005). The sample score tables provided here just demonstrates the process and can be used for identifying successful models in particular destinations. The numbers/scores are only indicative, in the absence of a focused participatory quantification effort.

Ecological Indicators (see Table 2 for scores)

1. *Topography* – alterations of the physical landscape during the inception and operation of the model.
2. *Air Quality* – activities like burning inorganic waste, fuels like kerosene, petrol, diesel etc.
3. *Noise*-Resulting from the use of generators, motors, engine, transport vehicles etc.

4. *Water Quantity* – per capita consumption of water and water conservation measures like rainwater harvesting.
5. *Water Quality* – activities like garbage disposal, runoff and wastewater discharge in local water bodies.
6. *Solid Waste Management* – scientific collection and disposal methods for solid waste.
7. *Terrestrial Flora* – introduction of invasive species like lantana, trekking, trampling etc, which affect the local flora.
8. *Terrestrial Fauna* – activities like excessive lighting, fire, smoke and noise, which affect the local fauna.
9. *Aquatic Flora and Fauna* – activities like angling, boating, fishing, water sports etc, which affects the aquatic biodiversity.
10. *Conservation Efforts* – reporting illegal activities to police, patrolling, energy conservation methods and generating awareness among locals.

Table 2: Sample Scoring of Ecological Indicators

Criteria	Indicators	Unweighted Score Across Models			
		Homestay	Public Sector	Co-Managed	Community Owned
Ecological	Topography	0	0	0	-1
	Air quality	-1	-1	-1	-1
	Noise	-1	-2	0	-1
	Water quantity	-1	-1	-1	-1
	Water quality	0	-1	0	0
	Solid waste management	2	1	-2	0
	Terrestrial flora	-1	-1	-1	-1
	Terrestrial fauna	-1	-2	0	0
	Aquatic flora & fauna	0	-1	0	0
	Conservation efforts	1	1	2	1
	Total	-2	-7	-3	-4

Socio-Cultural Indicators (see Table 3 for scores)

1. **Design** – habitat/tradition friendly design and materials.
2. **Local Art Forms** – support to local art forms like folk dance, music, theatre etc.
3. **Local Handicrafts** – promotion of local handicrafts by establishing gift shops etc.
4. **Local Cuisine** – emphasis on ethnic menu, using locally produced and indigenous ingredients.
5. **Culture** – impact of the activity on the overall life style of the local community, change in values and traditions.
6. **Education and Awareness of Guests** – on local resources by way of literature handouts, interpretation etc.
7. **Employment** – number of employees per bed/cottage.
8. **Leakages** – flow of benefits to outside communities e.g. purchase of commodities or services from outside the locality.

Table 3: Sample Scoring of Socio-Cultural Indicators

Criteria	Indicators	Unweighted Score Across Models			
		Homestay	Public Sector	Co-Managed	Community Owned
Socio/Cultural	Design	2	0	2	2
	Local art form	0	0	1	0
	Local handicrafts	1	0	0	0
	Local cuisine	0	0	0	1
	Culture	1	0	1	1
	Education/Awareness	2	1	1	1
	Employment	1	3	2	1
	Leakages	-1	-2	3	2
	Multiplier effect on local economy	0	1	1	1
	Equity in benefit sharing	0	0	2	0
	Domestic tourist	1	1	1	2
	Total	**7**	**4**	**14**	**11**

9. **Multiplier Effect on Local Economy** – activities generating indirect benefits like taxi/auto, shops etc.
10. Equitable distribution of direct and indirect benefits among the stake holding communities.
11. Proportion of domestic tourists to foreign visitors.

Economic Indicators (see Table 4 for scores)

1. Profit (% of average annual profits).
2. Gestation Period – number of years to break even.
3. Occupancy – average occupancy per year.
4. Living standards – change in public health, literacy etc.
5. Competition – number of competitors in the vicinity.

Table 4: Sample Scoring of Economic Indicators

Criteria	Indicators	Unweighted Score Across Models			
		Homestay	Public Sector	Co-Managed	Community Owned
Economic	Profit	1	3	2	2
	Gestation Period	2	1	1	2
	Occupancy	1	3	2	1
	Living Standards	1	1	2	1
	Competition	0	1	2	0
	Total	**5**	**9**	**9**	**6**

Scores for the three criteria can be compared between enterprises or models in and across any site. The decision on the cut-off level for each criteria and the relative importance of any of the criteria for making a decision on any venture needs to be discussed by concerned stakeholders in the specific context as discussed in the previous section. Table 5 provides the consolidated scores for demonstration.

Table 5: Sample of Consolidated Scores under the Three Criteria

Criteria	Homestay	Public Sector	Co-Managed	Community
Ecological	-2	-7	-3	-4
Socio-Cultural	7	4	14	11
Economic	5	9	9	6
Total	**10**	**6**	**20**	**13**

Role of economic criterion among the three selected criteria is only in ensuring that ET is not a loss making enterprise. Once this is ensured, this criterion need not be instrumental in making a choice between enterprises or models. Scores of ecological and socio-economic criteria should be the basis for decisions once the economic indicator is positive.

VIII. Concluding Recommendations

The paper recommends establishing National and State Ecotourism Directorates. National Ecotourism Directorate shall be mandated to provide uniform and inclusive definition of ecotourism across states, guidelines on multi-stakeholder constitution of state directorates, guidelines on criteria to monitor and on incentives. It will provide inputs on constitutional provisions for decentralized governance and international negotiations in ET. State Ecotourism Directorate is supposed to set up a management cell and streamline processes for the following tasks – of developing indicators for assessment and monitoring in line with accepted goals, of assessing proposals, registering enterprises, certifying and monitoring ET ventures, facilitating establishment of Institute of Ecotourism and designing a cess on natural capital used in high end tourism. SED can be instrumental in identifying and establishing exclusive eco-tourism zones in each state.

Acknowledgement

Authors wish to acknowledge the support provided by BHC, New Delhi and inputs from their colleagues at the Center for Conservation Governance and Policy, ATREE

Notes

1 The World Ecotourism Summit, Quebec, Canada (2002) Online document at URL *http://www.world-tourism.org/sustainable/IYE/quebec/anglais/declaration.html*

2 Nepal Tourism Board (2004): *National strategy and marketing programme of Nepal.* Online document at URL *http://discovernepal.com.np/pdf/national/Eco2004.pdf*

3 Tourism Authority of Thailand (1997): *Ecotourism Policy and Plans.* Available at URL: *http://conservation.forest.ku.ac.th/ecotourdb/english/P_P/PP.htm*

4 Sri Lanka Ecotourism Foundation. Online document at URL *http://www.ecotourism srilanka.net/pgs/about.htm*

5 Tsung-Wei, Lai (1995): Ecotourism in Australia. *Ecotourism Book.* (pp. 270-276)

http://www.apo-tokyo.org/gp/e_publi/gplinkeco/34chapter32.pdf

6 Marshall, V (2004): Assessing the possible local community benefits from ecotourism operations in Kenya. Online document at URL *http://www.uga.edu/juro/2004/marshall.htm*

7 Ministry of Tourism, Government of India. (1998): *Ecotourism in India –Policy and guidelines.*

8 Online document at URL *http://www.karnatakawildernesstourism.org/WLPolicy.htm* Wilderness Tourism Policy 203, Karnataka.

9 Online document at URL *http://www.keralatourism.org:8080/keralatourism/sidenews/ecokerala/Eco.htm* Eco-Kerala –Kerala Tourism Eco-Initiative 2004.

10 Online document at URL *http://www.keralatourism.org/index.php?zone=4&menu=29&* Conservation and Preservation of Areas Act 2005, Kerala.

11 Participatory Eco-tourism Programme undertaken by the Forest Department. Department of Tourism Government of Kerala. 2005.

12 Online document available at URL *http://www.tmi-india.org/sikkimtrekkingregulations.pdf* Sikkim wildlife (Regulation of Trekking) Rules.

13 Online document at URL *http://www.mptourism.com/wn/ecopolicy.pdf* Eco & Adventure Tourism Policy 2002, MP.

14 Online document at URL *http://hpforest.nic.in/eco3.htm* Policy on Development of Ecotourism in Himachal Pradesh 2001.

References

Batta, R N (2000): *Tourism And The Environment: A Quest for Sustainability.* Indus Publishing Company, New Delhi.

Brewer, G D and deLeon, P (1983): *The Foundations of Policy Analysis.* The Dorsey Press: Homewood, III.

Butler, R W (1980): The concept of tourism area cycle of evolution: implications for management of resources. *Canadian Geographer* 24 (1), pp 5-12.

Edward, S N, McLaughlin, W J and Ham, S H (1998): *Comparative Study of Ecotourism Policy in the Americas.* University of Idaho, Organisation of American States.

FAO (1997): *Ecotourism and other services derived from forests in the Asia-Pacific Region.*

George, E W and Reid, D G (2005): The Power of Tourism: A Metamorphosis of Community Culture. *Journal Of Tourism and Cultural Change.* 3(2), pp 88–107.

Heinz, E and Kenneth, P (1973): *Labyrinths of Democracy: Adaptations, Linkages, Representation, and Policies in Urban Politics.* Indianapolis: Bobbs-Merrill.

Jafari, J (1996): World Conference on Sustainable Tourism. *Annals of Tourism Research.* 23(4), pp 958-960.

Li, W and Han, N (2001): Ecotourism management in China's Nature Reserves. *AMBIO: A Journal of the Human Environment.* 30(1), pp 62-63.

Martin, B S and Uysal, M (1990): An Examination of the Relationship Between Carrying Capacity and the Tourism Lifecycle: Management and Policy Implications. *Journal of Environmental Management.* 31 (4), pp 327-333.

Naidoo, R and Adamowicz, W L (2005): Biodiversity and Nature based tourism at forest reserve in Uganda. *Environment and Development Economics.* 10, pp 159-178.

Patten, C V and Sawicki, D S (1993): *Basic Methods of Policy Analysis and Planning.* Prentice Hall.

Tandi, D (2004): Sustainability of Tourism in Bhutan. *Journal of Bhutan Studies* 3(1), pp 84-104.

The International Ecotourism Society (TIES) (1998): *Ecotourism Statistical Fact Sheet.* Online document at URL: *http://www.ecotourism.org/research/stats/files/stats.pdf*

World Tourism Organization UNWTO (2005): *Tourism Highlights.*

Online document at URL *http://www.world-tourism.org/facts/menu.html*

Wood, M E (2002): *Ecotourism: Principles, Practices and Policies for Sustainability.* United Nations Environment Programme, United Nations Publication. pp 1-32.

WWF International. (2001): Guidelines for community-based ecotourism development. pp 1-28.

6

Religious Tourism: An Overview

V Partha Sarathy

Religious tourism generates revenue in a way as no other kind of tourism does. It has a distinct edge over other kinds of tourism due to the pull of huge crowds in the form of tourists. There are various levels of religious tourism—international, national and regional. The article gives a perspective of religious tourism with respect to Hinduism, Buddhism, Islam, Christianity, Sikhism and Jainism.

Religious tourism has its own appeal, due to a variety of reasons. Firstly, it is widely believed that the places of worship have a special power, and what certifies this is the many miracles that are reported by people visiting these places. Secondly, the popular places of religion are pieces of monumental architecture and beautiful art. Many spiritual seekers, after reaching the religious centers, have obtained sublime levels of metaphysical consciousness.

Religious tourism is a big revenue generator for different countries. The tourism sector employs the largest workforce in the world. Religious tourism draws huge crowds in the form of tourists and hence has an edge over other kinds of tourism. No stone is left unturned when it comes to promotion of places having religious sanctity and significance.

Source: The Icfai Journal of Services Marketing, March 2006.

People of different faiths move to pilgrim centers during different occasions. There are various levels of religious tourism—international, national, regional and micro-level religious tourism. People of Islamic faith, for example, travel to Mecca in Saudi Arabia, from all over the world, as it is the holiest place for them. Similarly, Vatican City and Jerusalem draw Christians from all over the world.

When we talk of religious tourism, India must have the most prominent place, as it is the birthplace of so many faiths. It is the land of many famous temples and pilgrim sites, with religious tourism active throughout the year. Even then, it has been observed that pilgrimages peak only during the holy festivals. Rath Yatra in Puri is celebrated during the Hindu month of Ashadha[1]. Brahmotsavam, a religious procession in one of the richest temples of the world, i.e., Lord Venkateswara temple at Tirupati, is held in the Vaishakha[2] month every year. These two events attract lakhs of devotees every year. See Exhibit 1 for more details.

Exhibit 1: Indian Pilgrimage Sites where Devotees Assemble in Large Numbers for an Occasion

Place	State	Occasion	Sanctity
Basar-Saraswati[3] Temple	Andhra Pradesh	Around beginning of academic year	People make trips with their children to invoke the blessings of mother for speedy progress in academics
Kailash Mansarovar	Nepal	June-August	To pay homage to Lord Shiva
Amarnath Caves	J&K	July-September	To pay homage to Lord Shiva
Sabarimala	Kerala	December-January	To visit Ayyappa temple
Puri Jagannath temple	Orissa	June-July	The annual Rath yatra
Mantralayam	Andhra Pradesh	Month of Shravan[4]	Raghavendra Swami, a guru revered by Kannadigas, attained Moksha[5] during this month
Bhadrachalam	Andhra Pradesh	Month of Chaitra[6]	Birthday of Lord Rama, a Hindu God
Ajmer	Rajasthan	7th month of Islamic Lunar calendar	Urs festival to commemorate the death of the Sufi Saint Khwaja Moinuddin Chisti[7]

It is also observed that there is group travel. People of a particular community make elaborate plans and make visits to the holy places of their faith. Jains, for example, make such trips to Mount Abu and other important places.

There are again pilgrimage centers, which attract pilgrims throughout the year. These being Shirdi, Haridwar, Udupi, Kashi, Varanasi, Ujjain, Mathura, Golden Temple at Amritsar, Madurai Meenakshi temple, Srisailam, etc.

Private tour operators and tourism corporations run their customized package tours to help pilgrims. APSRTC[8] for example conducts South India, Shirdi and Tirupati tours in air-conditioned Volvo buses, which has drawn a favorable response from the pilgrims. The Indian Railways also chips in during the peak seasons, i.e., during festivals such as Brahmotsavam and Pushkarams by running special trains.

While a general overview has been presented so far, let us now look at religious tourism attractions of various religions, the initiatives of the state and some interesting facts about them.

Hinduism

Hinduism is the third largest faith amongst the world religions, but it has the largest number of religious places due to the multiplicity in the faith itself. There are many gods and goddesses in the religion, and hence, there are different temples and festivals that are celebrated with much fanfare.

From a tourism perspective, it has been observed that festivals such as Kumbh Mela (celebrated once in 12 years), Brahmotsavam (Tirupati-annually), Makar Jyoti (Sabarimala-annually) and Rath Yatra (Puri-annually) are big draws. In fact, the Kumbh Mela is said to be the largest congregation of humans in a single place. Such is the sanctity and popularity of this festival.

Melas

Melas are a vital part of the pilgrimage tradition of Hinduism. Celebrating a mythological event in the life of a deity or an auspicious astrological period, the melas attract enormous numbers of pilgrims from all over the country.

Kumbh Mela

Figure 1: Kumbh Mela

Source: www.zenzibar.com

The biggest of the melas, the Kumbh Mela (Figure 1), is a riverside festival held at four important places once every 12 years. The holy towns associated with the Kumbh Mela are Allahabad (at the confluence of Rivers Ganga, Yamuna and the mythical Saraswati), Nasik (on the banks of river Godavari), Ujjain (on the banks of River Sipra) and Haridwar (on the banks of Ganga). More than ten million pilgrims (13 million visited Allahabad in 1977 and over 18 million in 1989) usually attend the Allahabad and Haridwar festivals thus making Kumbh Mela the largest religious gathering in the world[9].

The year 2004 saw the Kumbh Mela, at Ujjain, attract 30 million people from across the world including saints, devotees and tourists[10].

Encouragement from the government has to be analyzed with respect to the arrangements made for the festival. For example in 2004, the arrangements made by Madhya Pradesh Government for the Kumbh Mela would be an interesting exercise in itself.

The sacred site near Ujjain Kumbh was divided into four zones and ten sectors for the devotees. Water supply was made through 74 kms long pipelines. Four power sub-stations were set-up for the Mela Township. Besides, new ghats[11] were constructed and old ones renovated on the banks of the Sipra. A signage system was also scientifically designed to facilitate easy movement of pilgrims.[12]

Ganga Sagar Mela

Held annually in West Bengal, is the largest fair held annually on the Sagar Island at the confluence of River Ganga and the Bay of Bengal at the time of Makar Sankranti in mid-January. Lakhs of sadhus and pilgrims congregate here from all over the country to visit the Kapil Muni Temple and to take a holy dip in the sea.

Exhibit 2: Godavari Pushkarams
Godavari Pushkaram takes place for a period of 12 days in Andhra Pradesh once in 12 years. In this connection, pilgrims from throughout India attend in large numbers, take a holy dip, do charity, perform rituals and visit temples at various places on the banks of the river in the East and West Godavari districts in Andhra Pradesh, besides some parts in Telangana like Bhadrachalam, Kaleswaram, Dharmapuri and Basar.
Source: http://apgodavaripushkar.nic.in

Exhibit 3: RTC Special Buses for Pushkarams
As many as 2,289 special buses were operated from various places in the State by the APSRTC during the recently concluded Pushkarams.
Source: http://www.hindu.com

Festivals

Onam Festival

Onam is the harvest festival, celebrated throughout Kerala in August-September, to welcome the yearly homecoming of the legendary King 'Mahabali' who was generous, just and kind. People decorate their homes, wear new clothes and hold special games and competitions.

Exhibit 4: Onam Festival

Onam is the most important national festival of Kerala and falls in the month of Chingam (August-September). It is the harvest festival of Kerala. There are several legends regarding its origin. The most popular legend is that Mahabali, the legendary king who ruled over Kerala in an age of plenty, was pushed down to the infernal regions by Lord Vishnu in the form of Vamana, returns to see his people once a year.

The celebration of Onam as a national festival was taken up as the Government initiative in 1961. The celebrations start formally on the day of Atham asterism[13] (13th star in the Lunar scheme of stars (There are 27 stars in a lunar month)). Onam has certain social aspects also. It provides an occasion for the family get-together for the Keralites. The head of the family presents clothes as gift (Onapudava) to the junior members, servants and tenants.

Apart from these social aspects of Onam, there are certain recreational and other aspects associated with the festival. Karadikali, Pulikali, Kuttiyum Kolum are some of the major recreational events performed by the people on the Onam occasion. There are some games peculiar to the womenfolk, such as Thiruvathirakali, Kummi, Mudiyattom Kali, Oonjal Swinging etc. The non-Hindus of the State also celebrate Onam with all the carnival spirit and therefore, it is a perfect example for the religious harmony of the state.

Source: http://www.kerala.gov.in/history&culture/festivals.htm

Onam being the state festival, the tourism week is also celebrated with it. The streets of the capital are illuminated. Various cultural and traditional programs are staged at Kanakakunnu Palace and selected premises of the city. The tourism week concludes with a grand and colorful procession where floats and folk performances from every part of Kerala are presented[14].

The state government conducts Tourism Week celebrations in connection with Onam, showcasing the gems of Kerala's culture. Onam resonates with carnivals, boat races, dance, music and feast[15].

Durga Puja

One of the most important and popular festivals is the Durga Puja. It is celebrated throughout the country, but with great grandeur in West Bengal[16]. The festival is connected to the legend of Mother Durga (the female goddess) who vanquished Mahishasura (a mythical demon). There are some ancestral houses in Kolkata, the capital city of West Bengal, where Durga Puja is being observed over decades and even over centuries. During Durga Puja, the West Bengal Tourism bodies conduct tours to traditional pujas at heritage houses in the mornings and afternoons and to puja pandals through the night.

Exhibit 5: Bid to Package Durga Puja as Tourism Event

An effort to package the Durga Puja festival of West Bengal and sell it as an event to the overseas tourist is being planned by the Union Tourism Ministry.

While corporates have shown eagerness to sponsor some of their clients as well as their staff to the event, a presentation has also been made at Baltimore on the occasion of the North American Bengali Conference. "Non-resident Bengalis have shown eagerness to send their children to be here during the Durga Pujas so as to experience the flavor of the land of their origin," M V Iyengar said.

The city's top hotels—Oberoi Grand and ITC Sonar Bangla—have agreed to be partners in this project while Indian Airlines and Air India have also agreed to promote it and publicise the event through posters and films on their inbound flights, M V Iyengar said. "If Mardi Gras and Munich Beer Festival can attract tourists, there is no reason why Durga Puja cannot do so with some planning and coordination."

The tourists would be taken around some of the 3,000 pandals that come up during the four-day extravaganza.

The product has been priced at $750 per head for overseas visitors and at Rs.27,000 for their domestic counterparts.

Tourist arrival at the city airport stood at 68,186 in 2003 calendar against 61,429 in 2002.

Source: The Hindu Business Line, July 17, 2004.

Navratri

Navratri, literally nine nights, is celebrated for ten days preceding the festival of Dussehra—usually in October. The most eagerly awaited festival of the year, which celebrates the harvest time, Navratri is an occasion when both rural and urban Gujaratis worship the nine incarnations of the Mother Goddess, Shakti, denoting cosmic energy.

The state government of the western state of Gujarat has been promoting the Navratri Festival in a big way to attract tourists and investment. In the year 2003, it organized[17] 'Vibrant Gujarat: Global Investors Summit', a three-day meet comprising a series of conventions, exhibitions and seminars aimed at creating awareness about investment opportunities in the state, to coincide with the International Navratri Festival (INF), pegged as the biggest cultural extravaganza.

Reliance Industries Ltd. tied-up as the main sponsors for the planned INF. TCGL (Tourism Corporation of Gujarat Ltd.) also undertook a major publicity campaign which included editorial coverage in leading travel magazines like *Conde Nast, Traveller, Natal, High Life* etc., in Europe, USA, South Africa, Middle-East and South East Asia to attract foreign tourists. Additionally, they also created a website *www.navratrifestival.com* for the event.

Exhibit 6: Singapore Airlines Pitches in for Gujarat Tourism

All set to become the first international airline to fly from Gujarat with direct Ahmedabad-Singapore flights from July 28, 2004, SIA plans to join hands with Gujarat's tourism department to pitch the state as a destination for the foreign traveler.

B K Ong, General Manager, India, Singapore Airlines (SIA), asserted that Gujarat would appeal not only to those looking for heritage tourism, but also adventure and eco-tourism thanks to various sanctuaries like Nalsarovar and Gir. It has a rich cultural heritage and can be pushed as a religious tourism destination through fairs and festivals like Navratri and the kite festival.

Source: Times of India, July 14, 2004.

Pilgrimages

Kailash Mansarovar Pilgrimage

Every year thousands of pilgrims make their way to the Kailash Mansarovar (Figure 2) which is located in the western region of Tibet. It is considered to be one of the most difficult pilgrimages in the world. The circumference of Mansarovar is 88 kms, its depth is 90 metres and total area is 320 sq kms[18].

The Ministry of External Affairs (MEA) of the Government of India organizes the pilgrimage to Kailash Mansarovar through the Indian side along with other agencies like the Kumaon Mandal Vikas Nigam (KMVN)[19].

Figure 2: Kailash Mansarovar

Source: www.shaivam.org

All those who would like to go on pilgrimage to Kailash have to apply subsequent to the call for applications published in leading dailies in the month of February. Yatris are selected at random from the received applications. The yatra is conducted in 16 batches, each batch having a maximum of 36 yatris. The yatra season starts in early June and the last batch starts the pilgrimage as late as end of August.

Amarnath Yatra

The annual Amarnath Yatra is a pilgrimage to caves of Amarnath accessible only during the months of June to August[20]. About a lakh and half pilgrims travel to the Amarnath caves passing through many obstacles. The caves are located in a narrow ravine at the far end of the Lidder valley and stands 3,888 meters above sea level. It is located 363 kilometers from Jammu via Pahalgam. One can also travel to Amarnath via Baltal, but that route is a little longer at 414 kms. The most commonly used route is via picturesque Pahalgam, located 96 kms from Srinagar. It takes about four or five days to cover the distance to the caves and back. About 3,500 yatris proceeded from Jammu towards the holy shrine, in 2004. Around 80% traveled via Pahalgam; the rest through Baltal. The Government of India makes elaborate arrangements for security, stay and travel for pilgrims.

The Temples

Sri Venkateswara (Balaji) Temple

Figure 3: Tirupati Temple

Source: www.indianslivingabroad.com

With a history that dates back to over 12 centuries, the shrine of Lord Venkateswara at Tirupati (Figure 3) is among the most visited temples in India and one of the world's richest.

Legend has it that Lord Vishnu (Venkateswara) had come down to earth in search of Lakshmi, his consort in a human form, to the hills of Tirupati[21]. The search culminates in marriage to his consort Lakshmi, who assumes the form of Padmavati.

It is said that at Tirumala, Lord Vishnu grants the wish of anyone who offers him their weight in something, be it gold, fruit, cloth, or whatever. Pilgrims who make such an offering and ask a boon or blessing generally return (after the fulfillment of their wish) and make another offering to the Lord, in acknowledgement of his kindness.

The worship in the temple is performed by Sri Sampradaya Vaishnava Brahmins, in the line of Ramanaujacharya[22].

It is the most visited temple in India and one of the most visited religious places in the world. This magnificent temple is located 20 kms up a hill from Tirupati. It is a very peaceful place and coming to this temple is a very awe-inspiring and devotional experience. On an average over 25,000 people visit daily, and on festival days the number goes up to over 100,000[23]. The temple administration has created many facilities to serve the pilgrims, such as:

- **Sudarshan Token:** It is a novel way of reducing the waiting period for darshan. Earlier pilgrims had to face hardships as they did not know the possible time of the darshan due to the long serpentine queues. The long queues also meant administrative problems for the temple administration.

The Sudarshan token system is a boon in such a scenario. Now the pilgrims can know well in advance the day as well as the time of the darshan. Pilgrims can also get the Sudarshan token from places outside Tirupati through online booking. Centers such as Hyderabad and Visakhapatnam have Tirumala Tirupati Devasthanam (TTD[24]) offices where tokens can be taken in advance (upto one month). Essentially, the Sudarshan token is a barcoded-computerized wristband, which is tied around the wrist of the pilgrims indicating the possible time when they could have their darshan[25] at Tirumala. The time is fixed by the Sudarshan counters set-up both at Tirupati and Tirumala, which would work in close tandem with the Tirumala temple in assessing the crowd level and the time factor.

- **e-Seva:** IT-based facility which the TTD has introduced, is basically a pilgrim amenity through which online booking of different seva[26] tickets and reservation of cottages could be done in advance by the pilgrims from their places. A particular percentage of tickets and accommodation is set apart for the pilgrims. It is a leap in the usage of IT by the TTD towards ensuring a hassle-free booking system.

The TTD also closely interacts with both individual management experts and IT gurus and also with corporate bodies and leading management consultants like Tata Consultancy Services, Indian Institute of Information Technology, Bangalore, ISO, CFTRI[27], RITES[28], L&T[29].

Puri Jagannath Temple

The Jagannath temple at Puri (Figure 4) is one of the oldest and most revered temples in India. It attracts thousands of pilgrims, but the highlight is the Rath Yatra. Devotees celebrate this day as it was on this day that Lord Krishna, vanquished his evil uncle Kamsa and then gave them darshan in Mathura in a chariot with his brother, Balaram.[30]

Figure 4: Puri

Source: www.vaisnava.cz

Rath Yatra (Festival of Chariots) is conducted once in a year at many places in the country, but the Puri Rath Yatra is one of its own kind in terms of participation and grandeur. Deities of Lord Jagannatha, Balabhadra and Lady Subhadra are carried out of the temple to their carts with the beating of drums. It is grand festival and the biggest event in the whole of Orissa. It is only during the 'Ratha Yatra festival', the big images of deities can be seen by all including non-Hindus[31].

About 5,00,000 people had gathered to take part in the festival in the year 2001[32] and it continues to rise every year.

Exhibit 7: Rath Yatra
The Rath Yatra of Lord Jagannath is also known as Yatra and Ghosha Yatra. These festivals are held on "Ashadha sukla dwitiya", i.e., the second day of the bright fortnight of ashadha (June-July) every year. This Ratha Yatra symbolizes that after a long time of separation, Lord Shri Krishna is going to Kuruksetra from Dwaraka to meet the inhabitants of Brindavan. Three different sizes of chariots are made for this Rath Yatra which begins from the Lord Jagannath Temple. The Chariot of the Lord Jagannath is called Nandighosh, the Chariot of Balabhadra is called Taladvaja, the Chariot of Lady Subhadra is called Padmadhvaja. Nearly one thousand devotees are needed to pull these chariots with the help of four ropes which are tied to each chariot and has no steering system on it.
Source: http://jagannathpuri.com/jprathayatra.asp

The Sabarimala Shrine

The Sabarimala shrine of Swami Ayappa[33] is situated in Kerala and is open only a few times each year. This being the Mandalam festival covering 41 days from November 15 to December 26, the Makaravilakku from January 1-14, on Vishu, the day of the vernal equinox in April, and during smaller festivals in May/June and August/September[34]. It attracts lakhs of devotees every year. The shrine is most famous for the Makar Jyoti[35] observed on the day when the sun starts its course from north (January 14).

Buddhism

Pre-eminent among all the Buddhist pilgrimage sites, both old and new, is Bodh Gaya, the place where The Buddha attained enlightenment (Figure 5). The other prominent places being Lumbini where Lord Buddha was born, Saranath, where he gave his first teachings; and Kushinagar, where he passed away.

These places attract a large number of tourists from China, Japan and the South-East Asian countries. There are some important pilgrim centers in Sri Lanka, as Sri Lanka was very much influenced from the halcyon days of King Ashoka who spread the message of Buddhism.

Figure 5: Lord Buddha Statue at Bodh Gaya

Source: http://sangha.net

Lumbini in Nepal, the birthplace of Lord Buddha, is a very important tourism attraction. The state capital of Magadha at the time of the Buddha, Rajgir was the place where the Mauryan King Bimbisara, was converted into Buddhism. The Buddha was especially fond of the beautiful Gridhakuta (Vulture Peak) for his meditations at sunset.

Promotional Efforts: The Government of India has formulated a comprehensive plan for the Buddhist circuit. It consists of important places in Bihar, Orissa and Andhra Pradesh. There are many important pilgrim centers such as Bodh Gaya, Rajgir, Kushinagar etc. Orissa, for instance, has a number of important Buddhist sites and the tourism department has developed a package for the "Buddhist tourism circuit". This package covers important Buddhist sites in Orissa, including Dhauli near Bhubaneshwar that was the site of the famous Kalinga war in 261 BC. The government is in the process of developing a 'Peace Park' in this region[36].

Exhibit 8: Buddhist Circuit

- The holy tree at Bodh Gaya (Figure 5), Sarnath, where the Buddha gave his first sermon, and Kushinagar where he attained Parinirvana.
- The ruins of Nalanda, Vaishali, the site, where he preached his last sermon, and announced his impending Nirvana.
- In Sanchi, the Great Stupa, temples and pillars.
- Amaravati and Nagarjunakonda in Andhra Pradesh, are the last destinations of the journey.

Source: www.hindunet.org/yatra/tourism/circuits/buddha.htm

Exhibit 9: Jet Airways Plans Buddhist Circuit Package

Private carrier Jet Airways is exploring the possibility of introducing a special Buddhist circuit tourist package covering India, Sri Lanka and Nepal.

Source: www.deccanherald.com/deccanherald/jun252004/n15.asp

Islam

Figure 6: Ka'abah—the Holy Center of Islam

Source: www.bible.ca

Founded by Muhammad Prophet, Islam has a worldwide following. Ka'abah (Figure 6) the holiest center of Islam, is visited by lakhs of pilgrims every year from all over the world. Muslims make it a point to visit Mecca at least once in their lifetime. The unique culture and understanding of the universe marks the architecture of the mosques. The concept of formlessness has been imbibed as can be seen by round domes.

The Holy Pilgrimage of Haj

This ritual represents one of the peak experiences in the life of a Muslim. The Haj or pilgrimage is made to the sacred places of Islam in and around Mecca (Holy City Mecca in Saudi Arabia with 1.4 million inhabitants—2003 estimate). Once in a lifetime every Muslim, man or woman, is expected (unless it is impossible) to make a pilgrimage (a Haj) to Mecca. The pilgrimage becomes special for the devotee when he enters into a radius of 10 kilometers from Mecca. This state of holiness and purity is also known as *Ihram*. The devotee dons special garments consisting of two white seamless sheets that are wrapped around the body.

The pilgrim should visit the holy center during the sacred month Dhu-al-Hijja[37] so as to enter with thousands of others into the annual mass observance of the circumambulation of the Ka'abah, the Lesser and Greater pilgrimages and the Great Feast[38].

Ka'abah, the center of Islam, is a rectangular building made of bricks. Around the Ka'abah is the great mosque, Al-Haram, and around the mosque, in between the mountains, are the houses that make up Mecca[39].

The principal ceremonies in Mecca begin with circumambulation of the Ka'aba. The pilgrims start at the Black Stone and run around the building three times fast and four times slowly, stopping each time at the southeast corner to kiss the Black Stone, or to touch it with hand or stick, or perhaps just look keenly at it, depending on the crowd.

The next observance is the Lesser Pilgrimage, which consists of trotting, with shoulders shaking, seven times between Safa and Marwa, two low hills across the valley from each other—this observance is in imitation of frantic Hagar[40] seeking in despair for water for wailing little Ishmael[41].

On the eighth day of Dhu-al-Hijja, the Greater Pilgrimage begins. The pilgrims in a dense mass move off towards Arafat (Muhammad linked certain of the ancient Meccan rituals with the Haj pilgrimage to Mt. Arafat and declared the city a center of Muslim pilgrimage. He also dedicated it to the worship of Allah alone[42]), nine miles to the east. They spend the night at Mina, at the half-way point. The next day, they all arrive at the Arafat plain. The pilgrims participate in a prayer service conducted by an imam.

Saudi Airlines does a commendable job in promoting the place and also has provided many facilities for the pilgrims who wish to travel to the holy city.

In India, The Haj Committee commonly known as Central Haj Committee[43] (CHC) has been established under the Haj Committee Act 2002, for making arrangements for the pilgrimage of Muslims for Haj. It announces the issue of applications; the committee also fixes up the quota for each state. The applications are closely scrutinized and then through the 12 embarkation points, sufficient arrangements are made for the safe departure of the pilgrims.

As per the latest developments for Haj Pilgrims, direct flights to Medina have been arranged. This means that 27,000 people can now fly to Medina from various Indian destinations unlike earlier when they had to come to Saudi Arabia's Jeddah airport and then proceed to Medina after visiting Mecca[44].

Subsidy

The Indian government has also given subsidies to the Indian Muslims traveling to Saudi Arabia for the holy pilgrimage. Tables 1 and 2 give more insight into the same.

In terms of percentage, the subsidy has increased from the year 2002 to 2003, but the important point to note is the steep rise in the price of travel fare.

Table 1: Amount of Subsidy Provided to Haj Pilgrims by the Government of India (2001 to 2003)

Year	Fare per Pilgrim (Rupees)	Subsidy Paid by the Government (per Pilgrim) (Rupees)	No. of Haj Pilgrims	Total Amount of Subsidy (Rupees)
2001	33,000*	21,000*	71,215	149.55 cr*
2002	35,300*	23,300*	70,298	163.80 cr*
2003	40,685*	28,685*	69,721	200.00 cr*

Note : * Provisional.

Year : Period of fiscal year in India is April to March, e.g., year shown as 1990-91 relates to April 1990 to March 1991.

Units : (a) 1 Lakh (or Lac) = 100000.
(b) 1 Crore (or cr.) = 10000000.

Source: Lok Sabha Unstarred Question No. 2811, March 10, 2003.

Table 2: Number of Haj Pilgrims Ferried by Air India/Indian Airlines and Saudi Arabian Airlines (2001 to 2003)

Embarkation	2003			2002			2001		
Point	Flights	Pilgrims	Operator	Flights	Pilgrims	Operator	Flights	Pilgrims	Operator
Ahmedabad	16	4448	SV	21	5997	SV	22	7215	AI
Bangalore	9	3619	AI	10	4076	AI	16	4988	AI
Chennai	7	2820	AI	7	2786	AI	10	2983	AI
Delhi	42	12175	SV/AI*	44	12884	SV/AI	87	26759	AI
Hyderabad	17	4900	SV	22	4648	IA	13	3847	AI
Kolkata**	15	5872	AI	15	5896	AI	18	5322	AI
Kozhikode	20	7986	AI	17	6951	AI	-	-	-
Kochi	-	-	-	-	-	-	21	6760	SV
Lucknow	38	7509	AI	34	6638	AI	-	-	-
Mumbai	39	10910	SV	49	14025	SV	47	13341	SV
Nagpur	5	1765	AI	-	-	-	-	-	-
Srinagar	36	7717	IA	30	6397	IA	-	-	-
Total	244	69721	-	249	70298	-	234	71215	-

SV : Saudi Arabian Airlines; AI : Air India; IA : Indian Airlines.

Note : * One AI Flight from Kolkata Routed via Delhi.
** Includes 1511 (Pilgrims from Gaya who traveled Gaya/Kolkata on Indian Airlines Flight).

Year : Period of fiscal year in India is April to March, e.g., year shown as 1990-91 relates to April 1990 to March 1991.

Units : (a) 1 Lakh (or Lac) = 100000; (b) 1 Crore (or Cr.) = 10000000.

Source: Lok Sabha Unstarred Question No. 2811, March 10, 2003.

Christianity

The Holy See (Vatican City)[45]

The Pope is the head of Christians and he is based in Vatican City. The Pope gives sermons and messages of peace through the altar of the same. Vatican City is one of the most important pilgrimage centers for the Christians.

Figure 7: Vatican City, Square

Source: www.bildungsservice.at

Vatican City is also called the Holy See (Figure 7). The Vatican City State is situated on the Vatican hill, on the right bank of the Tiber River, within the city of Rome[46]. Almost all of Vatican City's 458 citizens live inside the Vatican's walls. The Vatican includes high dignitaries, priests, nuns, and guards as well as approximately 3,000 lay workers who comprise the majority of the workers.

The chief attractions in the Vatican City are its museums. Over the last 20 years (from 1980-2000) the number of visitors to the Museums has doubled from a million and a half yearly to three million. Nearly 20 thousand people a day will be able to enjoy the art treasures housed by the Vatican[47].

Jerusalem

Jerusalem[48] is a religious center sacred to all three monotheistic religions: Judaism, Christianity, and Islam. Religious pilgrims from all nations continue to congregate in the Holy City and millions of people flow through the gates of Jerusalem each year. Today, Jerusalem is a city of religion, art, culture, and museums than an economically viable regional market place or a center of business activity. Jerusalem thrives as a city full of mystical attractiveness and endless fascination.

Sikhism

The Sikhs have utmost reverence for the ten gurus who spread the message of peace, love and brotherhood. Most of the pilgrimage centers of the Sikhs are the commemorations of the Sikh Gurus. The most important from tourism perspective are:

Sri Harimandir Sahib, Amritsar[49]

The Harimandir Sahib (Temple of God) is also commonly known as the Golden Temple or Darbar Sahib (Divine Court). It is situated in the city of Amritsar in Punjab. The Golden Temple is a living symbol of the spiritual and historical traditions of the Sikhs. It is a source of inspiration for all Sikhs and their chief place of pilgrimage.

Gurudwara Sri Hemkund Sahib

Figure 8: Gurudwara Sri Hemkund Sahib

Source: www.sikhtourism.com

Set amidst towering snow-capped mountains and lying beside a lake of pristine blue water, the Sikh shrine of Sri Hemkund Sahib (Figure 8) looks, even to the not-particularly-pious, a place of almost unbelievable beauty and peace. Seven peaks – known as the Sapt Sring surround the shrine, looming over lush green pastures. The lake's rocky shores are covered with snow through most of the year, but when the snow melts, the almost mythical yellow-green flower known as the Brahma Kamal, the 'Lotus of the Gods', blooms amidst the rocks. It's a place of a rather wild and untamed beauty and one of Sikhism's most important shrines.

Jainism

Jainism is a relatively less known religion, but at the same time one of the oldest in the world and finds its roots through the various Tirthankaras. The Shrines are beautiful pieces of architecture and splendor, and lakhs of Jain devotees visit them every year. Important centers are mentioned here.

Shatrunjaya Hills (Siddhagiri) in Gujarat is a major Svetambara site, an entire city of about 3,500 temples. Mount Abu in Rajasthan, with one Digambara and five Svetambara temples, is the site of some of the India's greatest architecture, dating from the 11th-13th centuries AD. In Karnataka, on the hill of Shravanabelagola, stands the monolithic 17 meters high statue of the naked Bhagwan Bahubali (Gomateshvara), the first person in the world believed by the faithful to have attained enlightenment, so deep in meditation that vines are growing around his legs.

Figure 9: Shri Shravanabelgola Tirth

Source: www.jaintirths.com

Shravanabelagola[50]: The town is 50 kms from Hassan and 10 kms from Chananrayanpatna. It has two hillocks, Indragiri and Chandragiri. The former one is also known as Vindhyagiri, and stands 143 meters high. About 500 steps lead to the top of this picturesque hillock where 58.6 ft high Bahubali (*Gomata*) (Figure 9) statue stands. It is a monolith carved around 980 A.D. and considered to be a landmark in the annals of world art. His broad shoulders are 26 feet across. He is a symbol of eternal value, absolute renunciation detachment, and a soul set free from material surroundings. The Gomateswara's head anointing (Mahamastakabhisheka) ceremony (Jain ascetics and laity participate in a purification ceremony in which the statue is anointed from head to toe[51]) is a visual splendor, which is performed once in 12 years.

Exhibit 10: Connect 2004 Discusses Major Plans for Karnataka Tourism

Another segment that the government plans to cash in is religion. Religious visits have brought in a number of tourists to the state. Destinations with a regious appeal have attracted visitors from both foreign nationals and Indian. A number of devotees visit Sai Baba's ashram in Whitefield, Bangalore and Sri Sri Ravishanker's Art of Living Institute which is also in Bangalore. Both these places are a stopover for pilgrims on their way to Tirupathi.

Source: http://www.expresstravelandtourism.com

(V Partha Sarathy, Consulting Editor, Icfai Books, Hyderabad. He can be reached at parthasarathy@icfai.org).

Endnotes

1 June-July, depends on the lunar year.

2 May-June, depends on the lunar year.

3 Saraswati: Hindu Goddess of learning and wisdom.

4 Shravan: July-August, depends on the lunar year.

5 Moksha: Emancipation from the cycle of birth and rebirth, the final liberation or Nirvana.

6 Chaitra: March-April, depends on the lunar year.

7 Millions of pilgrims from all over the world throng Ajmer to attend the death anniversary of the great saint every year. *http://tourism-of-india.com/ajmer.html*

8 APSRTC: Andhra Pradesh State Road Transport Corporation.

9 *http://www.sacredsites.com/asia/india/kumbha_mela.html*

10 *http://www.navhindtimes.com/stories.php?part=news&Story_ID=032936*

11 Ghat: The river side bank, bathing place, place of congregation of people along the river.

12 *http://www.mpinfo.org/english/articles/2004/180304a.htm*

13 *http://www.webindia123.com/kerala/festivals/onam.htm*

14 *http://www.indtravel.com/kerala/festival.html*

15 *http://www.hometown.aol.co.uk*

16 *http://www.westbengaltourism.com/fairs_festivals/durga.html*

17 *http://www.expresstravelandtourism.com*

18 *http://www.travel-himalayas.com/travel-to-tibet/mount-kailash-mansarovar.html*

19 *http://www.shaivam.org/pilkail2.htm*

20 Linga—a bell shaped figure, symbolic of the creative principle of Universe, also referred to the Diety Shiva.

21 *http://www.tirumala.org/opage52.html*

22 *http://www.vaisnava.cz/clanek_en.php3?no=167*

23 Ibid.

24 Tirumala Tirupati Devasthanam—the administrative body of the temple.

25 Darshan—visit to the holy center, visit to the Shrine, pay homage to God.

26 Seva-Service to the God.

27 CFTRI: Central Food Technological Research Institute.

28 RITES: Rail India Technical and Economic Services.

29 *http://www.mypurohith.com/Festivals/Brahmostavam_tirumala.asp*

30 *http://www.swaminarayan.org/festivals/rathyatra*

31 *http://www.vaisnava.cz/clanek_en.php3?no=175*

32 *http://www.rediff.com/news/2001/jun/23puri.htm*

33 The divine child of Lord Vishnu and Lord Shiva who are the two divine parts of the Trinity (Brahma being the third one).

34 *http://www.sacredsites.com/asia/india/sabarimala.html*

35 Makar Jyoti: A light seen at the time of Solar ingress day (January 14) on the top of shrine.

36 *Business Line,* October 20, 2003.

37 Dhu al-Hijja—the 12th month of the Islamic calendar and the season of the Hajj; it has one extra day in leap years—(*http://www.thefreedictionary.com/Dhu%20al-Hijja*).

38 *http://1stholistic.com/Prayer/ho1_islam-pilgrimage.htm*

39 *http://i-cias.com/e.o/mecca.htm*

40 Hagar was the Egyptian handmaid of Sarah, the wife of Abraham. When Sarah found herself unable to have children, she arranged to make Hagar the concubine of Abraham, to start a family through her. *http://www.keyway.ca/htm2000/20000820.htm*

41 One of the ancestors of Islam.

42 *http://www.sacredsites.com/middle_east/saudi_arabia/mecca.html*

43 *http://www.hajcommittee.com/glossary.html*

44 *Deccan Chronicle,* June 20, 2004.

45 *http://www.worldover.com/history/vatican_city_history.html*

46 *http://www.infoplease.com/ipa/A0108136.html*

47 *http://www.zenit.org/english/archive/0002/ZE000207.html*

48 *http://www.holylandnetwork.com/jerusalem/history.htm*

49 *http://www.sikhtourism.com/sikh1.htm*

50 *http://www.kamat.com/kalranga/jain/monu.htm*

51 *http://www.pilgrimage-india.com/indian-religion/jain-religion.html*

7

Medical Tourism
Positive Publicity is the Need of the Hour

Saji Salam

The article discusses the emerging competitive scenario of medical tourism in the World. It highlights where India stands out as against its competitors of Asia and America and how India can increase its share of medical tourists. Many of the medical tourists who visited India are basically from less developed Asian countries and African countries. Equally competitive medical technologies that India possess and the cost-effective rates at which these technologies are available drive many of these patients to India as against the well developed countries like USA and UK. The article further highlights the challenges and opportunities that this field holds and what competitive strategies can bring India the desired revenue flows.

What prompted me to write this piece is a news item in a financial daily which quoted 'experts' stating the medical tourism industry in India would bring in revenues worth US$25 billion by 2020.

Source: www.expresshealthcaremgmt.com, May 2006.

A Look at the Numbers

Let's look at some numbers to put this in perspective. The idea here is to not be precise but to give a sense of what numbers we are talking here and what it takes to the numbers projected. One of the best-managed healthcare groups in India with about 6,000 beds, has revenue of about US$125 million. I do not have the break-up of what percentage of these beds is owned vs managed. However, going with these numbers, my assumption based on crude mathematical projection is that, it would require about 60,000 beds, to reach US$1.25 billion revenue and 12,00,000 beds to obtain a revenue of US$25 billion exclusively from healthcare services.

Let us look at some of the actual numbers from the tourism industry as well. The numbers may be a little dated but this is what it looks like. In 2003, about 2,726,000 tourists visited India and the revenue from the same was US$3.5 billion. Well, if that many relatives of patients (about 3 million) travel to India, we could manage another US$3.5 billion from tourism services. Barring inflated projections like these, it remains a fact that medical tourism in India is a growing trend.

Segmentation of the Patient Population

Currently, the bulk of the patients come to India from neighbouring countries such as Bangladesh, Pakistan, other Asian countries, Africa and the Middle East. In many cases, the driver for cross border care is a question of quality of care than cost itself. The quality of care that we provide in India is simply not available in some of the neighbouring countries.

The second segment is the segment of patients sponsored by the governments in their respective countries such as Middle East and Africa. For those governments, India is relatively a cost-effective option compared to Europe or the US. Private patients (not sponsored) from these countries look at India as value for money option vis-a'-vis Europe and US. Moreover, post 9/11 there has been a dramatic drop in patients from Middle East to the US.

The market segment that the healthcare industry is targeting is the patient population from Europe and the US. There are several patients of Indian origin residing in UK and US, who are already using the services of hospitals in India, when they are on vacation etc. Apart from this we have the widely-publicised cases of patients from the US and Australia.

True, these countries do have an increasing population and the healthcare systems are on the verge of collapse. Even though it is economically viable for some of these governments to officially bless shipping of patients abroad, it is the political viability of such a decision that may need to be worked on. Would a political party in power in Europe/US would want to face the next election as the pioneer of shipping patients to 'third world countries'?

We may want to recognise that a strategy which works for attracting patients from Bangladesh may not work for patients from Britain, since the expectations and drivers are different. The industry think tank may want to recognise the diversity in the medical tourism patient population and devise niche strategies to tap into each of the segments.

Competition

What is a good reason for an average senior citizen in the US to fly 18-20 hours to get his hip replaced? Can he even travel with hips in such bad shape? Obviously if he is not covered by insurance and cannot afford the same in US he has to look at options. What if this can be done in Mexico or Costa Rica at comparable rate and a shorter flight?

I am not an expert of the patient flow patterns to competitor locations such as Hong Kong, Singapore, South Africa, Costa Rica, Mexico, the Caribbean and emerging destinations such as Dubai. Per Becca Hutchinson's article on a University of Delaware publication looks like this is what is going on in competitor markets.

South Africa draws many cosmetic surgery patients, especially from Europe, and many South African clinics offer packages that include personal assistants, visits with trained therapists, trips to top beauty salons, post-operative care in luxury hotels and safaris or other vacation incentives. Because the South African rand has such a long-standing low rate on the foreign exchange market, medical tourism packages there tend to be perpetual bargains as well. Bangkok Phuket Hospital is the premier place to go for sex change surgery. In fact, that is one of the top 10 procedures for which patients visit Thailand.

Argentina ranks high for plastic surgery, and Hungary draws large numbers of patients from Western Europe and the US for high-quality cosmetic and dental procedures that cost half of what they would in Germany and America. Dubai is scheduled to open the Dubai Healthcare City by 2010. Situated on the Red Sea, this clinic will be the largest international medical centre between Europe and South East Asia.

The Indian healthcare industry needs to examine the factors that have made these medical tourism destinations popular.

Challenges

There are definitely areas for improvement as the Indian healthcare industry starts marketing services to newer patient segments. A key difference in healthcare services in India, unlike the IT sector is the critical role the government has to play to utilise medical tourism opportunity to its best. Some of the areas for improvement, to make India a global healthcare destination are:

Image Makeover

Despite the success of India in the IT market, perception of India in the eyes of the target audience has to change dramatically. The predominant image of India the average senior citizen in Europe (who is a target customer) has in his mind the picture of pre-independent India. To transform those images and present an image of India where he can trust Indian surgeons with his heart, his face and hips is a challenge (outsourcing your heart surgery is a lot different from outsourcing a software code!). To the average senior citizen in the US, it is more of a challenge, since to many, India is still a land of snake charmers and cows in traffic, a land far far away.

Perception of Quality of Care

Though one may argue against this, an average patient half a world away perceives the quality of care based on the perception of the country's image as a whole. The patients may have a hard time comprehending that the quality of care in India can be comparable to the US. One way to get over this is for hospitals to follow international healthcare accreditation standards. Would a patient be willing to trust his heart, kidneys, hips and face if there is an iota of doubt regarding the quality of care? (This segment of high yielding procedures is where the Indian medical tourism market is looking forward to for better profits.) In fact, there have been cases of plastic surgery gone bad, particularly from Mexican clinics in the days before anyone figured out what a gold mine cheap, high-quality care could be for the developing countries.

Scalability of Healthcare Infrastructure

The first question that comes to my mind is whether India can scale up to address the increasing patient mass. Do we have enough specialists and super specialists? We may have enough and more of entry-level physicians, but how are we placed with regard to doctors with postgraduate qualifications? What is the reality on the group with regard to paramedical staff? How is the attrition among nurses due to demand abroad?

I am sure these questions are being asked. The other question is the sheer number of beds and physical healthcare infrastructure required. On a different note, from a social perspective, would there be enough doctors and infrastructure left to treat the not so 'profitable' Indian patient?

Role of IT Standards

Finally, adopting and adapting of IT systems and standards that are in vogue in the developed world would be required to ease the administrative processes involved in cross-border care and integration with the medical records in the country of origin.

How Can the Government Facilitate?

The role of the government is critical in various areas if we need to scale the existing model. Some of the areas where government can and should act are:

Medical Education

It is high time that the government really looked hard at the demand supply situation of human resources in the healthcare sector and recalibrated the supply of specialists and paramedicals in the country. This would mean changes to policies on post-graduate medical education, nursing education etc.

Infrastructure

Quality of healthcare service can be limited by traffic and hartals. The last thing the fledgling medical tourism industry in India wants is bad press on a couple of foreign patients in ambulances that were stuck in traffic for several hours due to a political party's rally. From airports, and high ways, and hassle free environments for patients' relatives, there is quite a bit where improvements can be made on the infrastructure side.

Law and Order

Law and order and general sense of security are definitely areas for improvement. For all the gold in the world, I might want to get my hip replaced in nearby countries, which are infested with and mines and missiles waiting to take off.

Legal Infrastructure & Ethics

What is the mechanism for international patients who seek legal redressal for service gone bad? How long would it take for resolving the same in India? Is our legal infrastructure geared up to handle healthcare specific issues in a speedy manner?

Privacy of Patient Information

One area that is understated in discussions around healthcare services in India is confidentiality of patient data and regulations related to privacy and security of patient data in India. A good start would be to adopt HIPAA standards in India.

(Dr. Saji Salam is Chairman of HL7 India. He can be reached at saji.salam@cognizant.com.)

8

Sports Tourism Flags Off in India

Bhavika Jhaveri

The emergence of sports tourism as a serious revenue stream for travel agents is symbolic of the industry's onward evolution. Bhavika Jhaveri reports on trends, opportunities and challenges that this new segment holds.

Sports has a universal appeal that traverses all geographical, cultural and class barriers uniting humanity in palpable excitement. Sports and travel share a symbiotic relation, whereby people are attracted to a particular destination as a sport event participant (active), an event spectator, or to attend sport attractions of that place (passive). In fact the concept started with British nationals travelling abroad for winter sports. The first such sports tourism package can possibly be traced back to 1898 when Sir Henry Lunn, a British travel agent, organised a 10-day skiing holiday in the Alps for a group of 10 for a princely sum of US$15.

Sports tourism today is a worldwide phenomenon billed in several billions of dollars. According to Sports Tourism International Council (STIC), sports tourism could well account for 32 percent of the total tourism market in coming years. While some Indian travel agents and tour operators have dabbled in sports tourism, it is only now that the market is witnessing an emergence of specialists and agents who are shaping it as a niche generating serious levels of revenue.

Home Turf, Stirring

India has been put down as a unidimensional country with its interest in sports restricted to cricket over the years. That, to an extent, explains why it is a late inductee to this growing worldwide trend.

The counter trend of Indians travelling abroad extensively has, to an extent, changed perceptions about their compulsion to travel, one of them potentially being for active and passive sports. Visible evidence of this is found in the promotion of golf packages, football and tennis tournaments by NTOs and Formula1 Grand Prix. Get Lionel India, a K K Birla group travel company, forayed into sports tourism last year, with a primary focus on the corporate segment. Gaurav Sundaram, CEO of Get Lionel India Ltd, opines, "In the next two to three years sports tourism will comprise approximately Rs.200 to 250 crore of our turnover. The segment hasn't been tracked by many companies but there has been a consistent trend in metros of large groups of people travelling abroad for a sports event."

Mumbai-based Trust Travels pioneered the trend of promoting Formula1 Grand Prix in India as a reason to travel abroad, especially to the Sepang circuit in Malaysia. According to Manoharan, director of Malaysia Tourism Promotion Board (Ministry of Culture, Arts & Tourism), the number of Indians travelling there has increased appreciably from around 600 visitors in 2004 to 1,200 in 2005 (100 percent increase). Tourism Malaysia, which actively promotes Formula1 in India, is encouraging corporate houses to use sport events as an incentive for their dealers and top performers. "Sports tourism is a small segment in India, but it ensures higher returns since a sports traveller is a high spender," he says.

Emboldened by the response of Indian outbound travellers, agents are now busy in promoting tours for the upcoming FIFA World Cup to corporate houses and incentive groups. Both SOTC and Thomas Cook have tied up with Emirates, the official carrier of the tournament, to avail tickets. P Srinivas, VP (Special Interest Tours) at SOTC-Kuoni Travel, explains, "Since India is not a participating country, one has to tie-up with Emirates to get distribution rights. We intend to send around 400 people from India." Majority of the booking was done almost a year ago since any world event leads to exorbitant room tariffs and shortage of accommodation. "Our sports packages have been created keeping logistics in mind. For the FIFA packages we have arranged for accommodation in the suburbs of the city that is hosting a match. Transportation worries have also been taken care of," Srinivas adds.

Thinking a step further, agents are also trying to position themselves to cash in on the upcoming ICC World Cup 2007 in the Caribbean for which generating enthusiasm is merely a matter of declaring that one has tickets. Cricket Logistics 2007, the official tour operator for the World Cup, has appointed Official Travel Agents (OTAs) who are required to adhere to the strict guidelines laid down by Cricket World Cup and the International Cricket Council (ICC) in terms of ticket prices and other conditions. Trust Travel & Tours Pvt Ltd, which is also one of the OTAs for the World Cup, has rolled out packages ranging from one week to three weeks and will soon release integrated cruise packages as well. Zakkir Ahmed, its MD, says, "We had 1,500 people travel to the World Cup in South Africa with us last year. This premier cricket event is perhaps the only one to draw so many Indians overseas at one time. This year, we are targeting close to 700 people. Unlike South Africa, visa and accessibility are an issue this time or the numbers would have surely been much higher."

Tour Operators and Travel Agents Dealing in Sports Packages
Air Cruise Travels Pvt Ltd: Cricket, Formula 1, Soccer (FIFA World Cup)
Friends Globe Travels Ltd: Cricket, Water sports, Golf, Soccer (FIFA World Cup)
Pyramid Travels: Cricket
Trust Travel & Tours: Formula 1, cricket
SOTC Sports Abroad: Cricket, Golf, Formula 1, Tennis and Soccer
Sports Services Pvt Ltd: Cricket, Golf, Formula 1, Golf, Soccer
GET Lionel India: Cricket, Tennis, Soccer, Formula 1

Specialist v/s All-rounder

Worldwide, the trend for sports tourism 'specialists' is a given trend. But in India, that profile is still more the exception. Sports Abroad, a Special Interest Tours division of SOTC-Kuoni Travel created three years ago, is driven by the conviction that there is a growing interest in new destinations. With several corporations sponsoring sporting events, the company too is showing keen interest in opting for sports holiday packages for its employees and clients. Srinivas says, "We have been taking Indian fans of Formula1 regularly to various international circuits and Sepang by far is the most popular one. Veteran Indian travellers are taking to it in a major way, packing their bags for events as far flung and varied as Wimbledon, the French Open, the Golf Dubai Desert Classic, the Spanish La Liga, sundry skiing competitions and the biggest draw – Formula 1 racing."

Bangalore-based Sports Services Pvt Ltd is rated as one of the few truly sports tourism focused outfits which is into club holidays, top sports events and counseling on how to create specialised packages. Shankar Vishwa-nathan, its director, explains, "We have ventured into sports travel because we are convinced that it will constitute a major part of the Indian travel trade. We have collaborated with south India-based Travel Tours and have the wherewithal to take Indians to any country to witness any sports event."

According to Vishwanathan, sports travel in India started to pick up after the Cricket World Cup in South Africa in 2003. "Cricket still constitutes nearly 70 percent of our total business. However, in the next three to five years, we see football, golf and Formula1 accounting for a larger share of our business." While major tour operators are vying for corporate houses, Sports Services is targeting the sports enthusiast who is fond of travelling. It is currently formulating packages for the Ryder Cup in Ireland and Asian Games in Doha. "We are testing the market. Our strategy is to cover a wide spectrum of sports and offer a wide array of choices," avers Vishwanathan.

NTOs Looking to Promote Sports Travel
Malaysia Tourism Promotion Board: Golf, Formula 1
South Africa Tourism: Cricket, Soccer, adventure sports
Visit Britain: Golf, cricket, tennis
Dubai Tourism: Golf, deep sea diving
Ireland Tourism: Golf
Sri Lankan Tourism: Cricket, golf
Singapore Tourism: Golf.

Untapped Potential

Active sports tourism, where tourists indulge in activities like adventure sports or golf apart from sightseeing, is still a largely untapped segment. While the Japanese and the Chinese constitute a major chunk of active sports tourists worldwide, Indians still have some way go.

Manoharan says, "Due to the rainy season in India from June to October, a good number of people travel to Langkawi, Penang to play golf. There are around 40,000 to 50,000 golfers registered in India so the potential is huge. We promote our golf packages through various tour operators."

Many travellers prefer to play golf rather than watch and this is a largely high-end tourism phenomenon. Major golf destinations like the Far East, Dubai, Ireland, Scotland and South Africa are emerging in the Indian consciousness. Carl Vaz, country manager for Dubai's Department of Tourism and Commerce Marketing (DTCM), says, "Our proximity to India makes a range of world class golf courses accessible to the Indian tourist. To begin with, we are looking to reach corporate golfers."

Game On

Tourism, like any other business, is vulnerable to the hazards of stagnation and the only way to pre-empt this danger is innovation. Tour operators and NTOs in India have been doing their bit to make sports tourism look like the next reliable bet to create a captive market to the extent that destinations, particularly in South East Asia, are already competing with each other for Indian tourists who don't want to sit on their hands through a sightseeing routine.

Besides sports tourism, both active and passive, is essentially a high-end tourism phenomenon with agents earning margins ranging from 10 to 15 percent as compared five to 10 percent on vanilla tour packages. Moreover, the segment of institutional sports travel, wherein students and domestic clubs travel to play sports at club level, has not even been tapped. Considering that betting is illegal in India, while it is a thriving multi-billion dollar business in Europe, live action suddenly holds a massive appeal for the older age group which has been identified as having the largest disposable income.

Racetracks, cricket grounds, golf courses and football stadiums across the Atlantic present innumerable avenues for travel agents to fly Indians to for an experience they haven't yet absorbed. Whether they are game or not hinges purely on how foresighted they are.

9

Message in Tourism Advertising: An Indian Perspective

Srividya Raghavan

The focus of this article is on 'tourism advertising' and the relevance of 'ad message' in this context. A case of how Oasis, an advertising agency, based out of New York, has helped to design a campaign for improving Indian tourism among North Americans has been described. Using this case as an illustration, the process of idea generation, importance of research, message design and format etc., are discussed.

Introduction[1]

There is an information glut in the market. The information ranges from television commercials billboards to logos on coffee cups. Studies have shown that this information overload adds up to an average of more than 500 messages daily. The bombardment of advertising messages for every individual is getting so high that threshold levels to receive advertisement messages are also increasing. Hence, most of these messages are perceptually blocked and only a few elicit a response, only a small proportion drive actual purchase. This phenomenon is making it essential for the businesses to manage advertising messages to increase chances of success in the travel marketplace. The local tourism promotion groups also need an awareness of advertising options as well.

In marketing, one aims to match the consumer preferences with their product. Advertising is only one aspect of the marketing mix which is used to effectively market the product. Advertising is essentially a persuasion tool used to target a specific target and convince them of the usefulness of the product. Advertising is defined as a non-personal form of communication where paid media is used and a formal sponsor is identified. The media forms used may be a myriad, such as TV, Radio, Billboards, Newspapers, Magazines, brochures and direct mails, and product endorsements. These days movies have also become a popular medium for carrying products and services with an advertising motive.

Advertising may be classified on the basis of the nature of the content and purpose of advertising: Brand, Information and Image.

Amongst these, Brand advertising is the most popular. It attempts to improve sales by building loyalty for a specific brand. It is competitive in nature and advertisers point out the advantages of the product over the competitor's, thus building some sort or differentiation and competitive advantage. In Information advertising, the main facts are highlighted and are most often used in introducing a new product. This can be used when a new tourist destination wants to convey information regarding its plus points to create awareness as well as the competitive message ("Incredible India"). This form of advertising can be used when first entering the marketplace and is often used when a demand does not exist as yet. Advertising can also enhance an organization's image and can also remind consumers to buy on a regular basis. For example, Coca-Cola is a brand which is at this mature stage.

While selecting a marketing strategy the following five issues must be kept in mind, of which advertising message is the focus of this article.

- Setting the main objectives of advertising.
- Determining the budget for the advertising (campaign).
- Creating the main message for the advertising.
- Selecting the most effective media depending on the target audience and nature of message.
- And finally evaluating the effectiveness of the advertisement.

Creating the Advertising Message

Traveling options when delivered in the form of a service can be very different from selling a tangible product like a toothpaste or refrigerator. Some lessons can be taken from how services are different from other products. One such elemental difference is that tourism is people intensive and people dependent and therefore it depends quite heavily on the personalities of the people who deliver the service and create the travel experience. Hence, controllable factors are divergent from the kind of control factors available at the point of tangible purchase.

Then, there is the issue of what people look for in their purchases in terms of rewards. These are different for different people and in the case of travel, people expect emotional rewards rather than purely objective rewards.Hence advertisements that aim to sell travel products must identify and address such complex expectations. Therefore it may be said that the personal nature of travel and its appeal go towards shaping the message.

A number of such appeals might be conceived of when attempting to create an appealing message. However, to set the specific travel business apart, it might be better to concentrate on one feature. Extensive exploratory research might be able to determine the distinction of the travel product compared to others.

Some suggestions made by Ogilvy and Mather, a leading advertising firm which handles many travel accounts are as follows:

- Aim the spotlight on the unique differences that the travel service offers.
- In most of the cases, facts are more effective than generalities. For example, "As low as Rs.2999" is more effective than saying "reasonably priced." If what the service has to say is important in selling the product. Image, then a copy heavy ad should not be a bother.
- In travel, it is important to alleviate anxiety about going to a new place, on the other hand the excitement of discovering a new place must be highlighted.
- Research can be used to try out various new ideas and since we never know what will work, we might as well trial using research as a tool.

- Quality is most important and hence the ad must reflect the quality of the service offered and hence the ad must demonstrate quality in appearance and content.
- People are always looking for 'bargains' and therefore must be used as much as possible. Point out that the deal is a 'steal'.
- Any positive news about the travel offer must be highlighted and produced as a new ad.
- When using coupons in an ad, make it the central focus. Not only can they be used to drive the sales, but can also be used as a good source of creating database.
- Advertisements are mostly evaluated on the basis of whether it is able to capture Attention, generate Interest, create Desire, and inspire Action on the part of the audience. This is popularly called the AIDA principle.

What Ails Indian Tourism?[2]

The Indian scriptures have always held the guest in high regard. As a child, every citizen in India, has been exposed to the concept of 'Athiti Devo Bhava' – The Guest is God. Recently, the government of India seems to have suddenly realized that we do not receive as many tourists as we should and that we have the potential, as an ancient country bestowed with abundant natural assets, to attract a large share of the world's tourism.

The tourism ministry's new initiative, called "The Guest is God," has been implemented throughout India as part of the 'Incredible India' campaign. As a part of this program, the ministry offers free training to all who come in regular contact with the foreign tourists – taxi drivers, tour guides, shop owners, waiters and customs officials. They are giving out a simple message, which states "behave nicely, and tourists will return with their money."

Inspite of the diversity in attractions – From beaches in Goa to trekking in the Himalayan range, yogic retreats in Kerala to the Taj Mahal in Agra, India attracts less than one percent of total tourism traffic in the world. And now, the Indian government has finally realised that to squeeze revenue from tourism is a challenging task.

The lethargic attitude towards marketing India's natural endowments besides the infrastructural problems such as bad airports, restricted flights and potholed roads are to blame for this state of affairs and since 2002, India has been promoting itself quite actively.

The Oasis Case[3]

In the words of Paul Bernasconi, Creative Director and Partner, Oasis Advertising which manages the India Tourism campaign, "It is the account that everyone in the agency wants to work on, because the more you learn of the country, the more you fall in love with it"[4] .The India Tourism office in New York hired Oasis. The Indian office was looking for a change and attempting to build a larger non-ethnic customer base in North America. In New York, Indian tourism, was trying to attract a better quality of tourists rather than the usual hippie style backpackers.

In order to gain insights for the India Tourism campaign, extensive web-based research and qualitative research was used by Oasis. According to Bernasconi, the first thing to do was to find a market that will be attracted to India and use it as a starting point to identify a target so that an appealing message could be devised and delivered. The challenging task was to sell India as a preferred destination to upscale Americans. It becomes a challenging task as the relationship of America with India is not as compatible with say, that of France. On the one side there is an issue of incompatibility and on the other side is the fact that Americans don't travel overseas for a holiday as much as some Europeans. Says Bernasconi, "Only about 11 percent have passports, and a few travel beyond Europe." Hence the target market itself was quite narrow. As oasis soon found out, that segment was made up of whom Bernasconi describes as affluent, educated and in their mid-forties with grown-up children. This market he says, however, has traveled to Europe before and is not keen on traveling again to the same place. As they are older, they seem to seek out more of a spiritual experience.

Bernasconi and his team soon found a significant increase in experiential spending on specific luxuries such as travel, spas and massages in the target segment and this indicated to them that they were on the right track. They decided to sell

India as a place that one would go to in order to transform themselves incrementally and not for just a vacation.

In 1997, the 'Eternally Yours' campaign was launched. At first only the TV spots were managed by oasis. However, soon it picked up the print category in 1999 and recreated it to mirror the TV campaign. The two 30-second TV spots were a montage of smiling, happy faces and that of landscape shots. These carried the title 'Jaded' and 'Reincarnation'. These were showcased on Discovery, History, Travel and Bravo Channels. The high-end publications such as *New York Times* Magazine, *Sophisticated Traveller, Conde Nast Traveller, National Geographic Traveller, American Express' Dreamscapes,* and in some Canadian publications carried the print advertising campaigns. The total ad spend was estimated at an astounding $1 million to $2 million for the advertising in both the media.

An ad reads, 'One billion people. One thousand languages. And a surprising number of places to seek inner peace.'[5] One visual is that of a boat decked with flowers on the Dal Lake, while another advertisement projected the visual ofthe Taj Mahal in the foreground and a field in the background. It reads – 'Many travellers to India claim to experience reincarnation. They come back as human beings'. The last of the ads depicts a sunset with elephants wading in a river and it reads – 'Only one country can change the way you see the whole world.' 'Eternally Yours', the punchline used, attempts to drill in the fact that 'India stays with the traveller forever'. The timing was so decided, such that the ads ran atleast for six months before the travel season started in November, so as to give potential clients, the time to plan and decide on their holiday.

Oasis decided that although the target audience were older, they would not make the ads look too old or ethnic. Instead they decided to make it resonate with traditional values. The idea was to connect American mindset with the cultural values of. The ads were made such that the words are not Indian but look Indian (Sanskrit) and the music sounds Indian (sitar) but is actually not. They attempted to evoke the feeling of India using traditional looks but connected using American themes.

The attempt on the part of Oasis was to approach the India tourism issue as a Branding exercise. They arrived at the core values and emotional connections and treated those as the crux on which to sell brand India to the target. The crucial questions were what does the Indian brand stand for and what benefits can it generate?"

To bring in the competitive issue, Oasis deliberately picked non-conforming images. While quite a lot of tourism advertising is about things that Travel service providers can do, such as offer great dining experience, amazing shopping facilities etc., it is important to include something more emotional and human – especially the peaceful images that one does not usually see, but experience.

America has a 60s connection with India, which was predominantly the era of the 'Hare Rama Hare Krishna' and the 'Beatles'. The spiritual connection with India is hence enduring and is rooted in the American historical mindset. While spirituality is still a focus for attracting tourists, travelers do not want to 'rough it out' anymore. They are looking for comforts and experiences while they also enjoy the sanctum of spirituality offered to them.

According to some estimates North America leads the pack among the fastest growing market in recent years for tourists visiting India. In 2000, the number of American travelers to India increased by 20 percent in same period compared with the previous year. According to K R Arya, Regional Director, Americas, at the Tourism Office in New York, "The US is the second largest market for tourists to India (next to the UK),"[6] according to him, among tourists arrivals in India, 12 percent of them are from the US.

In 2000, compared to China with 9 lakhs North American tourists, there were over three lakh tourists to India. Arya estimates about one million American tourists and says we can compete with China on all parameters such art, history, culture and architecture. He added that the Government's goal is an annual growth of 10% to 15% in American tourists.

According to Bernasconi, the advertising has received a favorable response. This was measured by Oasis using the redemption rate, which is nothing but the number of people who called the toll-free number listed in the advertisements (1-800-go-india) for a free brochure, and the number of hits to the Website (*www.tourindia.com*).

The other issues related to this kind of advertising are that the positive image of India has also been created. It seems as if the challenge for Oasis is to try and stay competitive. Israel and Thailand are now offering life changing experiences as an attraction and are gaining more and more travelers. According to Bernasconi, "The Americans understand a little bit about India from their memories, and India has its own emotional space in their hearts." The idea is thus, to make India a competitive destination – eternally.

Other Perspectives

The above case only illustrates the strength of a well created message in fulfilling its objective. However, India has the potential to sell itself on a number of other planks. For instance, the varied diversity in the landscape, food, clothing, lifestyle, etc., can each be harnessed as in the case of state-wise tourism. India can also sell itself as a medical tourist spot for the various types of treatments available for various health issues. Even the mainstream healthcare is much cheaper than in other advanced countries. Tourism in India can be sold on multiple planks and message can play a major role in determining the scope, target and medium of the advertising for each plank.

As a parting thought, one might think of selling tourism in India as:

- Medical Tourism: Dental Tourism
- Mystic Tourism
- Experiential Tourism
- Witness to History Tourism
- Variety and Diversity Tourism
- Nature Tourism

Some Images

God's Own Country: Kerala – An example of how the geography of India can change unpredictably from one state to another: Eternally Yours Campaign

Source:http://www.thehindubusinessline.com/catalyst/2002/02/28/stories/2002022800010100.htm

TourIndia Home Page

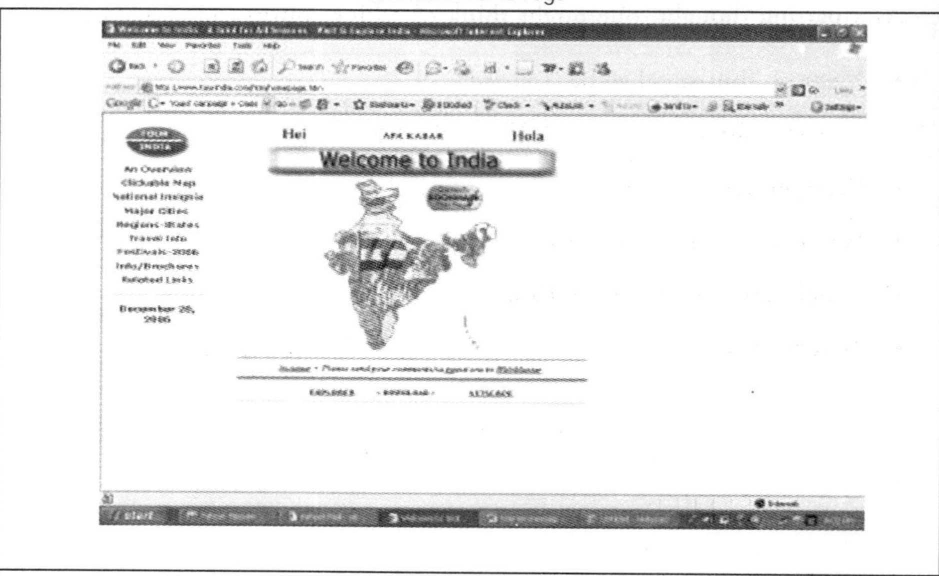

Source: www.tourindia.com

Incredible India Campaign

Sources: http://www.ourbollywood.com/uploads/Incredible%20India.jpp, http://www.incredible india.org/siteimages/IndianSunset.jpg, http://f.screensavers.com/migration/wp/Yoga_India_215.gif

India tourism – quality and content can be assured through easily navigatable websites.

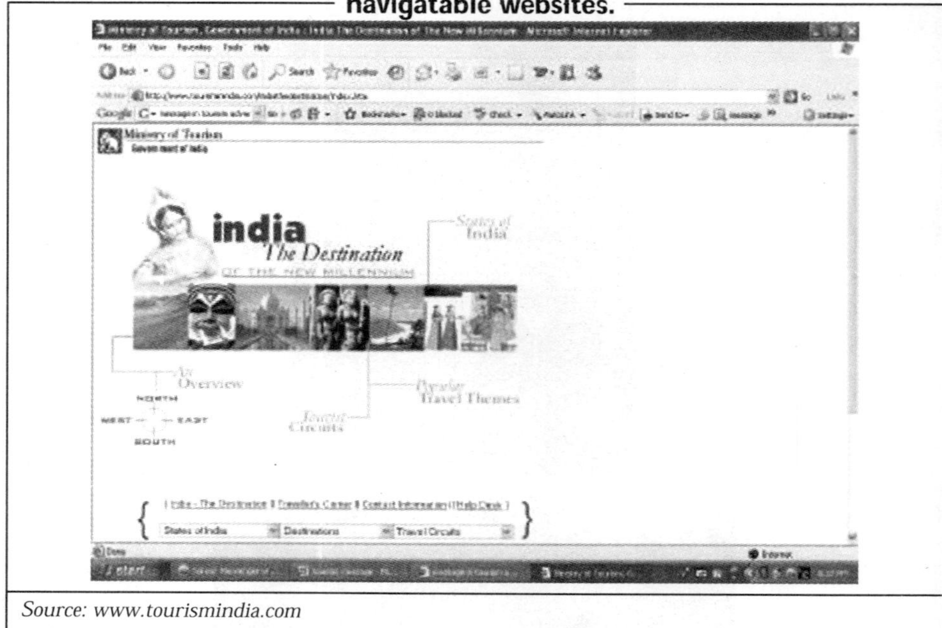

Source: *www.tourismindia.com*

Alternate plants for promoting tourism: This can take a different tone and language.

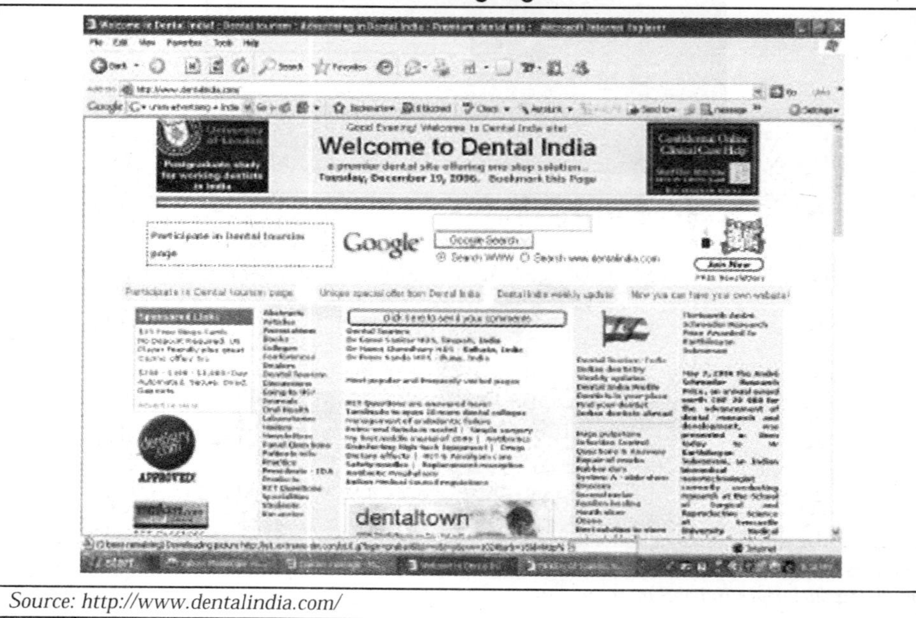

Source: *http://www.dentalindia.com/*

How tourism does not have to be center directed: The states can attract their own tourists competitively.

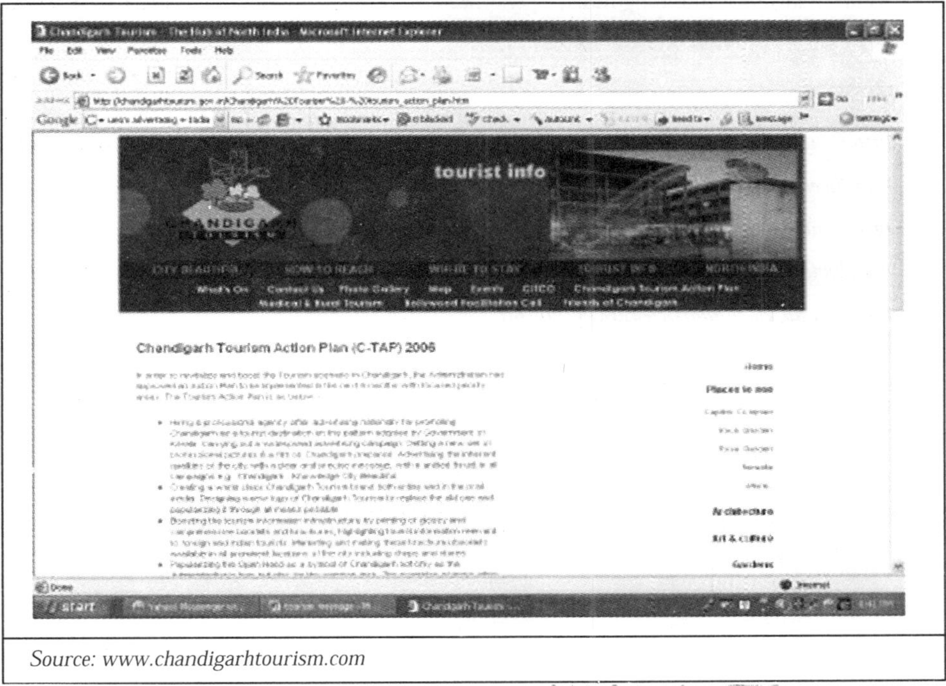

Source: www.chandigarhtourism.com

And so on and so forth.......

(Srividya Raghavan is with IMT, Hyderabad.)

Endnotes

1 The pertinent information in this section of the article has been referred from *http://web1.msue.msu.edu/imp/modtd/33710087.html*

2 The relevant information in this case study closely follows the report on: *http://www.iht.com/articles/2005/04/24/business/india25.php*

3 The relevant information in this case study closely follows the report on: *http://www.thehindubusinessline.com/catalyst/2002/02/28/stories/2002022800010100.htm*

Please note that the quotations of the Oasis spokesperson had to be borrowed verbatim since they were quotations.

4 Rina Chandran, "Branding India," *The Hindu Business Line*, Thursday, February 28, 2002, *http://www.thehindubusinessline.com*

5 Rina Chandran, "Branding India," *The Hindu Business Line*, Thursday, February, 28, 2002,' *http://www.thehindubusinessline.com*

6 Rina Chandran, "Branding India," *The Hindu Business Line*, Thursday, February, 28, 2002, *http://www.thehindubusinessline.com*

References

http://www.thehindubusinessline.com/catalyst/2002/02/28/stories/2002022800010100.htm

http://web1.msue.msu.edu/imp/modtd/33710087.html

http://www.tourisminindia.com/indiathedestination/index.htm

http://www.dentalindia.com/

http://www.iht.com/articles/2005/04/24/business/india25.php

10

Nowhere in the Picture

Reema Sisodiya

The Indian film industry has, for long, been the fancy of National Tourist Offices (NTOs) of various destinations promoting themselves in India but a closer probe by Reema Sisodiya reveals that their success has as much to do with the apathy of the bureaucracy of India's central and state tourism boards to recognise the opportunity in their own backyard.

They came, they saw, they conquered. This has been the case with India since time immemorial. It needs the world to recognise her true potential and in this case, it is clearly the NTOs of several destinations that have trained a keen eye on the Indian tourist. They have clenched the catchword 'Bollywood' with a firm fist and have encashed on it. They have realised the power and reach this industry has in showcasing their destination, which in turn leads to an increase in tourism traffic to their region. For NTOs, Bollywood is truly their golden goose.

NTOs on Top

Switzerland Tourism admits and accepts the contribution of Yash Raj Films in making their destination popular, while Korea Tourism Organisation (KTO) has thanked Vishesh Film for choosing Korea as the destination for the shoot of their film Gangster. Hyo Sik Jeon, director, KTO, on his recent visit to India, announced special support for film-makers to shoot in Korea. "In view of its wide reach and strong following both domestically and internationally, KTO intends to get the Indian film fraternity to shoot at its tourist attractions and showcase the same," he said. Harshad Mehta, honorary consul of the Republic of Armenia in India, has also expressed strong intentions of promoting Armenia through films and has also taken the efforts of showcasing the product to prominent film-makers from India.

All NTOs, right from Switzerland Tourism which was the first to tap the potential, to the other major players in the Indian market like Singapore, Australia, Mauritius, Malaysia, South Africa and recent entrants like Ireland, Korea, Armenia, Bavaria, Brazil, etc., are aggressively wooing Bollywood with strategic and meticulously planned marketing and promotional campaigns. Brazil, for instance, recently waived off visa fees for a film that was shot in Rio de Jenario. Seamless and hassle-free rules, easy permits and procedures coupled with attractive deals, benefits and incentives and much more are part of the package promoted by NTOs to lure Indian film makers to their respective destinations.

In a Nutshell, this is what NTOs have to offer in general

1. Single window clearance for all permits and rules for shooting.
2. Exclusive policy designed specifically for Indian film producers.
3. Free locations for shoots, concessions at sites.
4. State-of-the-art equipment and technical support provided free or at a highly subsidised rate.
5. Free airfare and accommodation.
6. Waiver of visa fees.
7. Support from airlines in terms of baggage allowance.

Says Kiran V Shantaram, producer, director and chairman, V Shantaram Foundation, "International destinations have gone all out to capture the attention of the Indian film fraternity. From user-friendly rules and procedures to a hassle-free functioning method, shooting abroad is far more pleasant than in India. Australia, New Zealand, Switzerland, etc, have provided attractive packages."

The Indian Scene

Correspondingly India, which is blessed with one of the world's most diverse topography, comprising breathtaking landscapes and rich culture, heritage and art, has not even looked at this potential. Each state has a plethora of diverse attractions and can easily catapult India as a top destination for film shoots both for the domestic and international market. Ideally, India should have done what the NTOs have been doing, using Bollywood as a tool to promote the country domestically and internationally. Though films are being shot in various parts of the country, film-makers are unanimous in voicing that shooting in India is a very difficult process. There is no single window clearance for the innumerable permits and other criteria that one has to get into place before starting work. Says Mukesh Bhatt, managing director, Vishesh Films, "It is a sad affair when it comes to shooting in India, especially in Mumbai. Bureaucracy, corruption and basically the entire system, is a nightmare for producers. Shooting abroad is comparatively economical and the product on offer is much more superior, such as beautiful streets, and clean and picture perfect locales as compared to the unclean streets of Mumbai. An international destination with their attractive packages is a dream for Indian film makers."

According to Shantaram, it is the high number of permits which one requires from various agencies for a film shoot that is painful. He says, "To shoot in a city like Mumbai, at say the Gateway of India, one needs to have permits from the following authorities – ASI, (Archaeological Survey of India), Navy, Police, the local police station (Colaba), MTDC (Maharashtra Tourism Development Corporation), BMC (Brihan Mumbai Municipal Corporation), RTO (Regional Transport Office), Traffic Police and host of others. Co-ordinating with all the authorities and the process of getting these permits can be a very lengthy and highly de-motivating." Bhatt goes a step further and totally blames the system for its bureaucracy, red tapism and corrupt practices. He says, "It is extremely frustrating to film in India especially in Maharashtra and Mumbai. We receive zero support from the authorities and over and above that have to bribe authorities for permits, which hikes up the cost of production. Unfriendly infrastructure, badly maintained locations also add up to the agony. It is high time we take a serious call on the system and have a straight and user-friendly system in place, like it is prevalent internationally." Bhatt is also of the opinion that the states only have plans and incentives on paper, if there are any in the first place.

Jayaraman, chief executive officer, Exotique Expeditions, a New Delhi based tour company, specialising in facilitating overseas film producers cites an unpleasant experience, while assisting a team of Philippines-based film makers to shoot their serial Extra Challenge at various locations in the Golden Triangle, including Fatehpur Sirkri and Taj Mahal. "The entire system is in a mess and we had to run in circles to get certain permits since ASI was involved. The run around for permits and sanctions was so tedious that the film-makers gave up and we have yet to recover our deposit of Rs. 50,000 from ASI. Further, the hotels are over priced, the entire infrastructure is an issue," states Jayaraman. According to him, encouraging international filmmakers to come to India for shoots is great business opportunity for the travel trade as well as tourism promotion of India at large. "The system has to change and requires vision from leaders and political will," opines Jayaraman.

Echoing a similar thought is filmmaker Ashok Pandit. Says Pandit, "The beauty of Kashmir is unmatched and used to be the most sought after destination for film shooting through the 60s and right till the time the state was rocked with insurgency problem. When the conditions were right, the destination was over priced, but then film-makers had to succumb to the demands. Today, the destination needs to make serious efforts to rope in film-makers. While the Kashmir government has invited film producers to shoot in the region, they have not supported the move with the providing the necessary confidence. I am extremely keen on shooting my next film there as the script requires a Kashmir background, and I am hoping for complete support from the authorities."

India has the Potential

India can adopt the thought process of the NTOs, of marketing the country through the medium of cinema in conjunction with the highly successful Incredible India campaign. This strategy would not only work wonders in providing the country much needed exposure, but also helps to increase the visitor numbers. Suresh Chablani, CEO, Rose Travels, which has been the official travel agency for a host of film producers and banners, opines that Bollywood and the regional cinema can be a vital tool in building brand India and destination marketing to boost tourism.

"Today, while the world is looking at India, it is the best time for India tourism and the state tourism boards to realise that films can be highly instrumental in showcasing the potential of the country to the world. We too have good locations and facilities like Ramoji Film City, for international film makers to come here and shoot," states Chablani. He further adds, "It is also a great business avenue for the trade as on an average a film unit comprises of 50 people depending on where the shoot is taking place. On an average there are about 24 films which are shot per year, if not more, and this can be a good mode of business. The increase in tourist traffic, both international and domestic, once destinations are popularised by films will also be a big boost of revenue for the trade."

Rajeev Talwar, additional director general tourism, government of India, agrees to the bureaucratic and technical bottlenecks. Says Talwar, "We definitely need to be more proactive and take the right steps to assist film-makers and make India a preferred location for shoots. It is unfortunate that film-makers have been facing difficulty in their work and it is important to provide the right environment which includes easy, smooth and time saving facilities for shooting. But I would like to state that more than concessions and subsidies emphasis should be first on making the process for film shooting convenient and easy."

Initiatives Taken in India

Very few in India have realised the potential of promoting the destination through films and unfortunately their efforts have been stuck on the decision table. In an attempt to capitalise on the tourism boom caused by cinema, Centre for Media & Entertainment Studies (CMES) had organised a cinematic conclave to promote Chandigarh and the northern states of Punjab and Haryana as ideal destinations for film shoots. Attended by stalwarts of the film industry, the conclave sought to ignite the imagination of the Mumbai film and television industry in opting to shoot in these regions and provide an impetus to cinematic tourism. A host of measures were announced which included setting up of an office in north India providing a single window clearance for film projects, access and information on the Web so that production houses in Mumbai can initiate and get clearances processed online, joint promotions by Chandigarh, Punjab, Haryana and Himachal in the form of consolidated cinematic tourism packages, etc.

During the conclave Jagjit Puri, managing director, Punjab tourism, said, "The aim of this conclave is to interact with the film and television industry, understand their needs and find out their problems. It is an integrated effort to promote north India. Punjab alone has 99 heritage sites. All these sites have been opened for shooting at nominal rates with a single window clearance. The state government provides 50 percent entertainment tax exemption for all films produced in Punjabi."

According to sources from Uttar Pradesh (UP) tourism, the film policy of the state called 'Film Bandhu' provides a rebate of 40 percent in the tariff of government tourist bungalows and 25 percent discount on Public Works Department (PWD) cottages. Free security arrangements, entertainment tax exceptions for films, which are shot 75 percent or more in UP and nominal charge for using the air strip for shooting are some of the other incentives offered by the film policy. Maharashtra has also set up subsidies four months ago, but only for Marathi films shot in Maharashtra. For a 35 mm cinemascope colour Dolby Digital Sound (DDS), the Maharashtra government gives 30 lakhs to the producer, while 25 lakhs are offered for non-DDS films. Jammu & Kashmir tourism has also announced special benefits for shooting in the state and Rajasthan is yet another state, which has a film tourism policy in place.

Though states have their policies in place, how effective and streamlined they are is yet to be seen. Pandit says, "All these policies are there, but they seem to be workable only on paper. We want policies that are real and completely free from bureaucratic hassles." Jayaraman sums up the bottomline for film tourism, "It will result in more business for travel agents and tour operators. In this light we are aiming to expand our business to promote India to international film makers and hope that the systems and infrastructure will improve to benefit tourism in India in the long run." Hence it's time India wakes up to this idea."

Initiatives to be Undertaken

An all-inclusive tourism policy specifically designed for the film industry needs to be formed to provide the right aid for film shooting.

- International film producers need to be encouraged.
- Promoting India through Indian films is also a resourceful proposition to boost tourism.
- An initiative in the form of 'Locations', a film tourism event, was sponsored by Chhattisgarh tourism board in 2003. This initiative did not materialise in concrete results. More such interactive meets should be organised.
- During his tenure, Jayatilak, former MD, Chhattisgarh tourism board, had suggested setting up of a specialised agency catering to the film industry, activation of the single window clearance system and drafting of a film policy. However, after his exit, his plans and initiatives failed to take off.
- Regional films can play a major role in intra-state tourism. Hence the states need to showcase their products to the regional film-makers.
- Infrastructure development, including increase in accommodation facilities, better transport systems will help to facilitate film-makers.
- Recently, the northern states joined hands to organise a cinematic conclave. More such activities should take place.
- Airfares need to be reduced, while railways need to give quotas for the film industry.
- No charge for cameras at historical sites.

11

ARTICLE SUMMARY

Application of Information Technology in Tourism Advertising Strategies

Venkatesh Tamlurkar

Information Technology plays an important role in the development of tourism for the countries all over the world. Its application in the advertising strategy proved very useful for the Destination Marketing Organizations (DMOs) who achieved the desired results by coordinating it with their organizational mission/goal. The World Wide Web formed as a new advertising medium offering extranets for the suppliers, intranet for employees along with a variety of sales and service links for customers. All this necessitated to go for an advanced study on the advantages of digital technology that helps us to understand it better and use it effectively especially in formulating the tourism advertising strategies.

This article tries to explore how the application of Information Technology helps to build up advertising strategies particularly in the field of Tourism that has been growing exponentially since past few decades. The following points have been touched upon that gives the readers a suitable corridor to follow while using the Information Technology for their advertising strategies for Tourism.

This is a summary of the Whitepaper "Application of Information Technology in Tourism Advertising Strategies". This paper was authored by Ulrike Gretzel, Daniel R Fesenmaier and Yulan Yuan.

1. ***The importance of Information Technology in advertising strategies related to tourism.***
2. ***The assistance provided by Information Technology to the Destination Marketing Organizations to promote tourism.***
3. ***The organizational barriers that impact the implementation and use of Web-based advertising and their implications to the organization.***
4. ***The new advertising strategies that Web offers to tourism organizations and its impact.***
5. ***The existence of various Web-based technologies that revolutionalizes the tourism advertising.***
6. ***The future of Internet technology in the tourism industry.***

Introduction

Tourism all over the world improved enormously in the recent years due to the publicity given by individual countries. The World Wide Web gained significance in tourism as it broke the boundaries across the nations and became easily accessible and available to everyone and everywhere. The strategies used by the advertisers to lure the potential segment got further enhanced with the application of Information Technology yielding promising results. The Internet was used by the tourism advertisers to create fully functioning business rather than just putting the banners of the destinations. A typical Website blended the publishing, real-time communication, broadcast and narrowcast presenting a variety of sales and service links for the consumers apart from offering intranets for employees and extranets for suppliers.

The open communication channel of Website allows free flow of information where technology and advertising strategies get integrated and coordinated. This helps the Destination Marketing Organizations[1] (DMOs) to effectively achieve their desired results to some extent in harmony with their overall organizational mission and goals. Acting as a personal, a niche, a mass and an interactive medium simultaneously, Websites do not involve any trade-off between richness[2] and reach[3] unlike the traditional media that would otherwise lead to inconsistency of information.

However, recent developments like the emergence of creative advertising strategies combined with new technology, vibrant consumer markets that are changing the business environment, globalization that is increasing the competition, etc., made it difficult for the DMOs to sustain their rhythm. Various factors like economic downturn, inadequate human resources, lack of hitech expertise and time limitations are making them struggle in the aggressive situations. Hence, efforts have to be put in to identify latest and effective strategies for tourism advertising on the Internet and change the existing business models by giving instant response to the market changes. Issues like different kinds of Web-based technologies that are available and their implications need to be understood apart from determining the various organizational hurdles that influence the implementation and use of Web-based advertising.

Latest Developments and Issues in Internet Advertising

With $267 million[4] in 1996, Internet advertising revenues reached $4.2 billion[5] for the third quarter of 2006 (more than 33% increase over $3.1 billion in Q3 2005). Travel and tourism which is an information-rich business and a very fragmented industry formed the most important business on the Web in terms of the volume of e-commerce with e-mail, wireless advertising and websites forming the three major vehicles for Internet advertising. Though the elements of other media are combined in it, it is more than their sum. As a new advertising medium, Internet has drastically changed the advertising industry giving rise to new sector like ad-serving business that provided greater online advertising expertise by using latest devices[6]. Internet formed as an important advertising medium for most of the industries as majority of homes had high bandwidth connections with television programs available online. This offered the consumers an opportunity to interact with the advertisement i.e., interactivity was not only *through* the medium but also *with* the medium thus making the old communication channels & models and business structures archaic.

The real opportunity on the Web lay in 'collaboration marketing' as it offered a great blend of two-way interactivity, flawless dealings, on-demand availability and customization that lead to enhanced relationships and superior personalization of goods and services. Interactive marketing demands a dialogue instead of one-way communication and the use of information will be *from* the consumer rather than *about* the consumer. This calls for allowing the consumers to interact with the website content by including interactive product demonstrations (like for example providing three dimensional view of the destinations, the infrastructure, the places of visit/stay, local attractions etc.,) apart from discussion groups on the Web advertisements. Otherwise, just the broadcast of information would lead to negative perception that Internet marketing is not entertaining thus reducing the number of prospective consumer hits. For this reason, organizations have to start rethinking by changing their business models that deliver value to the consumer and build upon relationship with the stakeholders. Parsons has framed an interactive marketing framework where he mentioned that Web marketing will be successful when the concept of Attract, Engage, Retain, Learn and Relate[7] is followed.

Interactive Marketing Framework (Parsons, *et al.*, 1998)

1. Attract

Applying the above framework to online tourism advertising strategy, the DMOs should first attract or expose the visitors to the site. Different strategies[8] that can be used are:

a. Advertising their Website to the Web search engines like Google, Yahoo, Alta Vista, Lycos etc., that index the Web.

b. Giving the visitors some good reasons or value to visit the Website like making the Website informative and entertaining.

c. Linking their Website pages within the industry to other's Websites with similar reciprocation.

d. Advertising their site on certain Web pages that have high traffic or its in order to create awareness about their presence in the market.

e. Being active in various Internet news groups that are frequented by potential consumers and participate in the discussions. This activity sometimes lead to spamming (getting tempted to send bulk e-mails to different news groups) that would not help in building any reputation in the long-run.

f. Including the e-mail and Website addresses on the company's print and electronic literature, stationery and display advertising.

2. Engage

DMOs should engage the visitors by generating interest and making them participate actively by turning the website into a live environment[9] that builds real relationship with the consumers. Some of the ways used to engage them are:

a. Providing online live help to the visitors as they prefer human interaction and this comes out more cost-effective than that through e-mail or phone.

b. Giving the potential consumers immediate access to someone at critical points of the buying process to solve any service-related issues and improve the chance of e-commerce.

c. Making the content more interactive that should be user-generated with spontaneous navigation and integrating the marketing campaign with surveys and live helps to make it more interactive and effective.

d. Using the e-mail to its best possibility as it the most effective marketing vehicle.

3. Retain

Generally people do not stay in a site beyond 30 seconds and DMOs have to pitch their idea and persuade in this short duration to make the visitors come back to the Website after their first visit. Retaining visitors involve more dynamic contents with good transaction capabilities and online communities. Some of the other strategies used to retain the visitors are –

a. Gaining a good ranking of the Website in the search engines and by removing the clutter through technically designing the page content.

b. Using catchy phrases, attractive graphics & images, highlighting texts etc., to arouse interest about the site that would finally attract and motivate the visitors to stay and investigate further.

c. Avoiding downloads that take too long time and distractions through advertisements, animated gifs that generally irritate the visitors.

4. Learn

Knowing the preference of visitors helps us to cater better to their needs. One can learn about a visitor by capturing information about them continuously. Most of the Websites ask personal details about the visitors whenever they visit the site for various reasons (may be to read an article, get some solution, know about a product etc). It is advisable to ask very little detail to avoid losing that visitor as not all will part with their personal information.

5. Relate

Whenever there is an online interaction with a visitor, customize the dialogue to his/her requirements that finally leads to delivering a valued service. This happens through personalized communications and offering products/services that are tailor-made to satisfy his/her needs.

It is worthwhile to mention at this point the sequence of stages through which the user processes the presented information. These stages consisting of exposure, attention, comprehension & perception, yielding & acceptance and retention are exactly followed through the above framework. Understanding the framework and the processing stages of the user helps the DMOs to design the Website according to the requirements of the consumers. Though Internet advertising for tourism requires innovative dexterity and distinguishing approaches, knowing the basics of traditional advertising enhances its success. There is high pressure on the management of tourism Websites as the time gap between the production and distribution of information is nil and timeliness of information and incessant updating of web pages plays a significant role. There are several barriers that are internal and external to the organization impacting the implementation and use of Web-based advertising. Some of them that limit the ability of DMOs to advance ahead are:

a. Facing the day-to-day operational challenges along with instantaneous absorption of changing technical knowledge and expertise.

b. Reluctance from some of the DMOs to invest in Web-based technologies causing difficulty in convincing the stakeholders to invest in online advertising and providing justification that such investment would yield potential results.

c. Deciding on certain activities like outsourcing or implementing internally the maintenance and updating of Website as it demands more money, time and people with technical and design expertise.

d. Designing and implementing of marketing strategies as Websites are global in nature catering to diverse groups of consumers.

e. Facing the problem of limited resources like smaller budgets when DMOs are small in size thereby affecting the adoption of effective technology.

f. Difficulty in justifying the advertising strategies if their effectiveness cannot be measured.

g. Imposing some government restrictions (like linking to other sites, privacy issues, online selling/transactions, etc.,) that needs to be in synchronization with the cyber laws.

Some web-based technologies that have the potential to revolutionalize the tourism industry are collaborative filtering[10], personalization software/profiling[11], knowledge-based service software[12], electronic payment[13], video conferencing[14], virtual reality and Web casting[15], Online Word-of Mouth monitoring[16], Networking software[17], etc. Innovative tools like palm pilots (Personal Digital Assistants) will serve the consumers with en-route information. There would be reduction of time between the awareness created and the action taken. Availability of rich and correct information through such technology helps to even arrange for trips without prior planning. The DMOs acknowledge the fact that the number of e-mails received by them is more than the toll-free phone calls. Though installing communication tools is easy, but it is very difficult to handle the increased volume of communication. To reach the full potential of the technology, one needs to dedicate the resources both for the development of the site as well as for the ongoing management of inquiries. The efforts by the organizations to use Web should be more to enhance both the knowledge capital and the social capital. Maximum advertising impact can be achieved by integrating both technology and non-technology products. The audience need to be specifically targeted with personalized ads as per their interest and this can be achieved by measuring the Web, ad-serving tools, and database mining.

Measuring Online Advertising

The return on the advertising investment can be known by measuring the Web advertisements. As the Web is interactive in nature that helps to track the consumer's behavior, new potentials open up that help in measuring the success of advertising. Since the Web is very complex in nature, standardization is very difficult and there are no standardized measures for knowing the traffic on commercial Websites. Even measuring the response of consumers to the Web ads is not standardized (other than Website hits say like the amount of time spent on the Website) and optimal media pricing models have no established principles. To know the effectiveness of a site, one has to evaluate the consumers who seek extra information (either online or offline) or depend on the site's speed, functionality, accurateness, and comprehensiveness of the information through proxy testing. Though 'log files' and 'cookies' provide huge information about the Web users, their intelligent and innovative use helps to gain better understanding about the consumer and design a better site. It can happen only when the advertising messages are more focused and mass e-mails are avoided as potential visitors get turned off soon. This not only controls the high transaction and coordination cost of losing the consumer but further reduces the prevailing low cost of online advertising.

Web Design for Tourism and its Importance

A Website for promoting Tourism should be designed in such a way that it reveals the personality of the medium, the consumers, and the environment. The Website should fabricate itself into the destination's culture and structure that helps it to position the place strategically. The main design parameters[18] that have to be reviewed are the Websites' content, graphical design, features and technology. It should be noted that the Website is made to entertain the user by providing the required information about the destination. It should not be complex, over-loaded or over-designed and the technology levels of the consumers have to be kept in mind while designing it. The people designing and developing the Website should have technical skills along with understanding of the advertising and the tourism industry. They should make the Website interactive allowing the user to do online transactions, make it user-friendly with a lot of consistency, creativity, and graphics apart from being educative. Keeping the Web page content accurate, attractive and easily searchable helps the DMOs to clearly understand the perceived image of the Internet users who apart from searching for information also seek a different kind of experience and expect interaction. An Internet users' positive experience makes them spend more time at the site that helps to create a better impact of the advertisement. The Web design of a tourism Website should focus towards the consumers where their information search behavior is understood to avoid any negative experiences. Otherwise, a simple negative experience like extensive downloading time would lead the users to jump sites. Such bad experience can be avoided by indicating beforehand the possible downloading time.

As Web is largely a pull medium unlike television and consumers seek the information actively, they would be in a lean-forward mode and get empowered through the Web. Hence, such situation demands 'permission marketing' where consumers are engaged in a dialogue creating a long-term interactive relationship. This would very soon lead to a situation where agents would be able to store the profiles on the client's browser, the cell phone or on smart cards that would enable them to access the profiles whenever a consumer enters an electronic or physical site. In addition, a network of sites would share the information about a particular profile that would make Web look like a push medium. The concept of reverse advertising should be in vogue where advertisements should be from the consumers demanding what they want instead of the suppliers offering their products and services.

The travel and tourism related Websites are promoted mostly through print and television ads (a successful way to direct traffic to a particular site), but search engines top in identifying and accessing the sites. While it is not easy to get the consumers to visit a site, turning them into repeat visitors is a far more complicated task. Many people visit a website or become loyal because of its brand name that is perceived as a mark of quality and assists them in saving their time in decision-making process. While there is no scarcity of shelf space on the Web, there is certainly a limited consumer attention. There need to be coordinated on and offline campaigns to build a brand that should be based on the understanding of the type of consumers targeted, rather than the traditional product-focused approach. Most of the Websites link themselves with industry partners like hotels, airlines etc., apart from having a strong presence in various search engines to build brand recognition and loyalty. Other effective ways used to attract people are word of mouth, magazines, consumer reports and this is the reason why most of the dotcom businesses are heavily investing in offline advertising.

Conclusion

Online advertising is changing the scenario of tourism industry as the strength of emerging technology is effectively exploited. The Web has certain distinct and inherent characteristics that make for online advertising with different skills and new approaches. It combines the characteristics of traditional media, offers unparalleled richness and reach growing into a platform for new form of communication, and a vast growth potential at a cost that cannot be matched by any other type of advertising media. In order to be successful, online advertising has to focus on attracting the attention of Internet users by providing both information and entertainment, otherwise they easily switch to other sites which catch their attention. Unless the new ideas are communicated and implemented, the web-based technology will never succeed. The database developed must integrate itself into the overall data management structure. There should be proper coordination among the suppliers of tourism products and services, satisfactory cooperation between the local tourism businesses and the DMOs, sharing of knowledge by the various organizational members for a successful online advertising. It is a known fact that the cost of not collaborating is much higher than the cost of coordination and an attractive Website can be built only through good teamwork. The concentration of DMOs should be on the consumers with proper market segmentation rather than on the content while developing the Websites. The DMOs should capitalize on the mass customization potential the Web offers by designing the communication strategies and programs that are tailor-made to the individual consumers' traits. Varieties of innovative technologies readily available in the market are used by the advertisers that help them to integrate interactivity and experience into the Website design. The application of Information Technology in tourism advertising strategies should mutually benefit the tourism destinations, the DMOs and of course the tourists who visit a place or stay there based on the influence of the Internet advertisement.

(Venkatesh Tamlurkar, Faculty Member, Icfai School of Marketing Studies, Hyderabad.)

Endnotes

1 DMOs promote tourism business by marketing the destinations and providing various services to the visitors in a country by creating greater advertising impact.

2 Richness – the quality of information like precision, bandwidth, currency, customization, interactivity, value, security.

3 Reach – the number of people who share the information.

4 E-marketing, 3rd Edition, Judy Strauss, Adel El-Ansary and Raymond Frost, Pearson Education, 2003 (page 367).

5 *http://www.iab.net/news/pr_2006_11_14.asp*

6 Latest devices – are the business intelligence tools that mine, analyze and use data about Internet users and their behavior.

7 Parsons A, Zeisser M, & Waitman R (1998) Organizing Today for the Digital Marketing of Tomorrow, *Journal of Interactive Marketing*, 12 (1), pp 31 – 46.

8 *http://www.wilsonweb.com/articles/attract.htm*

9 *http://downloads.velaro.com/livehelpbenefits.pdf*

10 A data mining software that uses the power of customer databases to identify customers who have similar profiles. The findings like preferences, interests, travel patterns etc are used for direct marketing. Eg: *Amazon.com*

11 A data mining software that rests on the belief that people live busy lives and want others to look after their needs.

12 A software that is based on the belief that people want more choices but they just do not want to be burdened with those choices.

13 This software enables electronic transactions

14 This software allows people to communicate with each other visually, regardless of their physical location.

15 VR software displays three-dimensional worlds. Web casting provides online live videos and events.

16 This contributes the most to the success of web-based advertising.

17 This software enriches the social capital of an organization facilitating the communication and knowledge transfer.

18 Werthner H & Klein S (1999) *Information Technology and Tourism – A Challenging Relationship*, Wien: Springer Verlag.

12

Advertising: The Wings of Tourism Industry

T Kalai Selvi

This article analyzes the potential of the tourism industry in India and evaluates the importance of advertising as a strategic communication tool.

Till recently Indian tourism has remained a lackluster industry which is unable to attract proportionate government and private investments. The post-liberalization era has opened up wide new vistas leading to a rapid expansion of travelers' base. It is important that the industry potential is tapped through suitable advertisements that inform the prospective tourists, attract and guide them.

Tourism accounts for 6% of world trade. Currently, in India, it is growing at 8.8% a year, next only to Monte Negro, a European destination which grows at the rate of 10.3%. Considering the cultural richness, diverse and strong religious heritage, superior quality of the higher education is offered, unperturbed natural wealth, pretty beaches and misty mountains, the pace with which the industry has grown is too slow. The chief reason for this poor state of affairs appears to be ineffective marketing and communication strategies. A well-designed and effectively implemented marketing communication strategy alone can make the industry flourish.

Source: Advertising Express, July 2005.

It is advertising among all the other elements of communication mix that creates a major part of the awareness about the product or service. Advertisements provide information and create awareness which further mould the consumer behavior favorably. All the other elements of the mix at one or other point of time require the support of advertising to make the marketing communication strategy a successful one. Advertising has the ability to reach mass markets and thus its ability to reach a large number of customers simultaneously makes it the most economical medium considering the cost of reaching an individual prospect.

There are four factors with regard to the advertising strategy identified and concentrated for tapping the full potential of the industry:

1. Advertising strategies do only the selling task rather than the marketing function.
2. The advertising pattern is seasonal and the continuous effort to understand the changing needs and to build the brand is lacking.
3. The advertisements are targeted only at a few segments and the potential majority is ignored.
4. The 'People factor' is given the least significance.

Advertisements do only the Selling Task rather than the Marketing Function

The marketing task involves educating people about the vast potential of tourism in an appealing way to specific target segments and further facilitating the relevant information to the segments, ensuring excellent service at reasonable rates and elevating the country's tourist attractions as the best in the world. The advertisements emanating from the tourism industry should inform, educate and reinforce the merits of all the elements of marketing mix. However, in India, the tourism advertisements mainly focus on offering informational services. 'The incredible India' website hosted by the Government of India and the other travel and tourism sites hosted by the State Governments give information about hotels available, their rates, the travel details (arrival and departure timings of buses and trains) and a brief narration about the destination with not much stuff to arouse interest.

A brilliant creative concept backing the advertising strategy is needed to get the attention and make the service memorable. It also serves as a thread to weave the entire tapestry (of the series of advertisements) in the campaign. Creativity in advertising requires empathy for the thoughts, feelings and values of the customers, that make them take notice of the advertisements.

To understand the customer, better research needs to be done which will give an insight into their needs, interests and preferences. The advertisements have to be planned accordingly to get the attention of the target audience. A traveler travels to a destination not for only one purpose. They look for opportunities for shopping, even starting new business ventures etc. And also allied services such as banking, insurance, laundry, insurance, transportation, hotel, entertainment etc., will have their impact on the traveler.

A better understanding of the travelers' minds and their travel objectives may make advertisements more meaningful and more successful. The traveler will be satisfied if he gets the value for the money he has spent. Maximum satisfaction is derived when the value is the highest. All these aspects have to be taken into consideration while planning for advertisements.

In the present scenario tourism and travel advertising is at a low offering information to only those who reach them. Whereas the industry has to be aggressive in its advertising as any other FMCG or durable goods company which will enable it realize its full potential.

Advertising Pattern is Seasonal

During 2000-03, there has been constant increase of advertising expenditure in the print media and it is an encouraging sign(Figure 1). Nevertheless, the advertising pattern in the print media (Figure 2) shows that there is heavy expenditure in the first quarter before summer holidays and the last quarter during which most of the festivals are celebrated. The advertisement expenditure declines during the second and third quarters and its pattern reflects the seasonal trend in tourism expenditure as well. However, it needs to be borne in mind that advertising expenditure spread evenly throughout the year has the potential of making the tourism expenditure graph smooth and continuous. As quality of work life is a

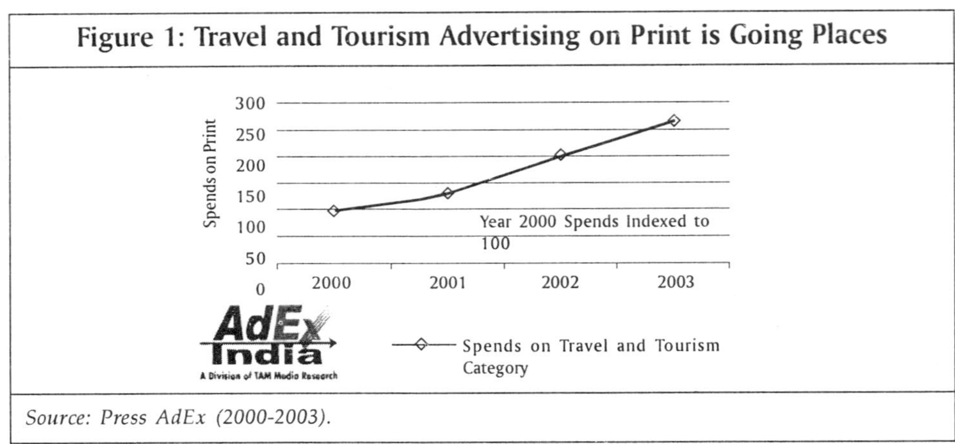

Figure 1: Travel and Tourism Advertising on Print is Going Places

Source: Press AdEx (2000-2003).

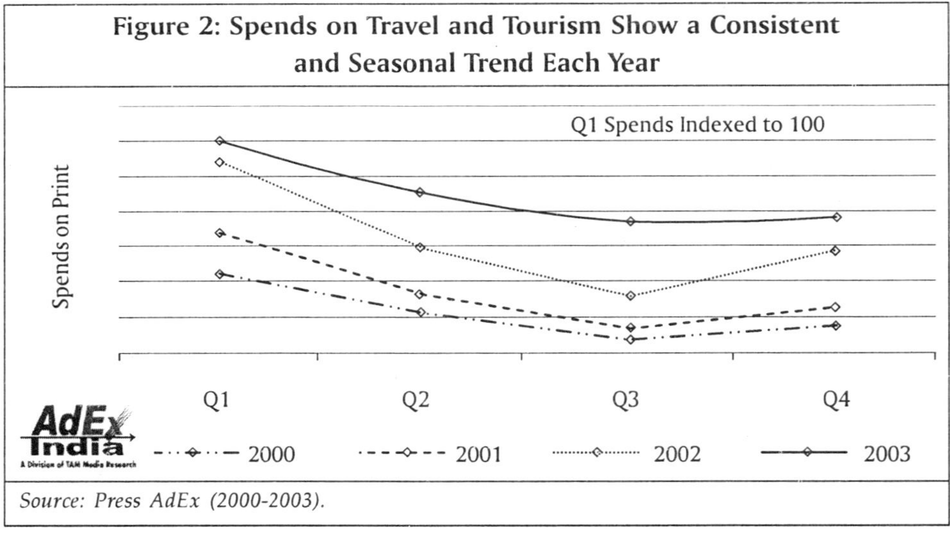

Figure 2: Spends on Travel and Tourism Show a Consistent and Seasonal Trend Each Year

Source: Press AdEx (2000-2003).

great concern for the organization and the organizations are moving towards virtual offices, the holidays are spread throughout the year. This potential segment which avails their leave and holidays during the off-seasons is completely ignored.

The Television (TV) advertising is much disappointing (Figure 3). During the period 2000-2003, the advertising expenditure reached the maximum of 124%. But there is a drastic decline to 27% in the year 2004. TV advertising has also shown no consistency (Figure 4). With regard to the share of spending in TV advertisement (Figure 5) 72% of the spending is by the International and Private agencies, State advertisements share 25%, and the rest 3% is the Ministry's share. Considering the fact that tourism is an emerging industry in India the proportionate advertising expenditure by the Ministry of Tourism appears to be very low. Tourism is still a fledgling industry and requires a lot of nurturing.

Advertisements are Targeted Only at a Few Segments and the Potential Majority is Ignored

Market segmentation enhances the focus and the effectiveness. As far as India is concerned, culture and heritage, sight-seeing, business, visitors friends and relatives, education, pilgrimage, wildlife, health and festivals are ideal segments.

Figure 3: Travel and Tourism Advertising Dips 27% in 2004 Compared to 2003

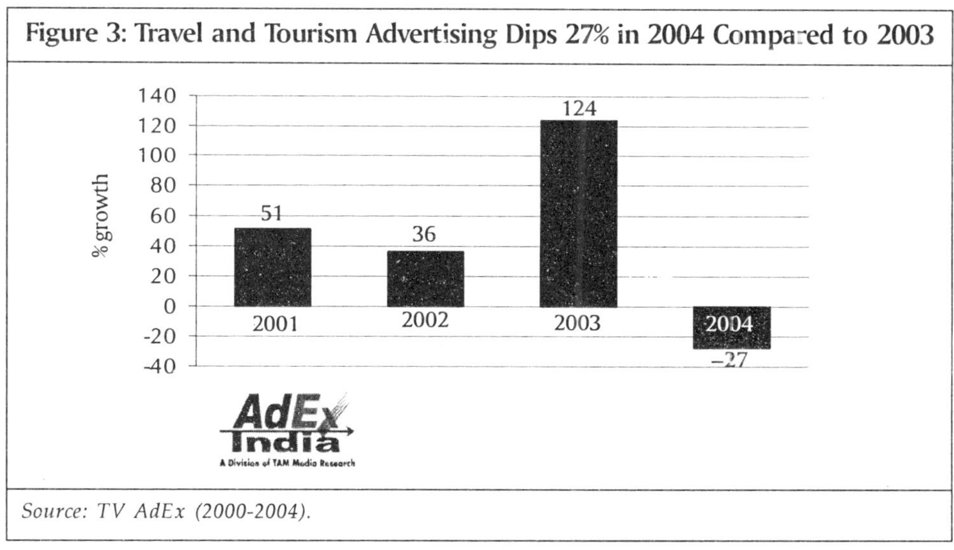

Source: TV AdEx (2000-2004).

As per the survey conducted on purpose to visit India (Table 1), sight-seeing is the major segment followed by business, official, visiting friends and relatives and education. Currently, advertisements focus more on culture and heritage. The potential sight-seeing segment is not given its due. The advertisements are also not directed to visiting friends and relatives and education segments. Well-planned and properly designed marketing strategies supported by effective advertisement campaigns can tap these segments well.

There is a myth that travel and tourism is only for the elites and upper-middle class. This attitude is revealed through the media and methods

Figure 4: No Consistency in Advertising Across 2000-04

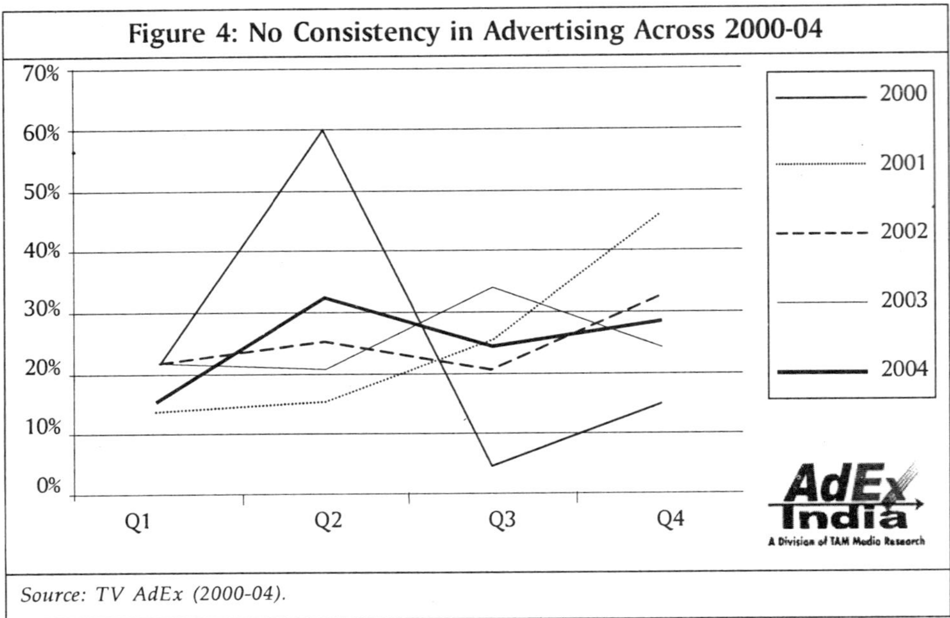

Source: TV AdEx (2000-04).

chosen for advertising. The Computer and English illiterates yet potential travelers are unable to view and understand the advertisements posted on the websites and in the national level-english magazines. There is minimal or no advertising at the regional level except in a few states.

Rural marketing is the buzzword in every other industry in India and it still remains alien to the travel and tourism industry. As discussed earlier, tour packages specially designed for this market can tap this potential majority in India.

The domestic segment is yet another less tapped segment. Tourism need not require a fat wallet of the traveler. Brief yet interesting tour packages could be designed to tap the so far untapped markets within India. Société Internationale de Télécommunications Aéronautiques (SITA) Holidays of India, launched for exploring and rediscovering India by Indians within India, is a welcome step towards promoting domestic tourism. Sitacare has tied up with Vedic India—a medical NRI Health Management tourism company to exclusively concentrate on healthcare is an initiative to promote health tourism. Only conscious efforts supported with aggressive advertising will enable to reach the desired target.

Figure 5: International/Private Tourism Spenders Spend Maximum on TV in 2004

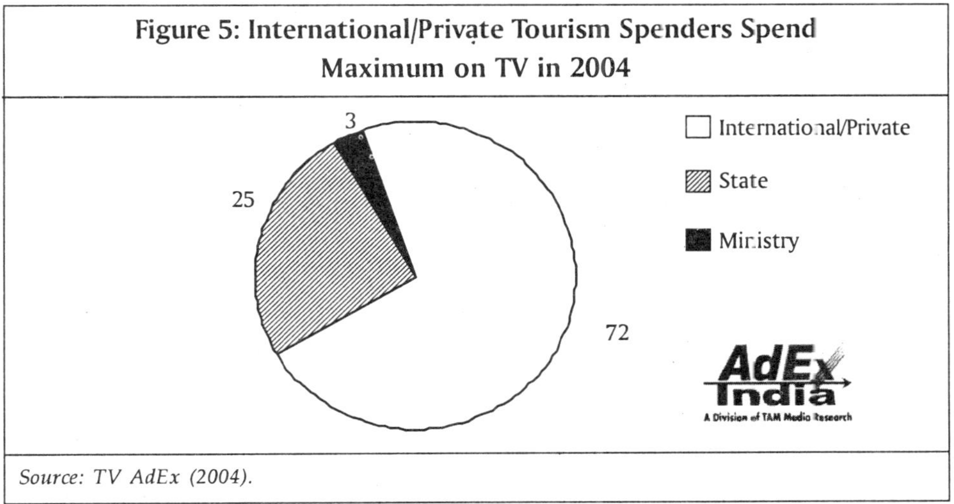

Source: TV AdEx (2004).

Table 1: Distribution of Tourists According to Main Purpose of Visit

	Age in Years			All Ages
Main Purpose of Visit	17-30	31-50	51 and above	
Seeing archaeological monuments	2.5	1.6	1.4	2.0
Visiting hill resorts	0.5	0.2	0.2	0.3
Visiting beach resorts	0.9	0.6	0.3	0.7
Sports and cultural events	1.0	0.6	0.1	0.7
Sightseeing	48.6	32.3	35.0	39.3
Business, official	11.7	36.0	29.1	25.2
Visiting friends and relatives	8.9	11.1	17.3	11.2
Study, education	6.6	3.6	2.3	4.6
Pilgrimage	3.1	3.3	2.9	3.1
Others	16.2	10.7	11.4	12.9
Total	100.0	100.0	100.0	100.0

Source: Data Bank, Courtesy: Marketing of Services IGNOU.

A Mckinsey report says, with thousands of people visiting India for medical treatment, the travel trade could earn around $2.17 bn by 2012. The reasons that attract them towards India are timely treatment, economical pricing and the high quality at par with any other developed country. The advertisements created for Medical tourism have to highlight these points.

Table 2: Perception of Tourists in Asia

Factor	Country/Ranking											
	Hong Kong	India	Indonesia	Japan	Malaysia	Pakistan	PRC	Philip-pines	Singapore	South Korea	Taiwan	Thailand
Rich in culture	-	I(71)	V(40)	IV(40)	VII(25)	-	II(68)	VIII(19)	-	VI(30)	IX(18)	III(57)
Pleasant and warm	-	IX(71)	VI(27)	V(32)	III(35)	-	-	II(37)	IV(33)	VIII(23)	VII(26)	I(57)
Shopping for visitors	I(79)	IX(13)	-	VI(27)	VII(25)	-	-	VII(24)	II(73)	V(34)	IV(36)	III(42)
Value for money	II(41)	IV(34)	V(32)	-	III(37)	-	IV(34)	IV(34)	IV(34)	VI(26)	-	I(53)
Offers good trading opportunities	I(56)	VIII(26)	VII(30)	V(45)	VI(42)	IX(7)	-	-	II(52)	IV(47)	-	III(48)
Easy to do business with	-	VIII(8)	VII(16)	VI(26)	III(30)	IX(3)	VI(18)	VI(18)	-	IV(27)	1(42)	II(35)

Numbers in bracket are percentage of respondents.

Source: Data Bank, The Economic Times. Courtesy: Services Marketing IGNOU.

The private hospitals have to tie up with the Government and the synergy can increase the inflow of the Medical tourists. Cooperative advertisements can be planned and executed.

The "People Factor" is Ignored

In a survey conducted on the perceptions of tourists in Asia among the 12 countries considered, India stands only in the ninth position with regard to Pleasantness and Warmth (Table 2).

The "People factor" is the most significant as far as the tourism industry is concerned. The allied industries such as hotel, laundry, travel, banking, insurance, entertainment, shopping etc., have an impact on the satisfaction of a tourist. Based on the segment of visitors, the tourism industry can have tie ups with the allied industries and they can go for cooperative advertisements focusing the advertisements on their synergies. A common "People policy" has to be framed and the same has to be uniformly and consistently followed. The advertisements have to emphasize on the "People factor" as their edge. Stories on how the tourism industry along with the other supporting industries prepares the people could also be focused on in advertisements.

Conclusion

The realities have been changing. The business networks are ever widening, incomes increasing and educational services are sought beyond borders and there has been a grown care for health and adoration for the tradition and culture, as never before. The country also offers an attractive ground for the global players. These changes have made one look at the tourism industry with a different perspective. With a fresh look, the advertising planning has to be reengineered in the industry to remind this dragon industry of its potential to fly.

(T Kalai Selvi, Faculty member, the Icfai National College, Salem.)

References

1. *Advertising Principles and Practices* – Wells, Burnett, Moriarty.
2. *Services Marketing* – Christopher Lovelock, Jochen Wirtz.
3. *Advertising and Promotion* – George E Belch, Michael A Belch.
4. *Advertising Communications and Promotion Management* – Rossiter and Percy
5. *Survey of Indian Industry* – 2004 The Hindu Publication.
6. Incredible India – a website hosted by the Ministry of Tourism and Travel and other Sites of State Travel and Tourism Ministry.

13

On the Right Track: Joyful Travel

Samita Bhatia

The article captures the joyful travel in these trains to different destinations of historical prominence and sightseeing. Trains such as Palace-on-wheels, Royal Orient, Fairy Queen, and Deccan Odyssey have been put into service to promote tourism and offer unique Indian Experience to the travelers. The luxurious traveling experience, high-quality service offerings, journey schedule have been narrated lividly in the article. The article also captures the experiences of Shahnaz Husain, a well-known beautician and Shruthi Seth, a Veejay.

To die-hard world travellers, train vacations are irresistible holidays, and there's nothing to beat the lure of chugging along on tracks that meander through laid-back or busy railway platforms. Trains that halt at destinations known for their historical past, ancient temples, stunning sea resorts, exotic wildlife and opulent or quaint hotels.

Be it the fear of flying or the hatred of crowded airports, the number of travellers opting for rail vacations is on an increase. The golden days of train travel are back as discerning holiday-makers discover the stress-free pace and smooth hospitality offered by the great train journeys of modern India.

Source: The Telegraph, November 6, 2004.

A Holiday on Wheels

One of the pleasures of boarding any of India's tourist trains is that you find yourself with plenty of time for various activities. Theres time for solitude and time for sightseeing; there's time to relax and time to enjoy the finer things in life; and above all, there's time to discover the company of new-found friends from across the globe.

The India experience is made complete by the myriad trains that criss-cross some of the country's best tourist locales. There are some jewels in India's tourism crown such as heritage tourist trains and narrow gauge 'toy trains' that get you to popular hill stations like Simla, Darjeeling, Ooty and Matheran.

In the Lap of Luxury

Royal India's love for luxury extended to its locomotives. The saloons of royal families used to be built at a huge cost and were extravagant to boot. Today tourists can live it up like the erstwhile royals by booking themselves on week-long tours on any of the luxury trains run by Indian Railways – The Palace-on-Wheels and The Royal Orient (which restarted its operations in 2005). The Fairy Queen, too, offers all-inclusive tours to Alwar from Delhi though it has a shorter run of two days. It finds mention in the *Guinness Book of World Records* as the oldest running steam locomotive in the world.

Your train holiday begins the moment you step aboard to be treated as a guest in a distinctive hotel. But travellers soon realise that no hotel can present them with the kaleidoscope of colours and panoramic scenery that flashes by the cabin windows.

The Palace-on-Wheels and The Royal Orient tours are packaged so that guests sightsee by day visiting palaces, forts, museums, temples, sanctuaries or beaches and retire to the train's royal saloons by night. The trains make quick time at night and arrive at the next destination just as travellers awake the next morning. A week on the train gives an idea of the lands varying topography.

The trains are fitted with all the modern conveniences one would expect of a first class hotel. Besides air-conditioning, each train is complete with restaurants, a library, a bar and lounges, where bartenders serve just the right amount of friendly banter along with your favourite poison. After drinks, make your way to the elegant restaurant car where liveried waiters guide you through a sumptuous menu.

Each saloon boasts of four large coupes with adjoining washrooms and a lounge with a television and video recorder. An attendant is on call 24 hours and the service is impeccable. Broad beds (only the lower bunks are used) with adequate storage facilities make for comfort while the running hot and cold water ensures a refreshing bath at the end of a day of sightseeing. A traditional welcome at every station makes you feel special.

The Palace-on-Wheels

The pride of the Indian Railways and Rajasthan Tourism, the train is the most luxurious way to travel through Rajasthan. It is, in fact, considered as one of the 10 best luxurious train journeys in the world. The coaches of the train originally belonged to the erstwhile rulers of the princely states of Rajputana, Gujarat, the Nizam of Hyderabad and the Viceroy of British India.

Since the coaches were very opulent they were not used by Indian Railways after Independence. However, they rolled into operation in 1982, as the spanking new Palace-on-Wheels with 14 coaches. All the coaches came with different names derived from the former princely states – Kota, Jaipur, Udaipur, Jaisalmer, Jodhpur, Bikaner, Alwar, Sirohi, Kishangarh, Bundi, Dungarpur, Bharatpur, Jhalawar and Dholpur.

The journey takes travellers into the heart of erstwhile *maharaja* country. It touches Jaipur, Jaisalmer, Jodhpur, Sawai Madhopur (to visit the Ranthambore National Park), Chittaurgarh, Udaipur, Bharatpur (for a visit to the Keoladeo Ghana Bird Sanctuary), Fatehpur Sikri and Agra.

The train has two restaurants, The Maharaja and The Maharani serving Continental, Chinese, Indian and Rajasthani cuisine. A satellite phone ensures that passengers can always be in touch – anywhere in the world. (Useful sites: *www.palaceonwheelsindia.com*)

The Royal Orient

In 1991, a new meter gauge Palace-on-Wheels was built on the lines of the original heritage train. The old train metamorphosed into The Royal Orient that now operates in Rajasthan and Gujarat. It is now undergoing some upgrades in its tracks and interiors and will roll out again in 2005.

The Royal Orient, the brainchild of the Tourism Corporation of Gujarat and Indian Railways, is a 13-saloon train. Its first halt is in Chittaurgarh and Udaipur in Rajasthan, from where its on to Gujarat. Before returning to Delhi it makes a halt in Jaipur. Like the Palace-on-Wheels, Oriental and Continental cuisines are served in rather natty dining cars, christened Sasan Gir and Velavadar. (Useful site: *www.gujarattourism.com*)

Fairy Queen

For a shorter journey, time travellers are opting for the two-saloon Fairy Queen, the train which makes an idyllic weekend trip between Delhi and Alwar. In 1855, the grand Fairy Queen had rolled out for the East Indian Railway.

Fairy Queen steams twice a month from October to February taking 50 passengers from around the world on a memorable weekend trip to Alwar. Travellers arrive in the picturesque town in Rajasthan the same day, and from there leave for Sariska Tiger Reserve for an overnight halt. (Useful site: *www.royalorienttrain.com*)

Deccan Odyssey

If a week-long train journey suits you best, then savour Maharashtra aboard the luxurious Deccan Odyssey. The seven-night, eight-day tour includes several exotic destinations covering the vast expanse of Maharashtra and Goa. It takes travellers to Mumbai, Ganpatipule, Ratnagiri, Sindhudurg, Goa, Pune, Aurangabad, Ajanta and Ellora.

The Joy of Hill Trains

Besides heritage trains, the toy trains of India have also grown to become tourist attractions. Rail enthusiasts always find the time to take a slow toy train up to the hill resorts as they offer panoramic views of little hamlets and terraced fields as they go through tunnels and over bridges. These trains, that puff along jungles of *sal* and teak, along steep mountain-sides, past boulders and wild flowers, are engineering marvels in themselves.

The trains, originally built to ferry British officials and their families from the sweltering plains to hilly retreats, are up and puffing today. The wondrous miniature trains that ply between Kalka and Simla and from New Jalpaiguri to Darjeeling are the most popular.

Kalka to Simla: The journey from Kalka to Simla is enchanting as the train stops at picturesque stations along the way. The Simla-Kalka railway has even completed a successful 100-year run. The track from the town of Kalka, that lies at the edge of the plains, to Simla, the former summer capital of British India, was built in 1889.

The track rises from 650m above sea level to a breathtaking 2,100m, passing through some 107 tunnels, 969 bridges, 919 curves and 18 railway stations along the way. The railway track was inaugurated by Lord Curzon, the British Viceroy in India, in November 1903. Tickets are heavily subsidised, as the train boosts Simlas economy with holiday-makers. A one-way ticket costs about Rs.125.

New Jalpaiguri to Darjeeling: The most famous of the little trains is the one linking New Jalpaiguri to Darjeeling. The 86km line with a two feet gauge, makes the Darjeeling Hill Railway the narrowest of the narrow gauges. The journey is regarded as among the most spectacular in the world. In July 1881, the track was opened to traffic.

Mettupalayam to Ooty: At a maximum speed of 33 km per hour, the train from Mettupalayam to Ooty crosses plains, plantations and forest clad hills. The 16 tunnels and tall girder bridges make for breathtaking views.

Neral to Matheran: Matheran is another hill resort that can be reached via a toy train. A narrow gauge toy train from Neral (87km from Mumbai) meanders up the mountain, treating tourists to some spectacular scenery. Getting from Mumbai to Neral by local train takes two hours, while the toy-train journey takes an hour and a half.

Riding one of India's luxury or tourist trains holds out the promise of a very different holiday experience and 'getting there' is just as enjoyable as being there. All in all, a magical journey that you will cherish for a lifetime.

Tour Programmes

Palace-on-Wheels (7 nights/8 days) Runs from September to April Places covered: Delhi, Jaipur, Jaisalmer, Jodhpur, Ranthambore, Agra, Udaipur and Bharatpur

Cost: Rs.1,05,000 per head

Booking: RTDC, Bikaner House, Pandara Road, New Delhi (2338 1884/ 2338 6069)

The Royal Orient (7 nights/8 days)

Places covered: Chittaurgarh, Udaipur, Jaipur, Junagarh, Somnath, Sasan Gir, Diu, Ahmedpur-Mandvi, Palitana and Ahmedabad

Cost: October to March $200 per day; April to September $150 per day. Indians pay the equivalent based on exhange rates.

Booking: Tourism Corporation of Gujarat, II Floor, A-6, State Emporia Building, Baba Kharak Singh Marg, New Delhi (2336 7050/4724)

FAIRY QUEEN (1 night/2 days) Starts every 2nd and 4th Saturday of the month from Delhi. Runs from October to March

Places covered: Departs Delhi Cantonment to arrive in Alwar. Next morning brings a visit to the Sariska Tiger Reserve followed by breakfast and return journey to Delhi.

Cost: Rs.10,000 per head

Booking: Tourism Directorate, Rail Bhavan, New Delhi (2338 3000)

The Toy Trains

Kalka to Simla: Simla is connected to Delhi by a broad gauge line up to Kalka. From Kalka to Simla, the train covers 96km in six hours

Mettupalayam to Ooty: Ooty is connected by a narrow gauge line from Mettupalayam, which serves as the railhead for mainline trains. The Nilgiri Express connects Mettupalayam with Chennai daily. Coimbatore, the nearest city, is 90km away and linked to all the major cities by rail.

New Jalpaiguri (NJP) to Darjeeling: NJP is the starting point of the hill train to Darjeeling and is directly connected to Calcutta, Delhi, Guwahati and other places in India by rail and air

Neral to Matheran: A narrow gauge line from Neral (87km from Mumbai) connects it to Matheran. The trip takes two hours.

14

Athithi Devo Bhava – Indian CRM Way

A V Bala Krishna

Athithi Devo Bhava has been a well-known maxim in Sanskrit language that has been pursued in its true spirit by Indians for so many centuries. Ministry of Tourism, Government of India in its latest endeavor to promote Indian tourism as a whole and particularly to bring home the Indian tourist service providers the necessity to treat foreign travelers well in order to increase the in-bound foreign tourist traffic, has picked up this slogan. Athithi Devo Bhava is a seven point training cum induction programme for the tourist service providers and people involved with the Indian Tourism such as taxi drivers, hotel service providers, tourist police and passport officials.

India has a great tradition of respecting parents, teachers and guests since times immemorial. History points out that this is one of the reasons why Indians were loved and respected throughout the world. Many foreign travelers who visited India during the ancient and middle ages mentioned the same in their travel accounts.

India, with its rich cultural heritage, drew heavily from the vedas and puranas for daily guidance in life. Sanskrit, which was the main medium of conveying the teaching transaction for thousands of years, is replete with many adages in this direction. "Matru Devo Bhava[1]," "Pitru Devo Bhava[2]," "Acharya Devo Bhava[3]," "Athithi Devo Bhava[4]," are a few well-known among them. As time passed on, they have become the guiding principles for leading virtuous and self-disciplined lives for thousands of years in India. Time and again this was emphasized by many spiritual personalities who have taken birth from time to time and advocated to follow these principles to lead organized and peaceful lives. While all other adages remained in their due places, "Athithi Devo Bhava," acquired prominence in the last few years, because of the Tourism Department of India's initiatives to attract foreign tourists. Department of Tourism in India, has picked-up this slogan in its latest campaign to sensitize all the stakeholders in tourism industry, about the importance of treating the in-bound foreign tourists, thereby aiming to encourage and increase foreign tourists' visits to the country. However, it may be puzzling for many, as to how a mere popularization of a slogan could attract tourist traffic to the country?

What is Athithi Devo Bhava?

"Athithi Devo Bhava," by which it means that, "Guest is God." It exhorts one to treat visitor as God. In other words, it implies that visitors' well-being should receive utmost priority. Government of India's tourism department has popularized this age-old maxim of Sanskrit language to initiate a nationwide campaign that aims at sensitizing key stakeholders towards in-bound foreign tourists through a process of training and orientation. It is a social awareness campaign aimed at providing the inbound tourists a sense of being welcomed to the country[5]. This is a capacity building program for tourist service providers and all the stakeholders of the Indian tourism industry. It aims at such key stakeholders of Indian tourism industry such as taxi drivers, immigration officials, tourist police, travel agents etc. 'Athithi Devo Bhava' is a nationwide campaign aimed at sensitising people about India's rich cultural heritage, its preservation, cleanliness, hospitality and bringing out an attitudinal shift among the masses towards foreign tourists."[6] As per Ministry of Tourism, Government of India, "It is a symbolic representation of India's age-old hospitality and with this campaign, we are trying to re-install in the stakeholders a sense of pride and responsibility towards tourists, while positioning India as a popular tourist destination worldwide[7]." "Welcome a guest, send back a friend" is the theme of the program[8]. It is seen as a complement to the "Incredible India Campaign," undertaken by Ministry of Tourism, Government of India.

The Need for the Program

India, despite being rich with a variety of tourist spots and abundant in different flora and fauna does not even figure among top 15 countries of the world in attracting tourist traffic. As per 2005 provisional statistics of Ministry of Tourism, Government of India, India's share in world tourism is 0.49% and in terms of receipts US$5.7 billion and stood at 0.89% of total world revenues[9]. Even though, tourism sector is the third-largest foreign exchange earner for the Indian economy and attracts about 3.92 million tourists per annum as per recent estimates[10], these figures are no match to its true potential and when compared to the figures of tiny Asian countries such as Singapore, Thailand and Malaysia. While Singapore could successfully attract 8.94 million tourists and revenue of $10.8 billion[11], Thailand hosted 15.3 million tourists and generated more than 5,25,000 million Bahts[12], while Malaysia attracted 16.43 million tourists in 2005 and generated revenue of 31,954.1million[13]. Furthermore, when neighboring China earns a share of 4.3% of world tourism's earnings, India, with equally diverse culture and heritage points, has a share of mere 0.89% in the world tourism's earnings[14]. This discernible difference and the huge untapped potential leave much to be expected both from Government (especially in the form of promotion) and other stakeholders of tourism industry. This low realization of true tourism potential is often attributed to a lack of cordial environment within India for in-bound foreign tourists. Charging exorbitant service charges, lack of hygienic environments and lack of awareness regarding sustained benefits of treating foreign tourists well are the pitfalls in exploiting the full tourism potential. "Often tourists are mistreated, cheated and rudely dealt with. This is perhaps the reason why in spite of an incredible wealth of tourist spots, cultural attractions, natural wonders and destinations for the soul, India isn't still amongst the top 15 tourist destinations of the world.[15]"

Eventhough the true potential of tourism sector, not only in earning foreign exchange to the country, but also as a major employment generator, has been recognized by different sections of the society, the necessary measures to remedy this situation fall short of expectations. The scenario can be remedied by initiating certain measures. Creating a better infrastructure, communicating right information, utilization of existing resources, creating a secured environment is expected of government. Inculcating a sense of responsibility to behave well with foreign tourists and encourage them to re-visit the rich cultural heritage of India in understanding as to how to treat the guests is expected of citizens, particularly by all the stakeholders of the tourism industry. The Government possessed with vast resources, and armed with necessary infrastructure may be able to tackle the situation supported by the necessary will. But, given the economic and social structure of India makes it difficult for tourism stakeholders, especially the stakeholders in the unorganized sector, to learn the things on their own. It extends the responsibility of the Government even to educate the citizens on the desired lines. This necessitates a major policy initiative on the part of the Government to stimulate the desired change in the perception of the public in general, and in particular and those who are directly involved with tourism industry such as tourism officials, travel agents, service providers etc., towards foreign tourists. It is heartening to note that government has begun to take cognizance of the full potential of the tourism sector and started employing measures to reverse the trend.

For instance, it has mooted and revived ancient motto of treating the guest as Gods by popularizing the ancient adage "Athithi Devo Bhava." "An initiative of this type has been taken for the first time since Independence[16]." Pointing to the need for it, Mrs Renuka Chowdhury, Minister of State for Tourism, Government of India states, The perception of what tourism means to a country needs to undergo a sea change in India[17]. India is the second such country after Egypt to implement such a kind of program.

Components of the Program

"Athithi Devo Bhava" program is a training and induction charter/catch line for all the stakeholders of the tourism industry. It is a seven point program (See Annexure I) aimed to achieve a perceptible shift in the outlook of the Indian citizens in their approach towards foreigners who visit India. As per Mr Amitabh Kant, Joint Secretary, Ministry of Tourism, Government of India, "The campaign will involve sensitization, screening, induction, training and orientation, certification and feedback of key stakeholders of the Indian tourism industry, including taxi drivers, tourist guides, operators, immigration officers, tourist police and others who have direct interaction with inbound tourists[19]." As per Standing Committee of Ministry of Tourism & Culture, "Capacity building for service providers scheme provides training through one to five day module to persons who are working in organized sectors and who come into contact with a larger number of tourists like those working in small hotels, dhabas, ticketing agents, travel agencies, police personnel etc.[20]"

The training program is to be carried out through a) provision of training and induction program to the stakeholders,b) organizing mass communication programs and c) conducting PR Road Shows.

Training program for the stakeholders emphasizes maintenance of personal and product/service/monument hygiene and cleanliness. It also lays stress on extending basic courtesies to the foreign visitors and behaving politely with them. It further emphasizes charging the foreign tourists a fair price for the services offered to them and not to indulge in cheating.

The training further stresses ensuring the safety and security of the visiting foreign tourists. Training is planned to be organized for various stakeholders of tourism industry based on their education, background and exposure to different levels of sophistication. Accordingly, trainees are divided into two levels and experts provide training to them. The first level covers taxi drivers, tourist guides, baggage handlers, porters and the second level caters to tour operators, shoppers, hoteliers, tourist police and immigration officials. While the first level of training predominantly involves nukkad training and organizing PR road shows apart from classroom training, the second level provides classroom training. After the completion of the training participants will be issued certificates that will be valid for a period of six months. They have to renew the certificates by attending re-training program. These trainees will also be given "Athithi Devo Bhava" logos by the department of tourism, which symbolizes the quality aspect. Taxis, restaurants and hotels whose staff attend the training program will display these logos. Foreign tourists will be encouraged to take the services from those service providers who display these logos. The training program also involves receiving feedback from the foreign tourists who visited India, about the kind of service they received and the behavior of the service providers during their stay so as to improve the training on a continuous basis.

Apart from training, emphasis will also be laid out on 'undertaking PR Road shows with the tourism trade'[21] and 'carrying out mass media communication in newspapers, TV, cinema and outdoors.'[22] The objectives of these programs are to communicate and create awareness among the general public about the importance of undertaking Athithi Devo Bhava program and the sustained long-term benefits they derive from it.

Implementation – Phase wise

The initiative was proposed to be implemented in two phases. While the first phase, which was started on January 19th, 2005 in selected cities such as Delhi, Mumbai, Goa, Hyderabad, Jaipur, Agra, Aurangabad and trained about 26,000 personnel[23], was completed in March 2005[24]. The participants were proposed to be re-trained between April 2005 and March 2006[25]. Tasting the success of the first phase of the training program, Ministry of Tourism, Government of India, initiated second phase of implementation in October 2005 targeting to train about 76,000 personnel and was to be scheduled to be completed in a year's time. The program is expected to be rolled out in a phased manner within a period of three years[26]. For the first year a budgetary sum of Rs.5 crores was allocated for the implementation of the programm[27]. For the year 2005-2006 a budgetary allocation of Rs.10 crores was earmarked for the project[28]. Mass media Campaigns were undertaken through television and print media. These campaigns that were aimed at building general awareness about the need to behave well with visiting foreign tourists also emphasized on fair price and minimum courtesies that needed to be extended to them. For example, a television ad released in the year 2005 aims to create a general awareness among Indian people about the necessity to conduct themselves well with foreign tourists and not to cheat them. This would result in long-term benefits to the country's prosperity in order to enjoy the long-term fruits. The ad commences by depicting a travel agent forcing a visiting foreign tourist to hire their services. The ad further shows that a responsible citizen reprimanding the travel agent not to do so in order to get the foreign tourist back to India. The television ad emphasizes the need for treating the guest equal to God - 'Athithi Devo Bhava'.

In order to give a major push to the 'Athithi Devo Bhava,' program, the tourism ministry convened a meet of nodal officers on 12th May 2005 in New Delhi. The meet was arranged to assign definitive roles to different ministries and departments of state governments and also to gear them up for the campaign.[29] In different states the programme was launched and implemented phase-wise. In Hyderabad, the state capital of Andhra Pradesh, the program was started by providing training to about 250 tourist service providers.[30] In Goa, the program started by Union minister of tourism Ms.Renuka Chowdhury, with a view to involving citizens groups to protect the historical monuments.[31] In Bangalore, the program aimed to train about 10,000 service providers in 2006[32].Trainees would also be offered a stipend of Rs.100/- and a certificate. The training program is structured to create an awareness about 'Athithi Devo Bhava,' campaign and to let the trainees understand their role and the safety aspects. In some of the states such as Andhra Pradesh, Maharashvtra and Karnataka, citizens who wanted to offer accommodation, boarding and entertainment facilities on a chargeable basis for the visiting foreign tourists got registered with the respective government bodies by paying the designated depository amounts. Citizens could provide these services to the visiting foreign tourists on a charge that is pre-fixed and intimated by the respective government bodies depending upon the class of city and the kind of services they offer such as lodging, boarding, provision of television, yoga classes etc. Moreover, the charges were so fixed that they would become quite cheaper when compared with a star hotel and at the same time offer a kind of unique homely experience to the visitors.

Issues/Challenges

For quite a long period, the Government did not provide enough budgetary support for promoting tourism sector. While Singapore, Thailand, Malaysia, China and the USA gave top priority for tourism sector, 'India earmarks only Rs.830 crores.[33]' Moreover, lack of sufficient infrastructure either in the form of developed public utilities or service facilities such as hotels, restaurants etc., is a major obstacle in attracting foreign tourists to the country. Added to this, the lack of will at a higher level with smaller neighboring countries such as Singapore, Thailand and Malaysia becomes a major hurdle in the development of India as a major tourist destination for the visiting foreigners of Asian continent. Moreover the reputation of India in the minds of foreigners especially that of Western countries needs to be improved before embarking on any major initiative. India is still viewed as a land of snake charmers and fakirs. This image needs to be changed positively by popularizing India's major tourist attractions and rich cultural heritage. Even though, in recent times, Incredible India campaign did this job reasonably well, much is believed to have been left undone. Often, Indian service providers, often, in the bargain of earning a short term benefit/reward earned notoriety as cheaters in the eyes of foreign tourists, which definitely worked against their long-term interests of earning huge foreign exchange. "Give the tourists what they want and they will come again and again[34]," says Murray Jones, a UK based tour operator and feels that most of the people in India are interested in getting maximum out of a foreign tourist's single and the first visit itself, but not interested in getting more from repeated visits[35]. In-bound foreign tourists feel the pinch, right from the moment they get landed on Indian soil, from the airport itself, from the non-cooperative attitude of immigration officials and with the existence of 'touts' which can have a negative impression with them, says Mr.Rajji Rai, Travel Agents Association of India's Vice President[36]. This apart, a slackness on the part of implementers of any new initiative like 'Athithi Devo Bhava,' the lack of appropriate infrastructure or inadequate awareness among stakeholders or inability to effectively communicate the message often work against the success of the initiative. Underutilization of the funds is another problematic issue. For instance during 2005-2006 the outlay for capacity-building for service providers program was not fully utilized.[37]

Future Perspective

As per Secretary, The Department of Tourism, Government of India, "We started Athithi Devo Bhava campaign and training programme. This has been well received. We will continue to do that in the current year. We will expand its scope. We are now equipping our institutes to take up this capacity-building in a much larger way."[38] With the program started in the first half of 2005 and scheduled to be rolled out in a phased manner in a period of three years, the campaign aims at leveraging the sustained benefits of "Athithi Devo Bhava," by bringing different stakeholders of tourism in India into its fold. With fast-increasing literacy levels and the ubiquitous presence of electronic and print media through the length and breadth of the country, this task should become easier. Moreover, the budget allocation for tourism has more than doubled between '2003-2004

(Rs.325 crore) to 2006-2007 (Rs.830 Crore)' with the rapid growth of airlines, especially, low-budget airlines, in-bound foreign tourists have more travel options to choose from within India. However, success of these initiatives in attracting foreign tourists to India depends upon how good our service levels are and how fair our deals are apart from how prudent are our travel packages. India, with the varied cultures poses a unique complexity for foreign travelers. India, a country having 22 different languages and more than 1500 mother tongues and its status of still a developing nation exposes visiting foreign tourists to different perplexities. They will be exposed to scores of service people speaking different dialects, while receiving their services. Any capacity-building program without specific address to these issues will leave much to be desired.

Also, the ability of the neighboring nations to attract the Asian-bound international tourist traffic to their respective countries by beaming unique themes from time to time such as 'Showcase Malaysia[39]' poses new competitive situations. Any new initiative to promote tourism should take all these aspects into consideration before embarking upon strategizing it. At the same time, new opportunities need to be identified by looking at the surrounding socio-economic developments. For instance, excessive growth of satellite television channels, scope for rapid growth of Indian cable television channels across the national boundaries, widespread proliferation of Internet and Web technologies opened up new vistas for Indian tourism industry. This results in more foreign people coming into contact with Indian Culture, 'Places of Prominence and Interest' through these channels and their exposure to real socio-political and economic conditions nullify the long-standing false impressions about India in the eyes of foreigners, especially Western travelers and creates new interest in India. This offers a new opportunity for tourism department in bringing out a positive shift in the perceptions of foreign tourists towards India.

Conclusion

India despite being very rich in variety of flora and fauna and having scores of historical and religious places could not claim the attention of foreign tourists for many decades. Instead, foreign tourists preferred the neighboring tiny nations such as Singapore, Malaysia and Thailand. Many factors are cited as the cause for the poor show by India on the international tourist map. Lack of appropriate tourism infrastructure, paucity of funds to promote tourism and non-congenial environment for the inbound foreign tourists are a few prominent ones among them. While most of the problems are being tackled the last aspect i.e., providing a welcoming environment to the visiting foreign tourists, was ignored for many years. However, the need to conduct 'Athithi Devo Bhava Program,' was to create awareness about the tourism's potential to create sustained benefits and the importance of behaving well with the visiting foreign tourists. With ever-changing realities in the tourism environment the program aims to achieve mutual satisfaction both for the service providers as well as the visiting foreign tourists. Capacity-building for the service providers is the core of the program, while receiving feedback from the visiting foreign tourist acts as the input to further improve the training inputs. With a prediction of more and more countries depending on tourism receipts for developing their economies in the coming decade, the ability to make the tourists repeat their visits holds the key for success.

Annexure I: The Seven point Athithi Devo Bhava Program

Athithi Devo Bhavah is a 7 point program of hospitality and training.

Samvedan Sheelta or Sensitisation

Here we will sensitise the various sections of the tourism industry about how each of them contribute for the growth of the tourism industry and how they will benefit from it.

Prashikshan or Training and Induction

This involves explaining to them the needs and expectation of the tourists, how they should respond and behave in order to satisfy their needs and meet those expectations.

Prerna or Motivation

This is motivation to participate in this program through various measures e.g., awards for the best worker in the segment. Because when you are enthused you can do wonders.

Pramani Karan or Certification

Certification to ensure standards shall be done at an appropriate stage in the training program.

Pratipushti or Feedback

Feedback shall be obtained from tourists about the service they have received and the experience they had, in order to improve the training program on a continuous basis.

Samanya Bodh or General Awareness

The mass media communication campaign will be undertaken to create general awareness among the public about the necessity and the benefits of the Athithi Devo Bhava programme.

Contd...

Contd...

Swamitwa or Ownership

The Atithi Devo Bhava programme is a movement we will urge all segments of the Indian society to adopt, and look upon as their own.

The Charter of Athithi Devo Bhava Training Program

Hygiene & Cleanliness

Hygiene & Cleanliness shall cover the areas of product for e.g., vehicles like taxies, hotel rooms, restaurants, shops, etc., personal hygiene & cleanliness of the person providing the service and cleanliness of the monuments /places of tourist interest.

Conduct and Behavior

The person concerned for e.g., the taxi driver /hotel employee shall behave in courteous and polite manner towards tourists.

Integrity and Honesty

The person providing service to the foreign tourists should display honesty and integrity.

Safety and Security

The safety and security of the tourists shall be ensured.

Source: www.incredibleindia.com

(A V Bala Krishna, Faculty Associate, Icfai Books, Hyderabad.)

Endnotes

1 Matru Devo Bhava means Mother is God.

2 Pitru Devo Bhava means Father is God.

3 Acharya Devo Bhava means Teacher is God.

4 Athithi Devo Bhava means Guest is God.

5 Tourism in India: Issues and Prospects, Current Economic Statistics and Review for the Week Ended January 28, 2006 (4th Weekly Report of 2006), *www.epwrf.res.in*

6 "Athithi Devo Bhava," *http://www.incredibleindia.org*

7 ibid

8 "Statement of Outlays and Outcomes/Targets: Annual Plan 2005-2006," Ministry of Tourism

9 *http://tourism.gov.in/statistics/Figure2005.pdf*

10 *ibid*

11 *www.asiatraveltips.com*

12 *http://www2.tat.or.th*

13 *http://www.tourism.gov.my*

14 *http://tourism.gov.in/statistics/Figure2005.pdf*

15 "Athithi Devo Bhava," *http://www.incredibleindia.org*

16 "New drive to boost tourism launched," *www.thehindubusinessline.com*

17 Tribune News Service, Thursday, January 20th, 2005, "Athithi Devo Bhava to be mantra of taxi drivers, immigration officials," *www.tribuneindia.com*

18 ibid

19 *http://www.incredibleindia.org*

20 Department-Related Parliamentary Standing Committee On Transport, Tourism & Culture One Hundred and Fourth Report on Demand for Grants (2006-2007) (Demand No.92) of Department of Tourism (Presented to the Rajyasabha On 22.5.2006), *rajyasabha.nic.in*

21 "Athithi Devo Bhava," *www.incredibleindia.com*

22 ibid

23 "Record Increase In Tourist Arrivals And Foreign Exchange Earnings: New Schemes of Tourism Infrastructure Upgradation And Human Resource Development Launched," Wednesday, December 28, 2005, *pib.nic.in*

24 Government of India, Ministry of Tourism, Rajya Sabha, Unstarred Question No. 3016, Answered on 20.12.2005, Programmes To Attract Tourists, Smt Renuka Chowdhury, *http://rajyasabha.nic.in*

25 "Athithi Devo Bhava," *www.incredibleindia.com*

26 Tribune News Service, Thursday, January 20th, 2005, "Athithi Devo Bhava to be mantra of taxi drivers, immigration officials," *www.tribuneindia.com*

27 ibid

28 Statement of Outlays and Outcomes/Targets: Annual Plan 2005-2006," Ministry of Tourism.

29 K V Kurmanath, "Centre Calls meet to rev up tourism drive," *The Hindu Business Line*, dated 12th May, 2005, *www.thehindubusinessline.com*

30 Tribune News Service, Thursday, January 20th, 2005, "Athithi Devo Bhava to be mantra of taxi drivers, immigration officials," *www.tribuneindia.com*

31 "Tax breaks planned for efforts to protect monuments," *The Hindu*, 8th February, 2005, *www.the hindu.com*

32 "Auto, taxi drivers to be 'cultural ambassadors'," *The Hindu*, 26th July, 2006, *www.thehindu.com*

33 "Tourism Demand No.29, Policy Note – 2006 -2007," *www.tn.gov.in*

34 Atul Sethi, "Where's Incredible India," *www.timesofinda.com*

35 ibid

36 ibid

37 Department-Related Parliamentary Standing Committee On Transport, Tourism & Culture one Hundred and Fourth Report on Demand for Grants (2006-2007) (Demand No.92) of Department Of Tourism (Presented To the Rajyasabha On 22.5.2006), *rajyasabha.nic.in*

38 Department-Related Parliamentary Standing Committee on Transport, Tourism & Culture one Hundred and Fourth Report on Demand for Grants (2006-2007) (Demand No.92) of Department of Tourism (Presented to the Rajyasabha on 22.5.2006), rajyasabha.nic.in

39 "Travel Fiesta for the Indian Traveller," *www.outlooktraveller.com*

SECTION III

CASES AND APPLICATIONS

15

Luxury on Wheels

Achal Dhruva

As the Deccan Odyssey commences its second season Achal Dhruva relives the memorable experience of enjoying the romance of the rails in royal comfort.

Humans are highly adaptable creatures, especially when it comes to comfort. All it took was probably an hour on-board the luxury train, Deccan Odyssey to throw all my romantic notions about unreserved and second-class train journeys, that have long been eulogised as the window to the heart of India, on to the tracks. After all, who wouldn't succumb to ostentatious luxury, beginning with a valet handing you a tall ice-cold glass of refreshing juice as you check into your suite on-board, the joy of unpacking your suitcase and arranging your clothes in the wooden closet followed by a long nice hot shower and then tucking yourself under the blankets on a soft bed in air-conditioned comfort to watch the latest 'Bollywood item number,' on the plasma television. And all this was just in my suite, the tip of the iceberg of the myriad and unique offerings designed to pamper you silly and make you feel like royalty.

Deccan Odyssey offers the best of both worlds – romance of the rails with five-star luxury, and attractive destinations showcasing the cultural, historical and scenic beauty of Maharashtra and Goa on its seven-day round trip from Mumbai. The Rs.32-crore train, a joint venture between the Maharashtra government, the Railway ministry and the Maharashtra Tourism Development Corporation (MTDC) was flagged off by the then Prime Minister, Atal Behari Vajpayee on January 16, 2004. Positioned against the great luxury trains of the world like the Orient Express and the Royal Scotsman, Deccan Odyssey is India's third and the eighth luxury train in the world. A flagship tourism product of MTDC aimed at placing Maharashtra on the map of premium tourist destinations, the train comprises 21 carriages hosting a total of 48 suites including four Presidential Suites and a staff of 50 with two valets per cabin catering to 96 passengers.

Emerging from my plush haven (suite), I began my exploration of the train but couldn't get further as I stumbled upon Mumbai Hi – the bar. The entire coach has been designed tastefully with easy chairs, sofas, small round tables, and a well-stocked bar with premium labels of liquor and the best wines. It was sheer delight to sip a drink out of a proper glass and smoke in peace on a train, after years of drinking surreptitiously out of a Coke or Pepsi bottle and fugitively having a smoke near stinking loos.

Dinner at Peshwa II, one of the two restaurants on-board was also a grand affair. The interiors of the restaurant, like the entire train recreate the opulence of Maratha royalty and have been designed by a firm that specialises in the interiors of heritage hotels. A three-course meal, comprising a selection of regional cuisine and continental dishes, was served by stewards dressed as Mavlas (Maratha warriors during the reign of Chatrapati Shivaji Maharaj). The catering and housekeeping on-board the train is outsourced to the Taj Group of Hotels. As I tucked in on the first night I was quite abuzz with anticipation of the excitement and pampering

Presidential Suite bedroom

Welcome at Bhoke station

The train boasts of a fully equipped spa

Pic: Mexy Xavier

View of the entrance of Sindhudurg Fort

Pic: Achal Dhruva

that would be dished out during the remainder of the journey.

The next morning we got down at Bhoke station before Ratnagiri on the Konkan Railway route to a rousing welcome of drums and 'tutari' (a kind of bugle) by the locals, a sequence which would be repeated at almost all the stations. We set off for Rai Jetty by an air-conditioned bus for a two-hour boat cruise on

Itinerary of Deccan Odyssey

Day 1 (Wednesday): Departure from CST at 16.40 for Bhoke. Dinner on-board

Day 2 (Thursday): Breakfast on-board and departure from Bhoke station to Rai Jetty by A/C coach. Two hour (approx) boat cruise to Jaigarh Jetty through the backwaters. Visit to Jaigarh Fort and then to Ganpatipule Beach by road. Lunch at MTDC Resort in Ganpatipule along with cultural programmes and free time. Post-lunch visit to Lord Ganesh Temple on the beach and departure to Ratnagiri. Visit to Ratnagiri Fort and then back to the train at Ratnagiri station. Depart for Sindhudurg. Dinner on-board.

Day 3 (Friday): Breakfast on-board and departure for Malvan Jetty by A/C coach to visit the sea-fort, Sindhudurgh. Then on to the MTDC Tarkarli Beach Resort for lunch followed by some leisure time. From Tarkarli depart for Walaval Jetty on a boat cruise on the backwaters of Tarkarli Creek. Journey to Sawantwadi by coach to visit Shilpagram and Art & Craft Centre for a cultural show, cooking demonstration of regional cuisine, etc. Return to train and depart for Goa. Dinner on-board.

Day 4 (Saturday): After breakfast on-board, depart from Karmali station for sightseeing by A/C coach to Old Goa. Visit Basilica of Bom Jesus, Se Cathedral, St. Francis of Assissi, the Goan Antiques museum and Fontanhas, the Latin quarters in Panjim. Lunch at Beach Hotel in South Goa followed by leisure time. Return to train at Madgaon station and depart for Pune. Dinner on-board.

Day 5 (Sunday): Breakfast on-board followed by sightseeing by A/C coach in Pune with visits to Raja Dinkar Kelkar Museum, Shaniwar Wada and Agha Khan Palace. Return to train after lunch and depart for Aurangabad. Dinner on-board.

Day 6 (Monday): Breakfast on-board followed by visits to Daulatabad Fort and Ellora Caves. Lunch at hotel in Aurangabad followed by a visit to Bibi-Ka-Maqbara and free time for shopping. Return to train and depart for Jalgaon. Dinner on-board.

Day 7 (Tuesday): Early breakfast on-board and departure from Jalgaon station for a visit to Ajanta Caves by A/C coach. Return to train and depart for Nashik with lunch on-board. In Nashik visit the Panchvati Ghats and Asian Temples. Dinner on-board and departure for Mumbai.

Day 8 (Wednesday): Breakfast on-board and check out at CST, Mumbai.

the backwaters to Jaighad Fort. The backwaters of the Konkan region, though relatively unknown, are as enchanting as the ones in Kerala.

Jaighad Fort, one of the numerous forts dotting Maharashtra, is rather small. Perched on a cliff it offers a breathtaking panoramic view of the sea on one side and the creek snaking through lush green foliage on the other. As is the bane of package trips, there is little time "to stand and stare," and we were off to MTDC's Ganpatipule Beach Resort for lunch. Ganpatipule Beach with its long strip of silver sands and blue waters has become a very popular weekend getaway.

	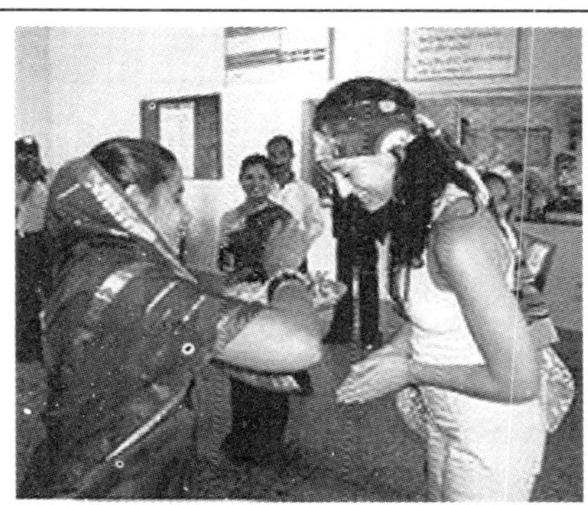
Conference coach, the only one of its kind on luxury trains in India	Traditional welcome of tikka and aarti

Guest participating in the folk programme during the boat cruise	Peshwa II, one of the two restaurants Pic: Mexy Xavier

Post-lunch, which was accompanied by a folk dance show and a visit to the famous Ganpati Temple on the beach, we were off to Ratnagiri to board the train.

Tariff		
Room Type	**October 2005-March 2006**	**April 2006**
Deluxe Suite		
Single Occupancy	Rs. 20,000	Rs. 15,000
Double Occupancy	Rs. 15,000	Rs. 12,000
Triple Occupancy	Rs. 10,000	Rs. 9,000
Presidential Suite		
Single Occupancy	Rs. 40,000	Rs. 30,000
Double Occupancy	Rs. 30,000	Rs. 24,000
		Contd...

Contd...

- All rates are per person, per night and for a leg of minimum three days.
- Tariff is inclusive of travel/catering/conducted sight-seeing/entrance fee at monuments/ parks/palaces/cultural programmes/boat ride. Guests have to pay for video cameras, liquor, laundry and other items of personal nature.
- Half fare is applicable for children between 5-12 years.
- 10% surcharge shall be levied on departure during Christmas/New Year.

Itinerary and terms are subject to change without notice

Reservation Contact details

Tel: 022, 202673/7762/7784; **Fax**: 022, 2852182

E-mail: info@mtdcdeccanodyssey.com

Website: *www.maharashtratourism.gov.in; www.mtdcdeccanodyssey.com*

It had been a long but exciting day in the sun and I decided to check out the health spa car equipped with steam, beauty parlour and gymnasium. After a good massage followed by a steam bath I was all set for a blissful night's sleep.

The sea-fort of Sindhudurgh, two kms from Malvan Jetty is an architectural marvel and was the first stop on the next day's itinerary of sightseeing from Sindhudurg station. Our next halt was at Tarkarli Beach, yet another gorgeous and relatively untouched beach. The boat cruise on the backwaters of Tarkarli Creek to Walaval Jetty was even more scenic than the one on the first day and the

Palace in Sawantwadi

Pic: Achal Dhruva

Aerial view of the Ganpatipule Beach

Contd...

Mumbai-Hi, the watering hole on-board Pic: Mexy Xavier	Boat cruise on the Tarkarli Creek

sight of fish leaping out of water had us riveted. From Walaval Jetty, we headed for Sawantwadi, the last major town before crossing into Goa. After a brief walk through the town, with a visit to the Palace and the Arts and Crafts centre to witness an enthralling cultural show, we were back on the train.

The next day saw us in Goa, and we did the rounds of the most popular tourist spots like the Basilica of Bom Jesus, Se Cathedral, Old Goa, etc. We boarded the train at Madgaon station rather early that evening for the long run to the next halt, Pune. One may have felt cheated about not being able to enjoy a night out in town in Goa, but the conference coach on Deccan Odyssey -- the only luxury train in India to have one – came to the rescue. The conference coach, Samvad, is equipped with a state-of-the-art LCD TV and audio system, and is designed in such a manner that it can be converted into a party zone, and that's exactly what we did, and rocked the night away.

While I had to hop-off at Pune station due to work commitments and miss the ensuing journey to Aurangabad to visit World Heritage sites of Ellora and Ajanta and Nashik, the three nights on-board were easily the most memorable of train journeys I have experienced till date. The cost of the Deccan Odyssey journey is as luxurious as the experience, and may not be for everyone, but oh what an experience! Also, those hard pressed for time can opt for the shorter version of the trip (either Mumbai-Pune, or Pune-Mumbai).

After the luxurious living on Deccan Odyssey it was tough getting back to the reality of normal train travel from Pune to Mumbai.

Se Cathedral in Panjim Pic: Achal Dhruva	Scenic view of the backwaters from Jaighad Fort Pic: Achal Dhruva

16

A Success Story

R Krishna Kumar

Kerala has developed a series of innovative concepts and projects to reinvigorate the State's tourism sector without diluting its commitment to conserve nature.

Kerala's swaying green palms, golden sands and languid backwaters once said it all. The occasional heat and dust-weary traveller needed neither advertisement nor invitation to bask in the coastal experience and embrace the rich natural and cultural diversity contained within its 38,863 square kilometres. Tourism promotion was an afterthought. Initial strategies to package the State as a tourism destination and develop the sector lacked focus and direction, met with scepticism and even derision, and were weighed down by the bureaucracy. Kovalam was Kerala's only claim to fame and it too was becoming jaded and a bit disappointing for its ill-planned, unsustainable growth and inadequate infrastructure.

Early morning in Munnar, one of the major hill stations in the State.

Source: www.flonnet.com © Frontline. Reprinted with permission.

The need to market and reposition itself and rope in the private sector to capitalise on the employment, revenue and foreign exchange generating potentials of tourism was too easy to recognise. Concessions and incentives were offered by the State government to woo private investment and promote tourism products after it was declared an industry in the late 1980s. But critics were sceptical of such aspirations, and decried efforts in this direction as being impractical in a State that remained economically sluggish despite impressive developmental indices. Though teething troubles were aplenty, but Kerala Tourism as a brand was developed with persistent, focussed effort, within a span of 10 years. There was a deliberate reorientation away from mass tourism, and towards projecting the State as an up-market, high-quality destination, identifying its inadequacies – minimal infrastructure and poor air connectivity, while capitalising on its exclusivity such as centuries-old Ayurvedic expertise and meandering sun-dappled backwaters.

The problem that niggled the State's tourism sector until then was whether to concentrate first on the development of infrastructure or on tourism promotion. The decision that came with the recognition that they both should go hand-in-hand blazed the trail for the travel and tourism boom in Kerala, making it one of its most economically viable industries today. According to figures of the State Tourism Department, the sector generated Rs.6,828 crores in total revenue, including foreign exchange earnings of about Rs.1,300 crores in 2004. Being a service industry, it employs about eight lakh people, directly and indirectly. Highly visible and targeted promotional campaigns and aggressive marketing ploys – including participation in travel marts, international and national tourism fairs, road shows, an enticing award-winning Website, CD-ROMs, a promotional film by ace cinematographer/director Santosh Sivan, colour-splashed succinct advertisements and the slogan that famously branded Kerala as "God's Own Country" have helped Kerala to leapfrog the status of being the most acclaimed tourist destination in the country.

Kerala is today India's benchmark for success in tourism, with the prestigious "Partner State" status conferred on it in recognition of its potential and performance by the World Travel and Tourism Council (WTTC). Commendations from the *National Geographic Traveller* as being one of the 50 "Must See" destinations of a lifetime and "one of the ten paradises of the world", other appreciative tributes from leading publications, including the coveted Super brand status, and numerous national and international awards have attracted both domestic and foreign pleasure-seekers in droves. Tourist inflow has increased exponentially over the years. The figures are impressive – Domestic tourist arrival in 2004 was estimated at over 59 lakhs (up from nine lakhs in 1990) and international tourist arrival at over three lakhs, more than 12 percent of the total number of foreign tourists arriving in India.

What has generated so much interest in such a tiny State? Apart from the famed 600 km coastline, enchanting backwaters, mist-laden hill stations, wildlife sanctuaries, national parks, historical monuments, pilgrim centres and awe-inspiring art forms, the "Kerala experience" now encompasses a variety of innovative tourism products – Ayurvedic rejuvenation packages, traditional houseboat holidays, cultural and religious festivals and celebrations, package tours, trekking, and increasingly popular concepts such as home stays, "farm and village tourism", "eco-agro tourism", "wellness holidays", "culinary holidays", and "working vacations" or "corporate getaways".

Kerala today can create experiences tailored to appeal to specific whims – a wedding in an exotic or traditional locale, a unhurried ride in a tinkling bullock cart, a stay in a tree house, or a walk through paddy field slush. The new age tourist can luxuriate or revel in the simplest of pleasures in exotic resorts, bask in the sunshine or refresh himself in the invigorating monsoon rain, gaze at the spectacle of caparisoned elephants or scramble atop one. It is "multi-destination tourism" at its best, offering a multitude of variegated experiences and attractions within a relatively small area, luring tourists into staying longer and spending more. The tourist visiting the State for an average of two weeks gets to see and savour more of Kerala than the laidback Malayali does in a lifetime.

The question before the State's tourism planners is, having once refurbished the sector's image and redefined its goals to facilitate such phenomenal growth, how can it be sustained? The tourism sector in Kerala continues to scan the world for prospective clients even as the world increasingly eyes the State as a dream destination. Along with the existing lucrative European market, great potential is in Australia. Efforts are on to woo clients from the West and South Asian regions. New tourism concepts such as monsoon tourism, medical tourism, adventure tourism, heritage tourism, pilgrimage tourism, eco tourism, and farm tourism are being developed and popularised, with a few private players keen on providing "experiential" holidays to discerning customers.

The rapid growth of the sector raises concerns. In encouraging creativity and private enterprise in the quest for innovation, norms must not be flouted, standards and quality must be regulated at periodic intervals, and exclusivity maintained. A handful of *kettuvalloms* (houseboats) may be a novelty, too many can spoil the lake. The total capital investment needed in tourism is projected to increase from Rs.1,800 crores in 2003 to Rs.7,500 crores in 2013, the lion's share of it expected to come from the private sector. The travel and hospitality industry has seen the pro-active involvement of private players, with the state playing the role of a catalyst and a facilitator, investing in critical infrastructure and formulating appropriate guidelines. The Oberoi, Taj, Mahindra Resorts, Casino and other national and international hotel chains have provided getaways throughout the State, helping to keep the tourist population dispersed. Local enterprises and private tour operators have been pivotal in helping showcase the essence of Kerala.

In order to strike a balance between the need to encourage further private sector investment and to conserve nature, a number of Special Tourism Zones are to be identified and developed under the purview of the Kerala Tourism (Conservation and Preservation of Areas) Act, 2005, which envisages the conservation, preservation and integrated development of such areas. The Act prohibits developmental activity, including construction in the special zones, except in accordance with its guidelines. The comprehensive development of Kovalam, Kumarakom, Fort Kochi and Munnar is proposed in the first phase of the project. Tour operators say there is a crying need to invest in expanding hotel accommodation and facilities for travel. Suggestions have been made to set up a novel "Heritage Home Protection Scheme" that provides incentives to convert traditional houses (*tharavads*) into tourist accommodations.

A view of the fireworks that mark the conclusion of the Thrissur Pooram festival.

More luxury cruises and houseboats would raise the revenue-generating potential per tourist, but the pollution of the backwaters is already a cause of concern. Common sanitation facilities have been proposed as a means to end such pollution. The preservation of the State's unique culture, art and heritage has been set as a priority. Work on heritage areas and structures has been undertaken by the State Tourism Department. Projects include the conservation of forts, restoration of mural paintings at temples and museums, and beautification of heritage buildings and premises. The Centre has allocated Rs.25 crores to the Tourism Department for schemes on heritage conservation in the State. Major projects for the conservation of forts in the Malabar region and the Thrippunithara heritage town are in the offing.

Hitherto unexplored or lesser-known areas, especially in the Malabar region, traditional skills, handicrafts, art forms, and new tourism products are to be developed and marketed to sustain tourist interest. Constant innovation is seen as the way to draw in the discerning tourist and prevent the frequent traveller from developing visitor-fatigue. The Tourism Department has drawn up a plan to develop pilgrim facilitation centres in association with the temple/church/mosque authorities concerned.

To solve the problem of lack of quality space in major town centres for tourists to congregate, town squares with public utility systems, information and facilitation centres and parking areas are proposed to be built in association with the local bodies. Wayside centres with minimum standardised facilities – restaurant, souvenir shop, public toilet, Internet/Automatic Teller Machines (ATM), public telephone – are to be set up through private sector initiatives. The *vazhiyoram* units are to be strategically placed so that there is at least one such facility within 10 to 12 km on roads leading to tourist destinations and on State and national highways.

Alappuzha is set to regain its lost glory as the "Venice of the East" with various schemes launched for the cleaning and beautification of its canals and backwaters, and establishment of various tourist-oriented facilities. The Bekal project envisages the development of the Bekal fort in Kasaragode district.

Generating the human resources needed for the burgeoning tourism industry is a challenge. The recommendations include exploring the possibilities of establishing more institutes to cater to the needs of the hospitality industry and travel and tourism sector as well as raising the existing standards in institutes, absorbing the educated unemployed into the sector after imparting specialised skills in tourism management to them, and making the host population "tourism friendly" by creating awareness about the need to interact appropriately with tourists.

In order to retain its competitive edge, Kerala needs to address its inadequacies in tourism infrastructure and ensure that its famed natural wealth and cultural heritage are not compromised by unbridled growth. The promotion of sustainable tourism through the rational use of resources is the aim of the industry, but efforts to diversify further the Kerala experience and use opportunities to cash in on the State's vast untapped potential carries with them the threat of ecological and cultural degradation. Paradoxically, the aggressive promoters of the land and its culture should also be its preservers. But it is a challenge boldly laid down in the slogan of Kerala Tourism Vision 2025: "Conserve Nature and Culture and Promote Tourism".

17

Marketing of Buddhist Destinations in Orissa: A Development Perspective for Tourism Services

Rajnandan Patnaik

Orissa, with its natural forests, rivers, mangroves, beaches and wildlife, provides a satisfying experience to tourists. Its ancient artistic temples, historic sites and embracing ambience exhilarate the spirits of tourists. The main highlights of the state are its capital city, Bhubaneshwar, the city of temples, Simlipal and Nandankanan sanctuaries, the mangrove forests of Bhitarkanika, the architectural marvels that dominate the landscape—Jagannath temple at Puri, Lingaraj temple at Bhubaneshwar, and Sun Temple at Konark, the golden sandy beaches at Puri, Konark, Gopalpur and Chandipur, and the natural port of Paradip. The Jagannath cult, which has been the core for Orissan culture, is believed to hold the 'tooth relics' of Buddha; and historians have long argued of Puri as 'Dantapura' or the 'land of tooth'. Some recent excavations have established Orissa as a center of Buddhist evolution. The tourism department of the Government of Orissa considers this as

Source: The Icfai Journal of Services Marketing, March 2006.

an opportunity to promote Orissa broadly on the lines of religious tourism, in general, and Buddhism, in particular. This paper studies the prospects of tourism services by identifying some of the critical elements that already exist, and provides a developmental perspective for the successful marketing of Buddhist destinations.

Introduction

Bordering the blue-green waters of the Bay of Bengal in the east of India, Orissa is bound by West Bengal and Bihar in the north, Andhra Pradesh in the south, and Madhya Pradesh in the west. The state is located between 17°48' and 22°34' North latitude and 81°24' and 87°29' East longitude. The topography is distinct with its eastern plateaus, Mahanadi river basin, eastern hill regions and the coastal belt. About one-third of the state is covered with natural forests, mines and minerals, which have the potential to provide vast economic development. The state has adequate water resources and power, yet lacks some of the essential hard infrastructure. The National Highways road networks in the state are in excellent condition, but the condition of the State roads is still poor. Some of the interior areas of the state are still not motorable. However, an optimistic view of the affairs is that the slackness of the development drive in the state has ensured low pollution levels and hence, conservation of heritage sites. This has increased the potential for natural tourism, much to the delight of the state government, which prides itself for the reasonably fair maintenance of the heritage sites.

Orissa has always been a vibrant cultural locus of Buddhist 'viharas and chaityas'[1], as has been established during the recent excavations of the Archeological Survey of India in 2002. Udayagiri, situated 10 kms west of Bhubaneshwar, with its elephant rock edict, was believed to be occupied by the Buddhist monks as early as the 2nd century BC. According to the historians, Emperor Ashoka led Magadha (ancient Bihar) against Kalinga (ancient Orissa) to Dhauligiri for the (in)famous Kalinga War. This bloody war, however, brought compassion in the heart of Ashoka, who embraced Buddhism there. Recent archeological excavations at Ratnagiri, Udayagiri, Lalitagiri, etc., have added new dimensions to the Buddhist establishments in Orissa[2]. The three forms of Buddhism—Hinayana, Mahayana and Vajrayana can be found with its range of sculptures that parallels the Buddhist art forms of Tibet, Nepal and China.

The 'remains' of Buddhist art and culture, at various places in Orissa provides a large scope to develop tourism in the state, based on the theme of pilgrimage of the Buddhists. The link-up (or circuit) of the places will have to be considered with respect to the infrastructural necessities and requirements, to start with. The purpose of this paper is two-fold – To briefly outline the archeological findings and its importance to Buddhism, and to suggest a strategy for establishing the essential elements for development of tourism and find out ways to establish marketing of Buddhist destinations in Orissa.

The essential factors and elements for marketing of Buddhist destinations are derived from various secondary sources, and a simple survey questionnaire is built on the Likert scale (see Annexure 1 for response scale). A preliminary primary survey was conducted at Bhubaneswar[3], based on the random sample of a hundred respondents, and their response is used here to provide some starting points (see Annexure 2 for summary of response). This paper precludes the actual market research and acts like a preceding market survey for establishing 'Buddhism tourism'. To make the reading interesting and pertinent, the method of stating illustration (of the history and archeological findings) and research (response of the market) simultaneously is chosen for each Buddhist destination. However, some may argue that undue weight is given to the factors of heritage importance and infrastructure development. However, it seems obvious that these two factors put sanctions on all other factors.

Archeological Significance and Development Parameters

Epigraphical sources are indicative of the rise of Buddhism in Orissa, right from the reign of Ashoka, the Great, to the end of the Somavamsi Empire. It is during this time that many mahaviharas, which were the centers of Buddhism knowledge and culture, came into being. Archeological excavations at Ratnagiri have revealed a continuous presence of Buddhism from the 2nd Century BC to the 12th Century AD. Although, the kind of Buddhism that emerged around the Ashokan period was Hinayana, yet the refinement to Mahayana and its flux into Vajrayana can be evidenced in Orissa. In fact, the study of Buddhist sculpture and art from the relics and monuments[4] in Orissá points to the gradual transformation of the Mahayana form of Buddhism into the Vajrayana form of Buddhism before 10th century AD, introducing the Tantric form of worship[5].

Looking at the richness, Orissa becomes undeniably one of the leading tourist points for Buddhist dominated countries such as Sri Lanka, Japan, China, Thailand, Burma Cambodia, Indonesia, and more. A brief outline of the five places of Buddhist heritage interests is given.

Dhauligiri

This is a hill on the river plains at the bank of the river Daya, a tributary of the river Mahanadi. Dhauli remains a site of special rock edicts of Ashoka, which were public orders of the ruler to the empires' administrators to rule with justice through gentleness[6]. The elephant gargoyle that protrudes from the rock also serves as a symbol of peace in Buddhism. The site is about 10 kms from Bhubaneswar by road, and falls on the well-connected Bhubaneswar-Puri road. The nearest major railway station and airport are at Bhubaneswar, with civic amenities like good hotels and boarding facilities. However, a small rest-house is at Dhauli[7], which is seldom used by tourists.

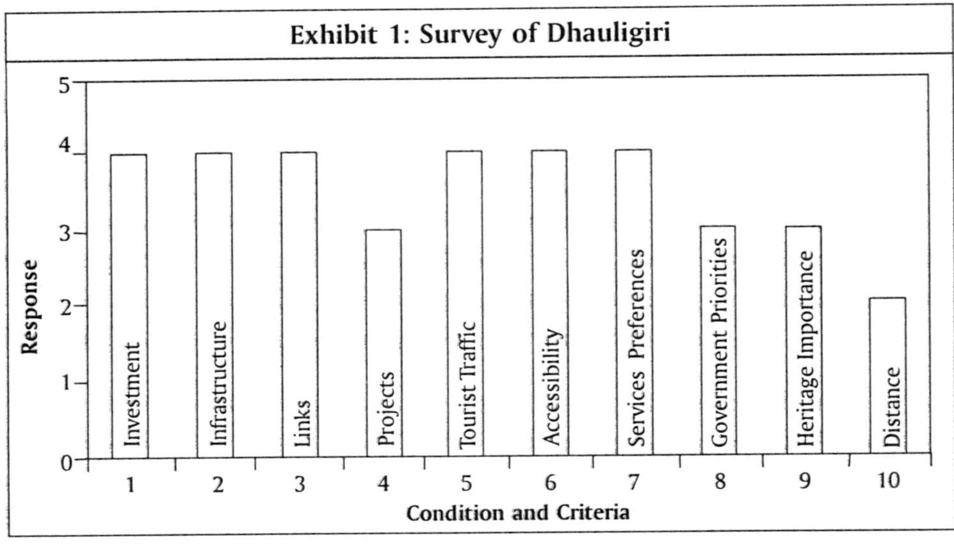

As is evident from the survey (average result shown in Annexure 3) and the Exhibit 1, the investments made in Dhauligiri have gone beyond the primary phase of development. Essential hard infrastructure of the area is present as it enjoys the benefits of being an agglomeration to Bhubaneswar. The place falls on the state highway connecting Bhubaneswar to Puri, the most popular tourist destination in Orissa, and thus, attracts the Puri tourists as a break journey place. Recent projects taken up by the Archeological Survey of India, the Department of Culture, the Government of Orissa, and some pressure groups such as Odissi dancers, are targeted to make Dhauligiri a place of Orissa's cultural advancement. Most of the tourists that go to Dhauligiri[8] see it as an en-route stop over to Puri and Konark, and thus, only demand for ease in accessibility. Nevertheless, some religious tourists have demanded for luxury housing at Dhauligiri. Moreover, the religious tourists, especially the Buddhist tourists, like to retain Bhubaneshwar as base for their tour, and like to visit the other four important places as a round tour in a day. The State Government's priorities have been very high on Dhauligiri, partly driven by acceptance and grants for development from the Buddhist nations. This makes the place highly important for cultural and religious heritage, compounded by its strategic proximity with other tourist attractions.

Ratnagiri-Lalitagiri-Udayagiri

The three neighboring hills in Kendrapara and Cuttack district, are on the seismic fault line bordering the River Brahmani, and includes incredible Buddhist hamlets. The Chinese pilgrim and explorer, Hieun-T'sang, discovered the area to hold a thriving Buddhist University by the name "Pushpagiri", and has chronicled the same. The ASI excavation findings[9] supports this, with Ratnagiri being the most advanced of the said Buddhist complexes. The area was a vibrant locus of Buddhism knowledge, religion and culture with its many planned chaityas and viharas. With this archeological and religious significance, a closer materialistic look at the three hills holds the potential to provide with the necessary tourism opportunities.

Lalitagiri

It seems like the earliest Buddhist complex, religious and educational center, which dates back to first century AD, as per the ASI excavations. Numerous brick monasteries, chaityas, stupas and other monuments[10] are spread over the region. Some sacred relics of Buddha in caskets were also discovered, making this a sacred and revered place for Buddhists in the world—especially the ones from South East Asian countries. With this, Lalitagiri (in the present Cuttack district) becomes the cornerstone, before one visits Ratnagiri and Udayagiri, located in the present Jajpur district. Lalitagiri is well connected with National Highway No. 5A that leads to Paradip Port. The site is about 80 kms from Bhubaneswar, has a rest house closely, but the same is not deemed fit for tourists. Further, the route on NH No. 5A does not have a single hotel or lodging/boarding place. Availability of food and other amenities are also difficult. Nearest major railway station is Cuttack, which is about 50 kms from Lalitagiri.

Exhibit 2: Survey of Lalitagiri

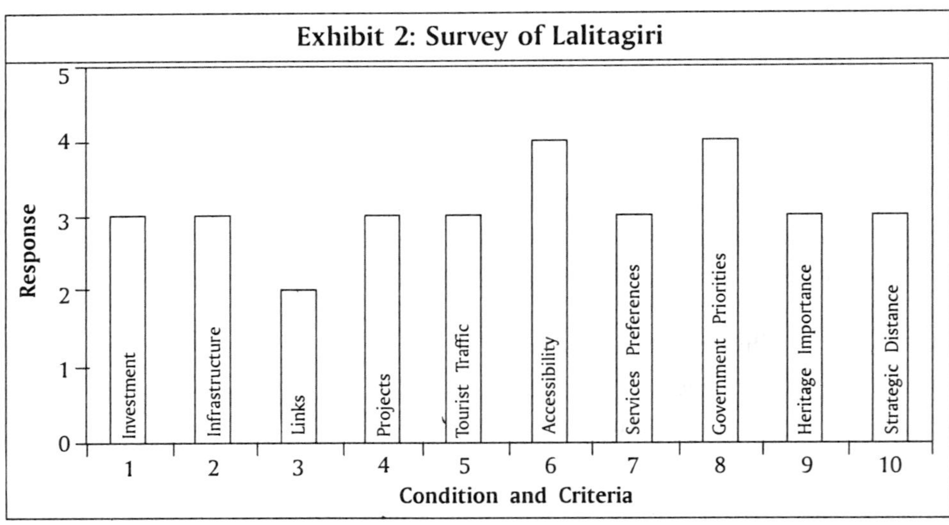

The investment made by the state government around Lalitagiri is almost in-existent. The site has only recently come into limelight with ASI excavations. It is not linked with any other tourism circuits, even the obvious linkage with Bhitarkanika[11] tour. The tourists visiting Lalitagiri, seek the place, and their number is very limited. As the site lays in the middle of the agricultural fields, a little away from the nearby town, the tourist's expectations of comfort from the place is very limited. After the ASI excavations, the State Government's priorities seem high, with its rise in heritage importance.

Ratnagiri

This lies in the valley plains of River Birupa, and is the third of the five important Buddhist sites in Orissa[12]. The ASI excavations have revealed two ancient large monasteries (mahaviharas), large stupas, and other sculptures. The place also holds smaller stone temple, numerous smaller stupas around the large stupa. Ratnagiri offers marvelous ruins in the form of sculptures, stupas and complex monasteries, which is a delight not only to the Buddhists, but also to any art and architecture lover. Ratnagiri is located in Cuttack district, at about 90 kms from Bhubaneswar near Paradip Road. As the place was almost unknown till recent, the infrastructure development and other investments in the area were never considered. Moreover, Ratnagiri being a little away from NH 5A route, so other tourism locations were never linked with it.

Exhibit 3: Survey of Ratnagiri

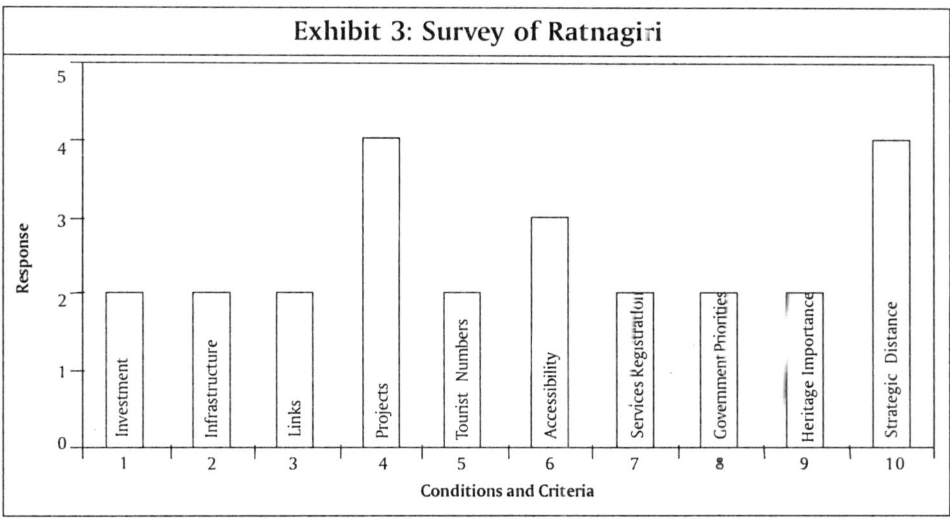

From the survey, it was evident that the tourists going to Ratnagiri are mostly serious tourists, who know the importance of the place. In some cases, they actually try to discover the place. However, the tourist inflow for the place remains low. Most tourists do not expect any convenience facilities at the site, and prefer only development of essential facilities in future. The place being a little distant from other convenient tourist sites, it has attracted few tourists, but situation is going to change with its rise in heritage significance.

Udayagiri

This is arguably the largest and the most enigmatic Buddhist site[13] in the district of Jajpur in Orissa. The ASI excavations have revealed a huge spread-out monastery with its share of stupas and sculptures. There is yet another monastery waiting to be excavated. The recent excavations have unraveled the mysteries of the past that have allured the religious Buddhists, archeologists, art lovers, relic hunters and adventure seekers alike, to the site. Udayagiri is at a distance of 85 kms from Bhubaneswar, at the foot of a large hill. The place is about 5 kms from the NH 5A on the other side (Jajpur district) linked by a single narrow road. A hilly, winding road approaches Udayagiri on the other side. The same road holds Ratnagiri at about a distance of 5 kms and Langudi at a distance of 10 kms. The place does not have civic amenities or any hotels.

Exhibit 4: Survey of Udayagiri

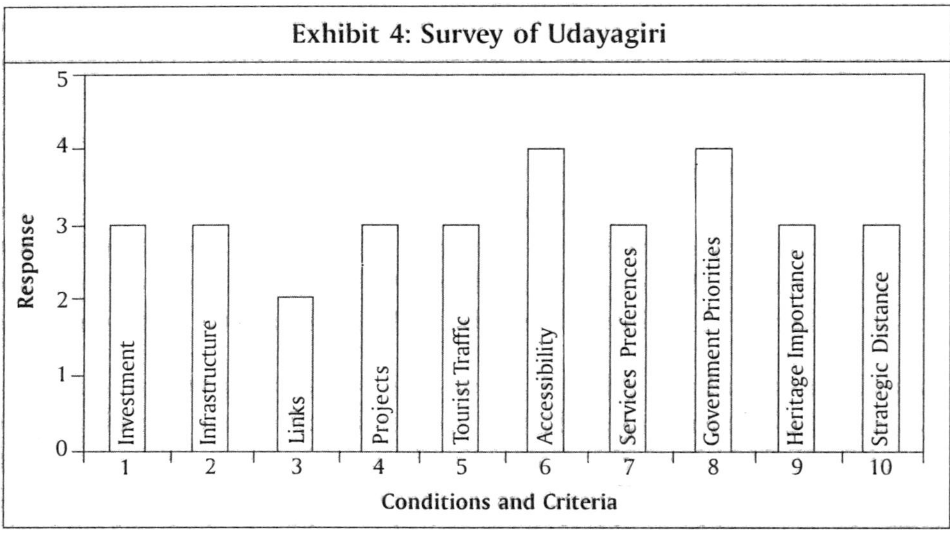

As per the tourist survey, the investments made in the area by the state government and the ASI have been primary in nature. Infrastructure till this point, has been largely in-existent, and the project is poorly liked with other excavation projects. The flow of tourists at the place has mostly been curious to find out what the ASI excavations unearth. The site is largely accessible from Bhubaneswar and the road for only the last 5 kms is rough. The site, although important, is yet to be established as a revered place for Buddhists. With potential rise in importance, the state government is expected to commit more on the development of Udayagiri.

Langudi[14]

This is a hillock in the plains of the Mahanadi Delta at about 90 kms from Bhubaneswar. With flat agrarian land all around the site, the numerous rock-cut Buddhist stupas and shrines include different postures of the meditating Buddha, "Dhyani Buddhas". Further, the rock-cut stupas resemble the 'Amravati' style, which is a refined form of Buddhist Art. Overall, Langudi hill is seen as a significant cluster or concentration of the three sects of Buddhism—'Hinayana', 'Mahayana' and the 'Vajrayana' all at one location.

Exhibit 5: Survey of Langudi

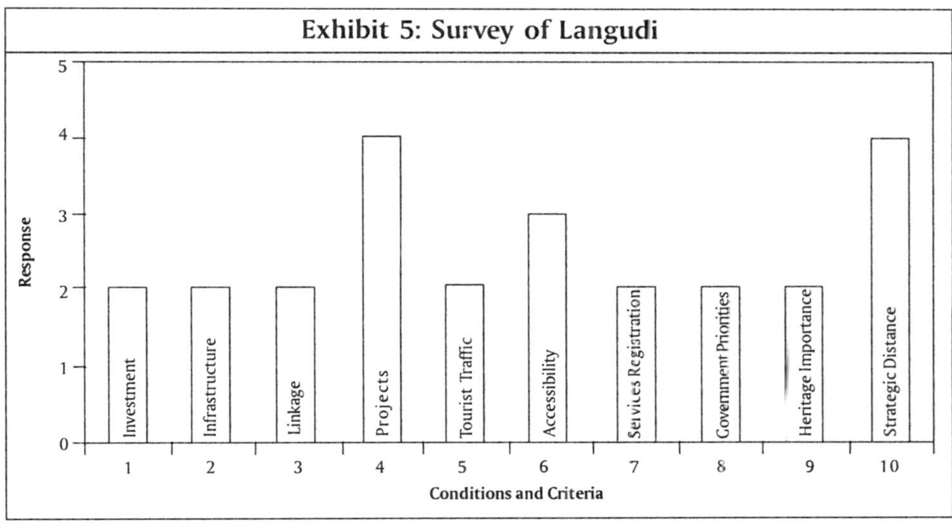

The tourist survey suggests that the ASI excavations has only provided some rationale for primary investments in the area. As the exploration is still on in the area, the expectations of tourists, regarding the facilities is very limited. The area is not at all linked with any other tourism circuit and the number of tourists flow in the area is also low. The state government has neglected the area till now, as it was most interior and recent of the other four sites. With its recent rise in importance, Langudi holds the potential to tell the evolution and propagation of Buddhism, which the tourists also perceive now.

Future Research

With the overall vision of developing an integrated Buddhist Tourism Circuit, the preparation of a Tourism Plan following the survey has to be undertaken by the department to identify and consolidate on the relative strengths of the destinations and suggesting ways for minimizing the apparent weaknesses for sustainable development of tourism in the region. A part of this is already indicated in this report, and taking cue from the same, further research needs to be done to establish the development and marketing criteria. The tourism plan, thus conceived will also identify and suggest strategies to seize the emerging opportunities and overcome possible threats.

The primary approach should be to identify the key areas as depicted in the Annexure 1, to evaluate the existing status of the destinations and to propose a comprehensive tourism plan for the Buddhism Circuit. This shall include the gaps in the existing facilities, infrastructure requirements, proposed sustainable projects with estimates and financial investment pattern over the next 20 years. Identification and sequence of the Buddhist Heritage Sites with focus on the five major centers of Dhauli, Lalitagiri, Ratnagiri, Udayagiri and Langudi will be the first step in the preparation of the tourism marketing plan. This will be followed by developing a Buddhism Tourist Circuit linking the prominent places of Buddhist importance with the nearby scenic spots.

The existing status of the infrastructure in these destinations and the nearest tourist attractions, shall be assessed keeping in mind the ecological balance and the environmental factors of the covered locations. Based on the primary survey findings and the infrastructure status (summary given in Annexure 2), the hubs and spokes of the Buddhist Circuits will be developed and financially viable projects for each of these destinations will be identified and proposed with detailed cost estimates inculcating various evaluation criteria.

The development and marketing plan for the proposed Buddhism Circuit shall be prepared with yearwise inflow of funds to the various identified projects in the chosen destinations focusing on the investment from private entrepreneurs, the UNESCO grants for heritage protection and conservation, apart from the State and the Central Government budgetary allocations.

A dedicated Project team comprising of a Team Leader who will be the overall incharge of the team, assisted by professionals who will include infrastructure engineers, tourism consultants and market research associates. The assignment will be executed in close coordination with the State Government's Department of Culture and the ASI, and it is proposed to interact closely with the other state institutions engaged in promotion and development of tourism related infrastructure and services.

Armed with the knowledge of preliminary survey, it is easier to propose a detailed study on the market. However, the sample chosen for the preliminary survey done here was random, with respondents from all walks and segments of the broad market. This becomes a limitation of this paper as the sample may be argued to be non-representative of the actual market. With this, it becomes essential to propose the subsequent implications of the proposed detailed market research as outlined.

Implications: Action Strategy

The researcher needs to commence extensive discussions with the Department of Tourism to understand the final objectives and the requirements from the tourism perspective. Thereafter, a detailed work plan needs to be prepared for undertaking the action research that will identify the roles and responsibilities, and the completion schedules for different parts of the Buddhism tourism project.

In the diagnostic stage, the researcher will extend the study of existing scenario in each of the five destinations in terms of tourist traffic, accessibility, existence of any unique heritage, proximity to other major tourist destinations, infrastructure status, carrying capacity, the State Government priority and other tourism-related aspects. This effort can be based on the preliminary findings of this report, and other data from the ASI and the other Government sources can be overlapped with. Further, it becomes imperative to interact closely with the state tourism department to gather details on tourist traffic in the past years and the specific efforts that have been undertaken for the promotion of tourism in the state. Tourism development models adopted abroad with specific attention on Buddhist pilgrimage centers, emerging trends in heritage and religious tourism, experiences in neighboring states with reference to Buddhist pilgrimage locations and their strategy in attracting foreign tourists and domestic pilgrimage travelers can also be studied.

This may be followed by undertaking extensive field visits spread over a year, to all the five proposed destinations, with a view to develop a complete inventory of tourist sites, infrastructure details and marketing requirements. A resource base can be prepared through interaction with the concerned Government departments and private agencies. During this detailed market research, care should be taken to interact with various stakeholders, state departments and facilitating agencies to gather their perspectives regarding development of the Buddhism Circuit in the State linking the five destinations and the perceived strengths and weaknesses of each of these destinations. The external tourism environment and the tourist traffic across Orissa, types of tourists and their preferences, average spending pattern and the number of days of stay will be studied by an extensive market survey amongst the visiting tourists with specific focus on the Buddhist pilgrims. Interaction is also essential with various facilitators such as travel agents, tour operators, tourism promotion bodies, eminent personalities, etc., to gather their views and perceptions on the proposed Buddhism Circuit. It is proposed to contact at least 260 contacts[15] during the field survey as per the following order and analyze the findings on infrastructure requirements and gaps, preferred circuits and potential projects from their responses.

Issues such as environmental impact assessment, carrying capacity of destinations, State tourism policies should also be studied in this part of research. To gain a wider perspective and to generate a consensus in the development and promotion of projects, efforts shall be made to organize a Focus Group Discussion (FGD) among the various stakeholders. Prospective tourism projects can be developed as a network whole for the five destinations and integration with other destinations/tourist attractions, along with associated development and marketing requirements. Such projects have the potential to address the inherent advantages and diversity of the Region as well as the State.

A detailed Development and Marketing Plan should be drawn for the integrated development of Buddhism circuit in the Region. This plan among others to include—(a) strategy for tourism development through coordinated regional and destination development; (b) private sector participation in tourism projects in the State along with the concessions and subsidies required from the state government; (c) identification of gaps in the development and other marketing activities that are required for integrated tourism development in the region and identify the agencies/institutions that will be required to undertake various development activities in the region; (d) identify the potential and scope for socio-economic development and development of local artisans, trade, etc., that will accrue to the state through the development of this circuit in the state; (e) long-term strategies for marketing, human resources etc., can also be suggested to ensure state's commitment on resources; (f) categorized projection of demand for each of the destination and that of the region; (g) identification of scenic spots of Buddhism heritage interest and other tourist sites near these five destinations so that they can be developed as spokes and conceptualize tourism projects that can be developed and promoted in each of the destinations; (h) detailed project cost and resource estimates with the investment requirements and the financial viability for the developed project profiles/for the next ten years; and finally (i) year-wise funding requirements for the next 20 years on development and marketing of the proposed Buddhist circuit destinations.

Conclusion

Some historians believe that the foundation of the great Buddhism religion and culture was laid in Orissa. Orissa has been the land of peace and tolerance (Dhamma), and shown the existence of multiple religions in ancient times, to the whole world. Even the legendary transformation that changed 'ChandAshoka to DharmAshoka'[16] can be felt with the evolution and growth of Buddhism in Orissa. The ASI excavations at the above major Buddhist sites reveal the importance of Buddhism in ancient Orissa and thus incite Buddhism Tourism in Orissa. The Department of Tourism, the Government of Orissa is poised to link religious tourism, such as Buddhism, Jainism, Jagannath Tourism, with natural tourism, such as On-sea tourism, Bhitarkanika-Gahirmatha, Chilika, and Simlipal Tiger Reserve. Although, the tourism department is exploring newer themes and destination circuits with unique attractions, an integrated development is essential to leverage the tourism potential of the state in a concerted manner. In this regard, this pre-market research proposes the Department of Tourism, Government of Orissa to contemplate and prepare a utilitarian Master Plan for Tourism, integrating the Buddhism Travel Circuit covering Bhubaneswar (Dhauli)-Lalitagiri-Ratnagiri-Udayagiri-Langudi and link the same with other tourism circuits.

All the five sites are located on hillocks, as Buddhism always wanted to build their centers of knowledge and religion on high grounds. The mahaviharas form of advanced Buddhist University was typical of the time, as conjured up by Langudi and Udayagiri. The society and architecture was also representative to Buddhism philosophies. Jajpur is another area that can be linked to the proposed sites as Jajpur historically has been a place of synthesis for Buddhism. On the other side, the road link to Jajpur is from Bhubaneswar to Panikoili, about 80 kms by NH 5A, then to Shantipur 6 kms, and then to Jajpur with 16 more kms through good state road. Although, this access is there, but it is very long. As there is no direct connectivity from Jajpur to Ratnagiri, a bridge over river Baitarani can be proposed, which can shorten the access distance by more than 20 kms. Further, widening and doubling of NH 5A is taken up by the National Highway Authority of India, under the port connectivity project. With such expressway, hotel/other facilities in the area will make commercial sense for investors and benefit the tourists who may intend to stay overnight in those areas.

Finally, taking the theme of Buddhism tourism a little further, the department needs to link the same with the evolution of Buddhism—Hinayana to Mahayana and finally to Vajrayana over the ages. Some of the sites still have a lot to offer after thorough exploration, which can feed to the element of curiosity amongst tourists. With this, it becomes imperative for the Department of Culture, the Department of Tourism and the Government of Orissa to keep a close tab with the Archeological Survey of India, to be current on recent discoveries. Further, the mystery of the unexcavated sites and every new piece of jigsaw information should also be marketed to the target market in real terms.

To know specifically about prospect tourism circuits, linkages with other themes, the target market, marketing mix, modes of service delivery and development requirement, it is imperative for the State Tourism Department to undertake a broad market research, not only locally, but also spread into important tourism entry locations in India and abroad (especially the Buddhist nations). The theme convergence plan is indicated above and approach of market research for the same, is proposed in the following.

(Rajnandan Patnaik, Faculty Member, the Icfai Business School, Hyderabad. He can be reached at rajnandan@ibsindia.org).

Endnotes

1 "*Viharas* are the dwelling places donated to the normally wandering Buddhist monks. *Chaityas* are the halls enclosing the stupas." At *http://www.saigan.com/heritage/architecture/* visited September 10, 2005.

2 This paper refers to five major Buddhist destinations in Orissa. Other minor ones include, Kuruma, Prachi, Banpur in Puri district; Choudwar, Jajpur, Lataharan and Kurukulla in Cuttack and Jajpur districts; Junagarh and Buddhakhol in Ganjam district; Sonepur in Sonepur district; Binka in Bolangir district; Ganiapalli and Melchamunda in Sambalpur district; Khiching, Udala, Ajodhya, Balasore, Baripada in Balasore and Baripada districts.

3 This is based on actual site visits of the author in his earlier capacity as an infrastructure consultant in 2004. The survey was conducted by his erstwhile colleagues, who contacted tourists (mostly foreigners) at Bhubaneswar airport in filling up the questionnaire. The author is grateful to all who have contributed in collecting this primary data.

4 Lokesvara image from Bhubaneswar, Buddha in "Bhumi-Sparsamudra" and "Avalokitesvara Padmapani" in standing pose from Khadipada, and many more colossal statues are displayed in the Orissa State Museum at Bhubaneswar. A colossal "Bodhisattva" at Lalitagiri, and many more at nearby Udaigiri and Ratnagiri, also adds to the archeological significance of the places. Further, "the back slab of a Buddha image at Solampur contains the story of Buddha, from his life to nirvana." At the site *www.indiantravelportal.com/orissa/ buddhist-heritage/buddhist-sculptural-art.html*, visited September 10, 2005.

5 This in itself remains a paradox, as Buddhism initially came into being as a reaction against Hindu form of Idol worship, but after the maha-nirvana of Buddha, used Buddha as Idol for worship. Moreover, embracing initially a form of pagan worship of nature, Buddhism in Vajrayana form resorted to unnatural Tantric forms of worship.

6 "The serenity of the place and the legacy of Buddhism motivated the Kalinga Nippon Buddha Sangha, to establish a Peace Pagoda or Shanti Stupa at Dhauligiri along with the construction of the monastery called Saddharma Vihar in early seventies of 19th century. Along with the Ashokan Edicts, the Peace Pagoda and modern Buddhist Monastery, Dhauli offers the visitors small rock-cut caves, Hindu temples of early medieval period and a renovated Siva temple known as Dhavalesvara on top of the hill are added attractions." At *www.indiatourism.com/orissa-tourism*, September 10, 2005.

7 "The Dhauli hill which is located on the banks of the Daya River stands a mute testimony to the epoch-making Kalinga war, fought in the 3rd century BC. The great wave of Buddhism, that overwhelmed the whole world, was born here. Dhauli is renowned for its Ashokan rock edicts, inscribed on a rock, crowned by a relief depicting an elephant. These contain 11 of the

14 rock edicts to be found, within the perimeter of the Ashokan Empire. Apart from these edicts, it also present two rock edicts that Ashoka had specially got inscribed, for the people of Kalinga." At *www.indiantravelinfo.com/bhubneshwar*, September 10, 2005.

8 Dhauligiri is also seen when one leaves by Rail or Road from Bhubaneswar to the Southern part of India. This has allured many tourists, who see the pearly white peace pagoda of Dhauligiri from a distance, to visit the place.

9 "The magnificently carved doorjambs of the Vihar and superbly finished Buddha images perhaps becomes the greatest concentration of Buddhist sculpture of the post-Gupta period." At *www.orissa-tourism.com/cuttack.html* visited September 10, 2005.

10 The site displays a large number of Mahayana sculptures consisting of colossal Buddha figures, huge Bodhisattva statues, statues of Tara, Jambhala and others. Interestingly, most of these sculptures contain short inscriptions on them. The standing Buddha figures, with knee length draperies over the shoulders remind one of the influences of the Gandhara and Mathura School of Art. At *www.orissa-tourism.com/bandjmonuments.html* visited September 10, 2005.

11 Bhitarkanika, with its mangrove forests and reptilian fauna spread over 670 sq kms, is one of the best forest sanctuaries in India. It holds a varied population of estuarine crocodile and Olive Ridley sea turtles (who come to nearby Gahirmatha beach for laying eggs), and other reptilian species like lizards and snakes. One of the entry points is through Rajnagar, which is assessed through NH 5A, the same road that connects Lalitagiri to Bhubaneswar.

12 Buddhism had developed at this place—unhindered from the first half of the sixth century AD up to the 12th century AD. The place was an important center of Mahayana form of Buddhism, which transformed into a great center of Tantric Buddhism or Vajrayana art and philosophy, during the 8th-9th century AD. At *www.orissa-tourism.com bandjmonuments.html* visited September 10, 2005.

13 The place was known as Madhavapura Mahavihara in ancient times. Recent excavation uncovered a huge complex of brick monasteries, housing several priceless Buddhist sculpture and it is believed through scientific evidences that some other treasures are buried deep within Udayagiri which have not yet been totally revealed to the outside world. Chronologically, the Udayagiri Buddhist complex is later than Ratnagiri and Lalitagiri and the monasteries probably flourished between the 7th and the 12th centuries AD. Interestingly, although the site is located close to Ratnagiri (about 5 kms), Udayagiri does not possess a number of Vajrayana sculptures. At *www.orissa-tourism.com/bandjmonuments.html* visited September 10, 2005.

14 "The description of Hieun-T'sang, the famed Chinese traveler of the seventh century AD, about the magnificent stupa on top of a hill at Pushpagiri Mahavihara which emitted a brilliant light because of its sacredness. On the basis of archeological materials including

inscriptions brought to light by excavation, Langudi hill in Jajpur district may be identified as Pushpagiri." At *www.orissa-tourism.com/bandjmonuments.html* visited September 10, 2005.

15 Based on experience gained from this paper and on issue of statistical significance, it is expected that the market research should cover: (a) Foreign pilgrimage tourists—100 Nos. (b) Domestic pilgrimage tourists—100 Nos. (c) Eminent local personalities residing in these destinations—10 Nos. (d) Service providers including tour operators, hoteliers and transporters etc.—25 Nos. (e) Development agencies—State department of tourism, PWD, Art and Culture, the Archeological Survey of India, Forest and Environment—10 Nos. (f) Private Investors—10 Nos. (g) Funding/financing agencies and institutions—5 Nos.

16 Chand Ashoka is the term given to the merciless and terrible Ashoka; and Dharm Ashoka is the epithet given to the reformed Emperor Ashoka, who was compassionate and just.

References

1. Baker, Priscilla, 1995, *Touring Historic Places: A Manual for Group Tour Operators and Managers of Historic and Cultural Attractions*. Washington, DC: National Trust for Historic Preservation.
2. Borocz, Jozsef, *Leisure Migration: A Sociological Study on Tourism*. Pergamon, NY: Elsevier Science, 1996.
3. Brass, Jane L, ed, 1996, *Community Tourism Assessment Handbook*. Corvallis, Oregon: Western Rural Development Center, Oregon State University. Website: *http://extension.usu.edu/wrdc/ctah/(html)* and *http://extension.usu.edu/WRDC/resources/tourism/ctah.pdf*
4. Burns, Peter, and Andrew Holden. 1995. *Tourism: A New Perspective*. London: Prentice Hall.
5. Dane, Suzanne, and Amy Jordan Webb. 2001a. *Share Your Heritage: Cultural Heritage Tourism Success Stories*. Washington, DC: National Trust for Historic Preservation.
6. Dutt, Nalenaksha. *Early History of the Spread of Buddhism and the Buddhist Schools*. With a foreword by Narendra Nath Law. New Delhi: Rajesh Publications, 1980.
7. Exploration and Excavation at the Archeological Survey of India at *http://asi.nic.in/activities.html* visited September 10, 2005.
8. Fa-hsien. *Travels of Fah-Hian and Sung-Yun, Buddhist Pilgrims from China to India (400 A.D. and 518 A.D.)*. Translated from Chinese by Samuel Beal, New Delhi: Asian Education Services, 1993.
9. Fesenmaier, Daniel R, Joseph T O'Leary, and Muzaffer Uysal, eds. 1996. *Recent Advances in Tourism Marketing Research*. New York: Hawthorne Press.
10. Garfield, Donald, ed. 1997. *Partners in Tourism: Culture and Commerce. Washington, DC*: American Association of Museums.
11. Green, Joslyn, Cheryl Hargrove, and Amy Jordan Webb, 1999. *Getting Started: How to Succeed in Heritage Tourism. Washington, DC*: National Trust for Historic Preservation.

12. Kotler, Philip, John Bowen, and James Makens. 1998. *Marketing for Hospitality and Tourism.* 2nd ed. Upper Saddle River, New Jersey: Prentice-Hall.

13. Land and People of Orissa at *http://orissagov.nic.in/people/peoplehome.htm*, visited September 10, 2005.

14. Major Buddhist Monuments at *http://www.orissatourism.gov.in/monuments.htm*, visited September 12, 2005.

15. Shields, Peggy O, and Timothy J Schibik. 1995. "Regional Tourism Marketing: An Analogical Approach to Organizational Framework Development," *Journal of Travel and Tourism Marketing*, Vol. 4, No. 1: pp. 105-113.

16. Vokoni, Boris. 1996. *Tourism and Religion*. Oxford, UK: Pergamon.

17. Wriggins, Sally H *Xuanzang: A Buddhist Pilgrim on the Silk Road.* With a foreword by Frederick W Mote. Boulder, CO: Westview Press, 1996.

Annexure 1:
Response Scale for Development and Marketing of Buddhist Destinations

Physical Condition of the Buddhism Tourist Destinations					
	1	2	3	4	5
Investments Made Till Now	None	Initial	Primary	Secondary	Advanced
Physical Condition of Infrastructure	Poor	Needing	Basic	Existing	Advanced
Linkage of Circuits with other Tourist Places	Not Linked	Poorly Linked	Fairly Linked	Highly Linked	Totally Linked
Physical Condition of Projects	ASI-Non Priority	ASI-Identified	ASI-Excavation	ASI-Exploration	ASI-Advanced

State of Tourism Market for Buddhism Destinations					
	1	2	3	4	5
Tourist Traffic Volume per year	Tens	Hundreds	Thousands	Lakhs	Crores
Accessibility to the Site	Walk Ways only	Non-Motorable	Part Motorable	Motorable	Express Access
Tourist Preferences of Services	No	Essentials Expectations	Basic Necessities	Comfort Requirements	Luxury Requirements
Government Priorities and Commitments	Very Low	Low	Medium	High	Very High

Marketing Requirements of Buddhism Theme and Sites					
	1	2	3	4	5
Heritage Importance with respect to Marketing	Very Low	Low	Medium	High	Very High
Strategic Location Distance from other Tourist Places	Extremely Close	Close	Reasonably Far	Distant	Very Distant

Annexure 2:

Compilation of Response of Primary Survey for Development and Marketing of Buddhism Tourism

	Lalitagiri	Dhauligiri	Langudi	Udayagiri	Ratnagiri
Physical Condition					
Investments	Primary	Secondary	Initial	Primary	Initial
Infrastructure	Basic	Existing	Needing	Basic	Needing
Circuits	Poorly Linked	Highly Linked	Not Linked	Poorly Linked	Not Linked
Projects	ASI-Excavat.	ASI-Advanced	ASI-Explorat.	ASI-Excavat.	ASI-Explorat.
Market State					
Tourist Traffic	Thousands	Lakhs	Hundreds	Thousands	Hundreds
Accessibility	Motorable	Excellent	Part Motorable	Motorable	Part Motorable
Preferences	Necessities	Luxury Req.	Essentials	Necessities	Essentials
Govt. Priorities	High	Very High	Low	Medium	Low
Marketing Requirements					
Heritage Imp.	Medium	High	Low	Medium	Low
Strategic Proximity	Little Far	Close	Distant	Little Far	Distant

Note: Average response is based on convenience survey of 100 respondents at Bhubaneswar Airport spread over October 2004.

Annexure 3

Average Response of Primary Survey for Development and Marketing of Buddhism Tourism

Dhauligiri

	Physical Condition of the Buddhism Tourist Destinations				State of Tourism Market for Buddhism Destinations				Mktg. Req. Buddhism Theme/Sites	
Resp	Invest. Made	Infras.	Linkage	Projects	Tourist Traffic	Accessi-bility	Services Pref.	Govt Priorities	Heritage Import.	Strategic Distance
100 nos.	4	4	4	3	4	4	4	3	3	2

Contd...

Contd...

Lalitagiri										
	Physical Condition of the Buddhism Tourist Destinations				State of Tourism Market for Buddhism Destinations				Mktg. Req. Buddhism Theme/Sites	
Resp	Invest. Made	Infras.	Linkage	Projects	Tourist Traffic	Accessi-bility	Services Pref.	Govt Priorities	Heritage Import.	Strategic Distance
100 nos.	3	3	2	3	3	4	3	4	3	3
Ratnagiri										
	Physical Condition of the Buddhism Tourist Destinations				State of Tourism Market for Buddhism Destinations				Mktg. Req. Buddhism Theme/Sites	
Resp	Invest. Made	Infras.	Linkage	Projects	Tourist Traffic	Accessi-bility	Services Pref.	Govt Priorities	Heritage Import.	Strategic Distance
100 nos.	2	2	2	4	2	3	2	2	2	4
Udayagiri										
	Physical Condition of the Buddhism Tourist Destinations				State of Tourism Market for Buddhism Destinations				Mktg. Req. Buddhism Theme/Sites	
Resp	Invest. Made	Infras.	Linkage	Projects	Tourist Traffic	Accessi-bility	Services Pref.	Govt Priorities	Heritage Import.	Strategic Distance
100 nos.	3	3	2	3	3	4	3	4	3	3
Langudi										
	Physical Condition of the Buddhism Tourist Destinations				State of Tourism Market for Buddhism Destinations				Mktg. Req. Buddhism Theme/Sites	
Resp	Invest. Made	Infras.	Linkage	Projects	Tourist Traffic	Accessi-bility	Services Pref.	Govt Priorities	Heritage Import.	Strategic Distance
100 nos.	2	2	2	4	2	3	2	2	2	4

18

Medical Tourism: India's Competitive Advantage

Dakshi Mohanty and T Phani Madhav

The case study discusses the potential of India in attracting medical tourists and its advantageous position as against its competitors. India equipped with sophisticated hospitals, skill-full doctors apart from possessing traditional medical knowledge is considered to be an attractive destination for many foreign patients. Rising medical costs in the western nations coupled with long waiting periods and availability of same kind of medical services at quite economical rates made India an attractive spot for the visiting western medical tourists. However for the underdeveloped nations the case is altogether a different one. Unavailability of appropriate medical facilities in their respective countries coupled with rising cost of medication in the other developed countries made India an attractive destination for the patients from these countries. Some surveys by eminent management consultancies point out that by 2012, India could earn major chunk of revenue through medical tourism. Against this backdrop, the case study further highlights role of the Government, the private sector in the development of medical tourism in India apart from the challenges ahead.

"Medical tourism is not new to India. Foreign and Non-Resident Indian (NRI) patients have been coming to India for the past 25 years. But the difference is that it was not structured as it is being done now."[1]

– Dr. Lloyd Nazareth, general manager,
Wockhardt Hospital.

"Compared to countries like the UK or the US, minor treatments like those for dental problems or major procedures like bypass surgery or angioplasty come at a fraction of the cost in India, even though the quality of doctors and medical equipment is comparable to the best in the world."[2]

– K K Aggarwal, executive vice-chairman,
Heart Care Foundation of India.

Introduction

A study on healthcare by the Confederation of Indian Industry (CII), a business lobby, and McKinsey & Co., an international management consultancy, estimated that "medical tourism"[3] could earn India an additional Rs.50 billion-Rs.100 billion ($1.1 billion-$2.2 billion) in annual revenues by 2012.[4] By upgrading its technology, gaining greater familiarity with western medical practices and improving its image in terms of quality and cost, the Indian healthcare industry began to emerge as a prime destination for medical tourists.[5] Though the quality of healthcare in developing countries like India was low, private hospitals offered advanced technologies and procedures on par with facilities in developed countries. Consequently, the country had attracted approximately 1,50,000 medical tourists in 2003. Most of the medical tourists to India were Indians living in US and Britain, residents of neighbouring countries like Pakistan, Nepal, Bangladesh, Mauritius and the Maldives, and citizens of African and West Asian countries. By all accounts, the high cost of medical care and long waiting periods for treatment and surgery in the western countries were major reasons for the rise of medical tourism in India.

Meanwhile, the Indian government along with the state governments (primarily Maharashtra, Gujarat, Tamil Nadu), travel agencies and tour operators initiated efforts to attract more foreign patients by promoting the country as a "global healthcare destination" and by offering tax breaks to hospitals. The Indian Healthcare Federation, an association of the healthcare delivery sector that included renowned hospitals like Apollo Group of Hospitals, Hinduja Hospital, Max Healthcare and the Fortis Heart Institute also promoted India as a destination for medical tourism. However, some industry experts opined that most of the foreigners would not think of India as a land of good health. They felt that the sight of the country's overcrowded public hospitals, open sewers and garbage-littered streets would unsettle most visitors' confidence about public sanitation standards in India.[6] Brushing aside the doubts raised about medical tourism in India, the private healthcare providers said that India's corporate hospitals could match world-class standards. "In a corporate hospital, once the door is closed you could be in a hospital in America,"[7] said P V R K Prasad, director-general of the Dr. Marri Channa Reddy Human Resource Development Institute.

Medical Tourism – The Global Scenario

Based on studies undertaken by various research groups, it was believed that the concept of medical tourism dated back to thousands of years. In ancient Greece, pilgrims and patients came from all over the Mediterranean to the sanctuary of the healing god, Asklepios at Epidaurus. In Roman Britain, patients took the waters at a shrine at Bath, a practice that continued for 2,000 years. From the 18th century, wealthy Europeans travelled to spas from Germany to the Nile.[8] By the turn of the 20th century, medical tourists[9] who mainly constituted people from UK, US and many other third world countries (where medical services were either expensive or not available), travelled to other countries in search of affordable health options and often combined it with a vacation.

The global healthcare industry was estimated to be worth $40 billion and was growing at a rate of 20% per year. Countries that actively promoted medical tourism were Thailand, Malaysia, South Africa and India among others (Exhibit I). Initially, many countries that wanted to become a healthcare destination focussed either on spas or on the "vanity" and the "exotic" surgery requirements. In South Africa, a number of travel agents with hospital connections focussed on the market for facelifts, tummy tucks and cosmetic dental surgery. Thailand was the preferred place for people who wanted to go for sex change operations. India's primary claim to fame was its ayurvedic treatment centres.[10] Gradually, many countries realised that a big opportunity lay in promoting the more conventional treatments. People from Mauritius, Bangladesh and the Gulf visited India for conventional surgeries and people from Japan flew to Singapore, Malaysia or Thailand for similar reasons.

Exhibit I: Countries Promoting Medical Tourism

Source: "Medical Tourism: Need Surgery, Will Travel", www.cbc.ca, June 18, 2004.

Analysts cited many reasons for patients to travel for treatment. The medical tourists were divided into four major geographical groups who travelled for distinctly different reasons. The first group of medical travellers was the Americans. Industry experts observed that though the US boasted of the best medical facilities in the world, Americans preferred to travel abroad for cosmetic surgery since cosmetic surgery was not covered by medical insurance in US. They opted to do their cosmetic surgery in countries like Thailand, Malaysia and South Africa, as it was much cheaper in these countries compared to their home country. A full facelift cost $8,000-$20,000 in US, whereas it cost $2,682 in Thailand and $1,252 in South Africa. According to the American Society of Aesthetic Plastic Surgery, in 2002, 6.6 million Americans went for cosmetic surgery in US itself. During the same period, the three countries (Thailand, Malaysia and South Africa) combined attracted approximately 1,00,000 Americans for cosmetic surgery. Some other Americans preferred travelling to other countries for treatment because the cost of medical treatment in US was quite high. Similarly, the Japanese usually travelled for medical treatment elsewhere because of the high cost of treatment in their own country.

The second group of medical travellers was from UK. Patients in UK travelled to other countries for treatment as they could not wait for treatment by the National Health Service (NHS) and also could not afford to consult a physician having private practice. The British healthcare system ensured free treatment to all its citizens. The only problem was that the NHS, which was set up in 1948, had a long waiting list for patients because of a shortage of doctors and hospital beds. Private medical facilities were available in UK, but they were quite expensive and also fewer in number. According to a study by the Vienna University of Economics and Business Administration, in 2001, more than one million patients in UK were waiting for inpatient treatment and half a million for outpatient treatment. Among them about 40% of the people requiring inpatient care needed to wait over three months and hip replacement and eyecare had the longest waiting periods.[11] Consequently, in 2002, the NHS started a scheme called "overseas treatment" to cope with its backlog cases in which patients were sent abroad for treatment to shorten the waiting list. NHS referred patients for treatments to countries like Austria, Spain, France and Germany, as the health service limited referrals to hospitals within three hours of flying time. Meanwhile, many British patients took initiatives to seek their own treatment abroad without waiting for the NHS to sort out the problems. Likewise, most of the Canadians preferred travelling to other countries for medical treatment to avoid long waiting times.

The third group of medical travellers was from West Asia. These people flew abroad to avail medical facilities that were either unavailable or in short supply in their own countries. Typically, patients from rich countries in West Asia travelled to US to avail top-quality medical care. An agency in Saudi Arabia estimated that every year, more than 5,00,000 people from West Asia travelled to different countries (Jordan, Saudi Arabia, Bahrain, US, India, Thailand, Malaysia) for medical treatment. It was estimated that in 2002, India had attracted more than 70,000 medical travellers from West Asia.[12] The fourth group of medical tourists was residents of underdeveloped nations such as Nigeria or Bangladesh. Because of the poor medical facilities in their home countries, they travelled to neighbouring country with better infrastructure for medical treatment. In 2002, it was estimated that about 50,000 people from Bangladesh and Nepal came to India for medical treatment. It was also found that around 1,26,000 medical travellers came to Jordan from neighbouring countries with poor medical infrastructure facilities.[13]

In 2002, five countries in Asia—Thailand, Malaysia, Jordan, Singapore and India attracted about 1.3 million medical travellers and earned over $1 billion in treatment costs only (Exhibit II). Other countries like Hong Kong, Lithuania and South Africa were also emerging as big healthcare destinations. The low cost of treatment in these countries had attracted medical travellers from all over the world (Exhibit III). Meanwhile, healthcare insurers in developed countries realised that the option of medical treatment in countries like Thailand and Malaysia could help them to reduce premiums and offer options to people who were uninsured. Industry analysts believed that insurance firms would provide a boost to the medical travel business. Many insurance companies in UK and the US already had accredited hospitals worldwide where visitors from western countries could seek emergency medical treatment. A few hospitals in Thailand planned to

Exhibit II: Global Medical Tourism

Country	No.of Foreigners Treated in 2002	From	Money Earned	Strengths
Thailand	600,000	US, UK	$470 m	Cosmetic surgery, organ transplants, dental treatment, joint replacements
Jordan	126,000	Middle East	$600 m	Organ transplants, fertility treatments, cardiac care
India	100,000	Middle East Bangladesh, UK, developing countries	N.A.	Cardiac care, joint replacements, Lasik
Malaysia	85,000	US, Japan, developing countries	$40 m	Cosmetic surgery
South Africa	50,000	US, UK	N.A.	Cosmetic surgery, Lasik, dental treatment
Cuba	N.A.	Latin America, US	$25 m-$50 m	Specialist niche treatment, vitiligo, night blindness, cosmetic surgery

Source: Datta, Prosenjit and Krishnan, Gina S. "The Health Travellers", www.businessworldindia.com, December 22, 2003.

Exhibit III: Cost of Treatment in Different Countries

(in dollars)

Procedure	US	India	South Africa	Thailand
Facelift	8,000-20,000	10,000-20,000	1,252	2,682
Hip Replacement	17,000	2,500	6,671	N.A.
Open Heart Surgery	150,000	5,0 00-10,000	13,333	7,500
Eye (Lasik)	3,100	7,000	2,166	730

Source: Datta, Prosenjit and Krishnan, Gina S. "The Health Travellers", www.businessworldindia.com, December 22, 2003.

get accredited by the Joint Commission Accreditation of Healthcare Organizations, which allowed the patients to qualify for the insurance if treated in those hospitals.[14]

India's Advantages – First World Healthcare at Third-world Prices

In the beginning of the 21st century, India was one of the leading countries to attract a large pool of medical tourists. The country had attracted about 1,50,000 medical tourists in 2003. In the international market, it lagged behind Thailand, which had attracted about one million medical tourists during the same period.[15] In the late 1980s and early 1990s, most medical travellers coming to India were from the Arab countries, Africa and Southeast Asia. However, by 2003, India had attracted tourists from all over the world. Most of the medical tourists to India were Indians living in UK and US, residents of neighbouring countries like Pakistan, Nepal, Bangladesh, Mauritius and the Maldives, and citizens of African and West Asian countries. Analysts opined that private hospitals in India were equipped with state-of-the-art medical infrastructure and a talented group of highly qualified doctors, which made it possible to offer world-class treatment at reasonable prices. As the treatment and the infrastructure at these hospitals were comparable with leading hospitals in the Western countries and the cost of medical treatment was much lower compared to the western countries, India emerged as a world class healthcare destination with the added lure of a holiday.

The low cost of treatment in India attracted many foreign patients. Research undertaken by industry experts showed that treatment costs in India started at around a tenth of the price of comparable treatment in UK or the US. A surgery and convalescence in a star hospital cost in India is cheaper to foreign nationals in comparison with medical care in their home countries. It was found that an open-heart surgery costs between $34,000 and $70,000 in UK. In US, routine open-heart surgery costs $150,000; with complicated problems it costs considerably more. In India, open-heart surgery costs between $3,000 and $10,000 in the best of hospitals (Exhibit IV). Analysts believed that effective marketing could divert patients from African and West Asian countries who were going to UK or US for treatment to India.[16] Harpal Singh, president of Indian Healthcare Federation and chairman of Fortis Healthcare Ltd., said, "India must leverage its competitive edge, especially its cost advantage. It is only one-fifth of the costs in the West. For instance, a heart surgery in the US costs $30,000, while it costs $6,000 here. Similarly, a bone marrow transplant in the US costs $2,50,000, while it is $26,000 in India."[17]

Exhibit IV: Treatment Costs in India Compared to UKandUS

Procedures	India	US and UK
Partial hip replacement	$4,500	US: $18,000
Full hip replacement	$3,000	US: $39,000
Orthopaedic surgery	$4,500	US: $18,000
Cardiac surgery	$4,000- $9,000 or £6,000	US: $30,000- $50,000 UK (private care): £30,000
Knee surgery	£8,000	UK (private care): £20,000
Gall bladder surgery	$7,500	US: $60,000
Tooth filling	$20 to $40	US: $300 to $400
Root canal	$200 to $400	US: $3,500
Heart surgery	Rs.2 lakh-Rs.4.5 lakh	Rs.11.5 lakh-Rs.23 lakh
Neurosurgery	Rs.2.3 lakh-Rs.3.7 lakh	Rs.7.8 lakh-Rs.13.7 lakh
Microsurgery	Rs.30,000	Rs.18 lakh
Joint replacement	Rs.2.3 lakh-Rs.4.5 lakh	Rs.9.2 lakh-Rs.23 lakh
Cataract	Rs.36,700-Rs.68,800	Rs.92,000-Rs.2.3 lakh
Preventive healthcare	Rs.9,200-Rs.18,400	Rs.69,000-Rs.1.4 lakh
Bone marrow transplant	$26,000	$250,000
Liver transplant	$69,000	$300,000
Cataract surgery	$1,250	$2,000

Source: Icfai Business School Case Development Centre.

Madras Medical Mission, a Chennai-based hospital, conducted a complex heart operation on an 87-year-old American patient at a cost of $8,000 (€7,000, £4,850) including the cost of his airfare and a month's convalescence in hospital. The patient claimed that a less complex operation in US had earlier cost him $40,000. At one private clinic in London a thorough men's health check-up that included blood tests, electro-cardiogram tests, chest x-rays, lung tests and abdominal ultrasound cost $574 (£345, €500). By comparison, a check-up at a clinic operated by Delhi-based healthcare company Max Healthcare cost $84.[18] A Hollywood agent, who was in India, went to dental surgeon, Dr. Anil K Mehta's clinic in Delhi for a check-up. She could not believe that dental care in India was so cheap. She said, "Wouldn't jaws drop when a doctor in India charges $150 (Rs. 6,877) for a procedure like root canal treatment that would have cost $2,000 in the US?"[19]

Industry analysts noted that unlike its western counterparts, which were saddled with prohibitive costs, India had the right mix of skills and value-for-money offerings.[20] As Indian corporate hospitals were on par, if not better than the best hospitals in Thailand and Singapore, there was scope for improvement, and the country was emerging as one of the preferred medical destinations.[21] Anupam Verma, director, Administration, P D Hinduja National Hospital said, "In terms of medical expertise and technology, these three countries are on par with the US, Europe or Australia. But while the cost of delivery may be 10 in the US, it is about 5 in Singapore, 3 in Thailand and about 2 in India. The idea is that countries at the lower spectrum of cost join together to promote Asia as a medical destination. It will be competitive, but promoting the region as an affordable healthcare destination will bring in more patients, than when the countries promote themselves individually."[22]

While Thailand and Singapore with their advanced medical facilities and built-in medical tourism options were attracting a number of foreign patients, India's state-of-the-art hospitals in addition to the latest technology in medicine had helped in attracting patients from neighbouring countries, West Asia and the West. Diagnostic centres in India were equipped with latest machines from multinational companies and the technology was also considered to be on par with other developed countries of the world. "We have well equipped, state-of-the-art hospitals and we can offer the same level of care as anywhere else in the world. There is no reason why we should not become the healthcare destination of the world,"[23] said Dr. Prathap C Reddy, chairman of the Apollo Group of Hospitals, the world's third-largest private healthcare provider. In 2003, a report published by Dr. Vinay Kothari, the managing director of Hospihealth, a hospital and healthcare planner and management consultancy, mentioned that a decade ago, India was roughly 50 years behind US. However, over the last 10 to 15 years the gap had begun to close fast, with hightech super-specialty hospitals coming up all over the country. Many Indian private hospitals made efforts to improve quality by employing quality manpower, better salary structure, training and providing facilities to their doctors for continuing their education.[24]

Analysts opined that while quality remained an issue for India in the past, it seemed to be improving since India's economic liberalisation in the early 1990s. Private hospitals were finding it easier to import hightech medical equipments. Therefore, medical technology, which used to differentiate the healthcare facilities available in developed countries with that of India, did not exist. "For instance, for our cardio unit, we have been able to acquire a new solid-state, flat-panel detector, the Digital Cathlab System, that gives the best image quality with very few side effects to the human body. This is at par with what is offered in the best hospitals in the West, and now at least five major (Indian) hospitals have this system,"[25] said R Basil, chief executive at Bangalore's Manipal Hospital. The corporatisation of the sector had also helped in boosting the image of healthcare in India. "Now it is not only the clinical talent and the technology here that is world class, but also service standards, the way hospitals are being managed, patient services, administrative services, etc.,"[26] said Vishal Bali, general manager of the Bangalore-based Wockhardt Hospital and Heart Institute.

Realising the economic benefits of medical tourism, the Indian government announced its plans to reduce import duties on medical equipment resulting in the reduction of purchasing costs of medical equipments. Dr. Prathap C Reddy said that even companies producing medical equipments also recognised India as a potential market. When medicated stents for angioplasty came to market in 2001, they were launched in India barely a month after their initial launch in Paris and even before they were launched in US.[27] Analysts said that although Indian hospitals were equipped with state-of-the-art technology, they were able to charge far less than their US and European counterparts because pay scales were much lower and patient volumes were quite higher. Moreover, in New York, a heart surgeon would typically spend $1,00,000 a year towards malpractice insurance whereas the amount was $4,000 in India.[28]

In addition to the state-of-the-art healthcare facilities in India, the country possessed a talented pool of highly qualified and experienced medical professionals. Dr. S K Sama, chairman of Sir Ganga Ram Hospital in Delhi said, "Professional expertise in the country is as good as in the best hospitals abroad. We give personalised attention at much lower costs, at the same time we provide top-of-the-line services. In five years, things would be totally different. Europeans would be seeking healthcare here."[29] India's medical schools produced a large number of skilled professionals. There were more than 35,000 specialist doctors of Indian origin in US alone. Doctors in India had excellent clinical knowledge and the quality of doctors was comparable to the best in the world. Many Indian doctors had American or European credentials. India had established world class expertise in practices such as cardiac care, cosmetic surgery, hip replacements, knee replacements, joint replacements, organ transplant, angioplasty, cancer treatment, infertility treatments, skin problems, laser eye surgery, orthopaedic surgery, gastroenterology, ophthalmology, transplants, urology and dentistry.

According to Hari Prasad, vice-president of Apollo Group of Hospitals in Hyderabad, foreigners should have confidence in India's medical system because many Britons and Americans were accustomed to the treatment by expatriate Indian doctors.[30] "Nobody even questions the capability of an Indian doctor, because there isn't a big hospital in the United States where there isn't an Indian doctor working,"[31] said Anupam Sibal, a British-trained paediatrician and Apollo Group of Hospitals' director of Medical Services. It was observed that doctors at Indian hospitals had corrected problems that had gone wrong when treated in the West. A patient from Nigeria, who is a businessman of Indian descent, had lost his index finger. He went to Europe to correct it at a huge cost but the problem deteriorated. However, Apollo Group of Hospitals fixed the problem within ten days.[32] Dr. Devi Shetty, a surgeon at Narayana Hrudayalaya, a top cardiac care provider in Bangalore believed that in the next 10 years, doctors of Indian origin would define the way surgical procedures would be done. He said, "When a surgeon in the US retires, he would have done 2,500 operations. At Narayana Hrudayalaya, we have surgeons in their 30s who have already done 3,000 procedures."[33]

Some of the established hospitals in India were Apollo Group of Hospitals, Escorts Hospitals in New Delhi and Jaslok Hospital's in Mumbai. Corporate hospitals such as Global Hospitals, CARE and Dr. L V Prasad Eye Hospitals in

Hyderabad, The Hindujas in Mumbai, were also attracting a lot of foreign patients. The success rate in Indian hospitals was comparable to that at the world's top hospitals. For example, at Apollo Group of Hospitals, surgeons had 98 5% success in the 50,000 heart operations they had performed. Of 138 bone marrow transplants, 87% was successful, and of 6,000 kidney transplants, 95% was successful.[34] Similarly, at Escorts Heart Institute and Research Centre, a leading private healthcare provider, the death rate for coronary bypass patients was 0.8%. By contrast, the 1999 death rate for the same procedure at New York-Presbyterian Hospital, where former US president Bill Clinton underwent bypass surgery, was 2.35%, according to a 2002 study by the New York State Health Department.[35]

As healthcare salaries and medical facilities improved in India, many Indian doctors who had left their country for more-developed countries were returning back to their home country. The familiarity of the Indians with English language and diverse tourism options in India had also attracted patients from western countries. Medical treatment in UK was free under the NHS, but because of the long waiting periods (ranging from six to 18 months), some patients opted for expensive private care. Patients who could not wait or opt for private insurance preferred coming to countries like India where they could obtain high quality care at bargain prices without any waiting list.[36]

One such patient was 68-year-old British pensioner James Campbell who suffered from osteo-arthrititis of both knees. He was told that he would have to wait for three years for an operation in UK. He opted to come to India to get his surgery done and saved £12,000 in the process.[37] Another patient, Tom Raudaschl, an Austrian who lived in Canada and earned his living as a mountain guide, was suffering from osteo-arthritis in his hip. Raudaschl decided to undergo "hip resurfacing", a new procedure that involved scraping away damaged bone and replacing it with chrome alloy. He learned that he would have to wait as long as three years if he wanted to have the operation done under Canada's national health plan, a delay that would have cost him his job. In US, the procedure cost $21,000. So Raudaschl opted for a surgery at Apollo Group of Hospitals in Chennai, which cost him $5,000, including all hospital costs. Dr. Naresh Trehan, cardiologist and executive director of Escorts Heart Institute and Research Centre said, "If you can wait for two years for a bypass surgery, then you don't need it or you're dead—one of the two. Similarly, if you're wobbling on your frozen joints for two years because of a waiting list, it's a human tragedy."[38]

Medical Tourism – India's Potential

Industry experts believed that the inflow of medical tourists in India was on a rise due to cost difference or affordability of the treatment coupled with international standard of the hospitals and quality of doctors. In addition to patients from other developing countries, top Indian hospitals attracted a significant share of foreign business from people of Indian origin who lived in developed countries but maintained close ties with their homeland. Only in Britain, there were about 1.5 million Indians. Harsh Srivastava of the CII said that since India was well qualified and reasonable in every aspect of healthcare, from new-drug discovery and testing to surgery, the obvious solution for rich countries was to outsource their medical needs.[39]

Indian government's data indicated that from January 2004 to October 2004, India had received 2.62 million foreign visitors as against 2.12 million in the corresponding period in 2003. Foreign exchange earnings through tourism also increased from $2.8 billion during the ten-month period in 2003 to $3.85 billion in the corresponding period in 2004.[40] According to India's Ministry of External Affairs, the $17 billion Indian healthcare industry comprised roughly 4% of the country's GDP. Hospital services, healthcare equipment, managed care and pharmaceuticals were expected to grow by 13% annually till 2010. According to the Insurance Regulatory and Development Authority, India's healthcare industry could grow exponentially like software and pharmaceuticals in the 1990s. The government believed that only 10% of the market potential was tapped. With global revenues an estimated $2.8 trillion, healthcare was the world's largest industry.

According to the "Frost & Sullivan Indian healthCare Industry Forecast 1996-2006", the industry's growth highly depended on India's continuing macroeconomic liberalisation, including further tax cuts, a broader tax base and reduced interest rates for borrowers. The forecast said that the introduction of product patents in India was expected to boost the industry by encouraging multinationals to launch specialised life-saving drugs. Some analysts believed that India's natural advantages of lower production costs and its skilled workforce would attract multinationals to set up research and development and production centres. The export of bulk drugs and formulations was set to increase at a compounded annual growth rate of 20% and 10% respectively between 2002 and 2006.[41]

According to a report by Confederation of Indian Industry (CII) and McKinsey & Co., medical tourism, which was growing at a rate of 30% could generate revenues of Rs.100 billion ($2.1bn, €1.9bn, £1.3bn) by 2012 (compared to an estimated $333 million in 2004) and would account for 3%-5% of the total healthcare delivery market. According to CII, India was unique as it offered holistic medicinal services. With yoga, meditation, ayurveda, allopathy and other systems of medicines, India offered a unique bundle of services to an individual that was difficult to match by other countries. In addition, the clinical outcomes in India were on par with the world's best centres and the country possessed internationally qualified and experienced specialists.[42] A case study done by CII revealed that Thailand with a population of 60 million was successful in attracting one million health tourists in 2003 because of the development of world-class infrastructure. According to CII, the success story behind Thailand tapping the health tourism market was the aggressive international marketing by the tourism authority of the country. It had also integrated traditional medicine and service integration with tourism. CII believed that India should also replicate the Thai model and capitalise on its inherent strengths to become a world player in medical tourism.[43]

CII also suggested that Indian government should encourage medical tourism by increasing air connectivity linking major cities like Delhi, Chennai, Bangalore, Hyderabad and Kolkata, and create health support infrastructure. There was also a need to undertake an international marketing campaign targeted at selected countries, besides establishing one-stop centres in key markets to facilitate the inflow of foreign patients. CII proposed the government to streamline immigration process for medical visitors. CII recommended the government to build adequate health infrastructure, create speciality tourist packages to include medical treatment and promote hospital accreditation and standardisation. The study indicated that private healthcare would be the largest component of medical tourism in 2012, reaching Rs.1560 billion from the existing level of Rs.690 billion.

CII along with Indian Healthcare Federation worked closely with the Indian Government to develop a strategy to project India as a world-class healthcare destination. CII along with Indian Healthcare Federation worked with tour operators to bring out attractive packages for medical tourism. Together they suggested a list of reputed hospitals in major cities, which had good air connectivity, with details of their service to the Indian government to promote them for medical tourism. CII suggested uniform price band in major specialties, which were indicative pricing to the government. Industry experts believed that the initiatives would facilitate foreign patients seeking treatment in India.

Government's Role in Promoting Medical Tourism

The Indian government initiated efforts to promote medical tourism in the country. Union Minister of State for Tourism, Renuka Chowdhury said in Parliament that medical tourism was an evolving concept and some states like Andhra Pradesh, Kerala, Karnataka, Maharashtra and Delhi with medical facilities of international standards were promoting it. The tourism ministry developed a logo to mark out ministry-approved centres of healthcare. The department also brought out a CD on ancient healing methods.[44] The Federation of Indian Chambers of Commerce and Industry (FICCI) and the Federation of Indian Exporters Organization visited Singapore, Malaysia and Indonesia in August 2004 to showcase medical facilities in India.

A team of CII, FICCI and representatives from private hospitals also toured Thailand and Singapore to understand how they transformed medical tourism into a paying proposition. A seminar was conducted to discuss India's chances to emulate Thailand. "The Thailand formula involves close coordination between the government and the healthcare industry, especially after a study revealed that each medical tourist brings in a revenue of $600 as against $230 from an ordinary tourist,"[45] said Sushil Jiwrajka, the head of FICCI's western India council. In eastern India, government-owned domestic carrier Indian Airlines teamed up with leading city hospitals in Kolkata to give air passengers a 30% discount on diagnostic and therapeutic services in city hospitals. The state governments also initiated efforts to promote medical tourism in their respective states. Kerala attracted patients from Gulf countries, Canada and the Maldives, while Mumbai attracted tourists from European countries. Gujarat emerged as a prime destination for medical tourists with cardiological problems.[46]

The Karnataka government set up Bangalore International Health City Corporation, which catered to patients with a wide variety of healthcare products and treatments. Bangalore was a hot destination as medical aid was the cheapest among the metros. For instance, a cardiac surgery at Hrudayalaya cost Rs.75,000 to Rs.1.10 lakh. A bypass at Manipal Hospital cost Rs.94,000 (if the patient was admitted in the general ward). The Maharashtra state government launched the Medical Tourism Council (MTC) of Maharashtra in collaboration with the state's business sector and private healthcare providers to promote medical tourism in the state. It unveiled fixed price treatment packages for foreign patients including costs such as medical, transport and accommodation. The brochure produced by the MTC included a table listing the comparable costs of procedure. For example, the average price of private heart surgery in the West was $50,000 whereas in Mumbai, it could be done for $10,000. It also used the state's more conventional tourist attractions to woo medical tourists. One of the slogans being considered was "open your new eyes on the beach of Juhu"—a reference to the five-star Arabian Sea resort 30 kilometres (20 miles) north of central Mumbai.[47]

The Gujarat government also set up a medical tourism council to facilitate medical tourism in the state. Aiming to showcase Gujarat and its cultural heritage as the best in India, the state government rolled out its ambitious Vibrant Gujarat Navratri 2004, which was used as a platform by the government to promote tourism on a global basis. Two major events were organised during Navratri 2004 to promote medical tourism in the state. First was an exhibition on medical tourism, where leading hospitals of the state displayed their facilities. A seminar on the issues and concerns related to medical tourism was also conducted. Kerala, another state in India, had also pioneered health and medical tourism in India. The state's focus on Ayurveda and its wide array of treatments and medications attracted foreigners. Kerala Ayurveda Centres were established at multiple locations in various metro cities highlighting the advantages of Ayurveda in health management. Kerala participated in various trade shows and expos to showcase the advantages of this traditional form of medicine.

The Tamil Nadu government also initiated efforts to woo foreign patients. The state held talks with the Airport Authority of India for a separate counter for people visiting the state for health tourism. Tamil Nadu Tourism Development

Corporation (TTDC) joined hands with Apollo to launch a traveller's privilege coupon called the Apollo Hospitals—TTDC Preventive Health Care Package. The package provided the tourist a 15% discount on Apollo preventive health check. The tourists, who opted for TTDC tour packages could use the coupon and a health check could be conducted at any of the Apollo Hospitals or clinics across the country. This coupon came along with the ticket purchased for any of the tour packages organised by TTDC.[48]

Private Sectors' Role in Facilitating Medical Tourism

Private hospitals, travel agencies and tour operators took initiatives to promote medical tourism in India. The Indian Healthcare Federation, an association of the healthcare delivery sector that included private hospitals like Apollo Group of Hospitals, Hinduja Hospital, Max Healthcare, the Fortis Heart Institute projected India as a healthcare destination. The private hospitals offered services such as airport pick ups, Internet-equipped private rooms and package deals that combined standard medicine with yoga and other forms of traditional Indian healing to attract foreign patients. Private hospitals coordinated with airlines, tour operators and car rental businesses to offer tourists a package deal that encompassed medical costs, hotel tariffs, airfares, airport pickup and tours to nearby popular tourist spots.

Among the private hospitals, Apollo Group of Hospitals (Apollo), the third largest health service provider in the world and the largest in Asia was the choicest destination for patients from Southeast Asia, Africa and West Asia. The group tied up with hospitals in Mauritius, Tanzania, Bangladesh and Yemen besides running a hospital in Sri Lanka, and was managing a hospital in Dubai. "We've just entered into a partnership to provide operational management services to Lagos-based Hygeia Nigeria, one of the largest healthcare groups in West Africa. We've also bagged a project consultant job for a 100-bed multi-speciality hospital in Ghana. Projects in Kuwait, Yemen, Sudan, Ethiopia, United Arab Emirates (UAE), and even Bangladesh, Nepal and Malaysia are also at various stages of association,"[49] said Dr. Hari Prasad, vice president, Apollo. Of the 5,200 hospital beds run by Apollo, foreign patients, mostly from West Asia, Africa and countries of south Asia, usually occupied about 100 beds. Apollo had treated about 95,000 international patients, many of whom were of Indian origin.

It has also planned to open some "tele-medicine" booths in Britain, where family doctors could consult specialists in India, and eventually, refer patients to them. The hospital joined hands with hotel groups to offer a combined medical as well as tourism package where patients could undergo treatment as well as visit some tourist destination in India. The group had entered into a tie-up with Sita, the Kuoni group's inbound travel arm, to launch a jointly developed project – Sita Care. Apollo Gleneagles partnered with Hyatt Regency to offer its foreign patients a comprehensive medical-cum-tourism package. Apollo's chairman Dr. Prathap C Reddy suggested the Indian government to include special flights targeted at international travellers. He felt that improving the connectivity of Mumbai and Delhi (where most international flights land) with Hyderabad or Chennai (where there were many private hospitals) could help in attracting medical tourists.

In addition, Apollo also initiated efforts to persuade Britain's NHS to bring patients from UK to India. Apollo was represented at a London meeting that was attended by a UK government's health adviser and private healthcare providers from South Africa, Australia, India and the UK. The consensus at the London meeting was that UK needed consultants and registrars to come over on short-term contracts before returning to their home countries. The Apollo team responded with a counter offer of a medical tourism package that would bring down waiting period for surgery in UK and offer sub-contracted healthcare at vastly cheaper rates. Recognition from the NHS ensured international standards in terms of patient care, quality improvement and patient safety Furthermore, Apollo was in the process of getting accredited with Joint Commission International, which facilitated better response from Europe and the US.

To attract patients from foreign countries, many hospitals focussed on providing more value to their customers. Escorts Heart Institute and Research Centre based in New Delhi provided airlift facilities for its patients from neighbouring countries like Nepal and Bangladesh. It also provided lodging facilities for its overseas patients. The hospital had two medical centres with limited diagnostic capabilities in Bangladesh and it planned to open two more medical centres in Kabul and the UAE. The Mohali-based Fortis Health Care, awarded the Best New Hospital Designed Worldwide by the American Association of Architects in 1999, had four facilities in operation and planned to add three new hospitals in and around Delhi. Fortis Hospital also entered into a mutual referrals arrangement with

Partners Healthcare System that included hospitals like Brigham Women's Hospital and Massachusetts Hospital, Boston.

The Hinduja hospital had a coordination centre in London, which facilitated registration of patients from Europe. Manipal Hospital had set up information centres in several countries, including UK and UAE. The hospital planned to include two floors exclusively for foreign patients. Manipal Hospital was in the process of getting accredited with the US Joint Commission International Accreditation, an industry certification for quality standards. It already had an ISO certification for meeting European quality standards. Narayana Hrudayalaya had a tie-up with the government of Kenya, besides information centres in Bangladesh and Malaysia. It has also increased its bed count from 460 to 780, and the number of operating theatres from 10 to 30. Vedic India also planned to set up medical townships across different states by partnering with Britain-based international property consultants, Chesterton Meghraj. Apollo and Manipal charged between 10-12% surcharge on foreign patients. Hinduja charged a 25% surcharge on foreign patients. Wockhardt Hospitals had partnered with US private health insurers Blue Cross and Blue Shield to insure patients treated at the group's hospitals. The British health insurer Bupa also insured the costs of treatment at Wockhardt hospitals. Wockhardt was also in talks with Britain's National Health Service about outsourcing the treatment of British patients to India.

In addition, travel agents were aggressively promoting India as a destination for medical tourism. "This sector has a lot of potential and we are planning to tap it. As it is not just tourism we are being careful. We are planning to come out with a brochure on it so that we could promote it in Germany, the US and the UK,"[50] said Rajeev Kohli, marketing director of Pacific Asia Travel Association. Thomas Cook appointed leading surgeon Padam Sanghvi as its medical tourism project adviser and planned for a deal with a leading hospital chain in India. Cox & Kings partnered with Vedic India and Omkar Trust. Cox and Kings India had a 2004 winter package that helped the patients anywhere in the world for visa arrangement, airport pick-up, transport, hotel and hospital. The Mumbai-based Jaslok Hospital had an informal tie up with Air-India and the Taj group of hotels. Mumbai-based Dr. Batra's Positive Health Clinic also had a tie up with Cox & Kings, Brightland Holidays and Sterling Resorts, which offered discounts to its members.

Challenges Ahead

While on the one hand the tourism ministry, state tourism boards, travel agents, tour operators, hotels and private hospitals were taking measures to attract foreign patients, some industry experts felt that the price advantages, state-of-the-art facilities, infrastructure and talented pool of highly qualified and experienced doctors were not enough to attract them. According to them, health and tourism industries needed to pool their resources to improve medical standards, clinical expertise, insurance coverage and appropriate infrastructure.[51]

Some industry experts observed that lack of standardisation and accreditation were major hurdles in drawing patients from abroad. Though rating agencies like Crisil and the Indian Credit Rating Agency had graded a few hospitals for setting standards, certification from international agencies like the Joint Commission on Accreditation of International Standards was considered an important aspect to attract foreigners. Some industry analysts felt that the FICCI and the CII were not taking serious measures to promote medical tourism. The FICCI said that the "Medical Tourism Council of Maharashtra" website contained "all the details". However, the site contained jumbled up addresses of hotels and tour operators (including an unusual spelling error of the word "doctors") and missing contact details. Oberoi Towers in Mumbai, part of the Oberoi luxury hotel chain, was listed as a member of "Medical Tourism Council of Maharashtra". But Priya D'Cunha of Oberoi's marketing department told *Asia Times Online* that they had no idea whether they were part of any medical tourism council.[52]

Some others thought that differential pricing was not a good practice. As different hospitals charged different rates for the same procedure, it left international patients confused. Moreover, India also lacked qualified specialist nurses and paramedics and qualified hospital administrators.[53] Trained nurses preferred to work in gulf countries due to higher wages offered there. A study undertaken by CII revealed that specialist nurse training would become vital as the number of single-superspeciality and multi-superspeciality hospitals increased.[54]

There were also serious concerns regarding the image of India that made it hard to compete with other Asian countries. Analysts stated that most foreigners would not think of India as a land of good health. Many private hospital owners revealed that as India continued to suffer from an image of poverty and poor hygiene, it discouraged many patients. However, private healthcare providers felt that foreigners could be sheltered from such poor conditions and that the quality of India's corporate hospitals was world class. Vishal Bali, vice-president of Wockhardt Hospitals, pointed out the fact that US private health insurers Blue Cross and Blue Shield insure patients treated at his group's hospitals, was a proof of quality.

India's poverty made even some Indians squeamish about medical tourism. About 43% of the population lived below the poverty line and had no access to basic healthcare, adequate nourishment and clean drinking water. The country accounted for 20% of the world's pregnancy and childbirth-related deaths among women.[55] According to the World Bank, India had only four doctors for every 10,000 people, compared to 27 in the US. Healthcare accounted for just 5.1% of India's GDP, against 14% in US.[56] The country had 1.5 beds per 1000 people while China, Brazil and Thailand had an average of 4.3 beds. Though the bulk of India's population lived in the rural interiors, about 59% of medical practitioners was located in the cities.

Some analysts felt that with the increase in number of foreign patients in India, quality medical service might become unaffordable for resident Indians. However, hospital sources opposed this estimation of the analysts. Anupam Verma, one of the directors of the Hinduja Hospitals assured that domestic patients would not run out of hospital beds, as 30% capacity of private hospitals was not utilised and that could be offered to medical tourists. Dr. Nazareth of Wockhardt believed that a large inflow of foreign tourists would not affect local patients; with many corporates such as Apollo, Fortis, Max, Wockhardt and Escorts entering the medical services industry, infrastructure was bound to expand. As *The Economist* wrote, "In the long run, medical tourism, like software exports brings money into the country and may ease the lot of India's poor, who have little access to healthcare. In the short run, however, medical treatment is both more easily understood and more transferable than software, and envy is harder to avoid."[57]

(Dakshi Mohanty, Associate Consultant and T Phani Madhav, Team Leader, the Icfai Business School Case Development Centre. The authors can be reached at dakshi@icfai.org and phanimadhav@icfaipress.org, respectively).

Endnotes

1 M, Raja, "India's Medical Tourism Injection", *www.atimes.com*, August 31, 2004.

2 Kohli, Shweta Rajpal, "Medical Tourism Growing at 30% a Year: Study", *Business Standard* (*www.rediff.com*), November 12, 2002.

3 Medical tourism is the practice to visit countries with low prices and buy services in their private hospitals. *www.encyclopedia.thefreedictionary.com*

4 "Get Well Away", *www.economist.com*, October 7, 2004.

5 Neelakantan, Shailaja, "India's Global Ambitions", *Far Eastern Economic Review*, *www.globalpolicy.org*, November 6, 2003.

6 Marcelo, Ray, "India Fosters Growing 'Medical Tourism Sector", *The Financial Times* (*www.yaleglobal.yale.edu*), July 2, 2003.

7 Ibid.

8 "Medical Tourism: Need Surgery, Will Travel", *www.cbc.ca*, June 18, 2004.

9 Medical tourists were the people who visited a particular country primarily for a medical procedure.

10 Datta, Prosenjit and Krishnan, Gina S. "The Health Travellers", *www.businessworldindia.com*, December 22, 2003

11 Ibid.

12 Ibid.

13 "The Health Travellers", op.cit.

14 Ibid.

15 "Get Well Away", op.cit.

16 Hasan, Shehla Raza, "India Bids for Healthcare Tourism", *www.atimes.com*, July 19, 2003.

17 Baxi, Amitabh, "It's Advantage India in Medical Tourism, says CII", *www.economic times.indiatimes.com*, October 30, 2004.

18 "India Fosters Growing 'Medical Tourism' Sector", op.cit.

19 Bajeli-Datt, Kavita, "Get Well Soon... in India", *www.the-week.com*, October 31, 2004.

20 Dutta, Rumi, "Healthcare Chains on Tourism Map", *www.business-standard.com*, December 1, 2004.

21 Somasekhar M, "India Eyeing Share in Medical Tourism Pie", *www.blonnet.com*, May 11, 2004.

22 "India may Join Hands with Singapore, Thailand for Asian Healthcare Hub", *Business Line*

www.networkindia.iesingapore.com, November 2004.

23 Bhatia, Shyam "India can Earn $1 billion from Medical Tourism", *www.us.rediff.com*, December 6, 2003.

24 "India bids for Healthcare Tourism", op.cit.

25 "India's Global Ambitions", op.cit.

26 Ibid.

27 Ibid.

28 Lancaster, John "Surgeries, Side Trips for 'Medical Tourists' ", *www.washingtonpost.com*, October 21, 2004

29 "Get Well Soon... in India", op.cit.

30 "India Fosters Growing 'Medical Tourism' Sector", op.cit.

31 "Surgeries, Side Trips for 'Medical Tourists' ", op.cit.

32 "India's Global Ambitions", op.cit.

33 Ibid.

34 Ibid.

35 "Surgeries, Side Trips for 'Medical Tourists' ", op.cit.

36 Shrinate, Supriya, "Healing the World", *Business Today, www.india-emb.org.eg*, September 16, 2004.

37 Ram, Arun, Bezbaruah, Supriya, David, Stephen, Unnithan, Sandeep, Ghosh, Labonita, Vinayak, Ramesh and Radhakrishnan, M G. "Hospitality Industry", *www.indiatoday.com*, November 24, 2003.

38 "Surgeries, Side Trips for 'Medical Tourists' ", op.cit.

39 "Get Well Away", op.cit.

40 "India Fixing Star Rating for Hospitals", *Indo-Asian News Service* (*www.in.news.yahoo.com*), November 5, 2004.

41 "India Bids for Healthcare Tourism", op.cit.

42 "It is Advantage India in Medical Tourism: CII", *www.ibef.org*, August 16, 2004.

43 "Leverage Cost Benefit to Promote Medical Tourism: CII", *www.newstodaynet.com*, August 17, 2004.

44 "Get Well Soon... in India", op.cit.

45 Iyer, Malathy, "India Out to Heal the World", *The Times Of India*, *www.healthlibrary.com*, October 26, 2004.

46 "'India: Attractive Destination for Medical Tourism", *www.blonnet.com,* June 26, 2004.

47 Wright, Ben, "Maharashtra Woos Medical Tourists", *www.news.bbc.co.uk*, February 10, 2004.

48 Subramanian, Lakshmi, "Medical Tourism: Tamilnadu's Top Agenda", *www.express travelandtourism.com*, October 2004.

49 "India's Medical Tourism Injection", op.cit.

50 "Get Well Soon... in India", op.cit.

51 Saxena, Supriya, "India Gears up for Medical Tourists", *www.domain-b.com*, September 3, 2004.

52 "India's Medical Tourism Injection", op.cit.

53 "Medical Tourism can Contribute Rs.100 bn by 2012", *www.indiainfoline.com*, April 13, 2004.

54 Ibid.

55 "India's Global Ambitions", op.cit.

56 "Surgeries, Side Trips for 'Medical Tourists' ", op.cit.

57 "Get Well Away", op.cit.

19

Health Tourism in Kerala: The Ayurvedic Way

Priyaa Ravikanth

This industry focus looks at the enormous potential for "ayur-tourism" in Kerala. The charm of Kerala is well-known and so is the practice of ayurveda healing. What is interesting to note is that when these two aspects merge, i.e., ayurveda and tourism, a new facet of tourism opens up with many opportunities. Different therapies are also outlined here.

"Ayurveda has given a big boost to the state's tourism industry and has put Kerala on the world tourism map. Of the foreign tourists, who visited the state this year, over 40% had combined ayurveda in their package."[1]

Pierre and Hélène had flown all the way from France to Kerala (Exhibit I) during the monsoon season for their "*Ayurveda holiday*"[2], something that this couple had not missed for past three years. What brought them to this state on the tropical Malabar coast of southwestern India was the healing effect of Ayurveda. Hélène's got relieved of migraine, and the couple went back

[1] According to Rajendra Prasad, President of Thambu, a tribal organization in Kerala, "Ayurveda Cuts a Healthy Deal for Kerala Tourism", *Business Standard*, February 28, 2006.

[2] Ayurveda Holiday refers to a holiday or vacation for Ayurvedic treatment.

revejenuated. Kerala also enthralled the couple with its endless beaches, tranquil backwaters, mist clad hill stations, lush green forests, delightful wildlife, incredible art forms, unique spicy cuisine and rich cultural heritage.

Exhibit I: An Overview of Kerala

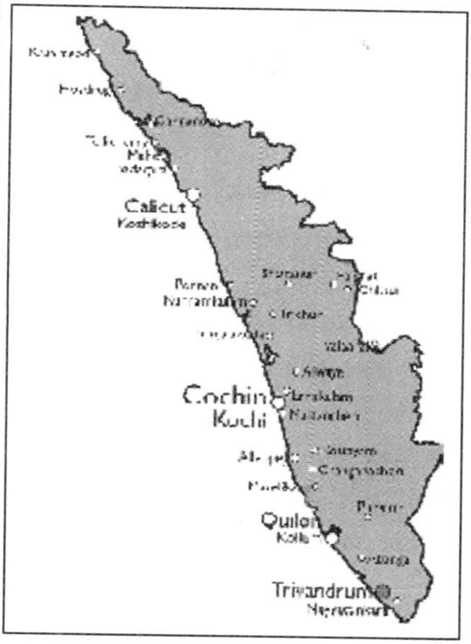

Kerala was known for its spice trade for several millennia. Traders from Arabian countries and Europe came here to trade in spices. The spice trade dated back to three thousand years. Located at the extreme southern tip of the Indian sub-continent, Kerala with 38,863 sq.km. area (1.18% of India's landmass) is sandwiched between the Arabian Sea to the west and the Western Ghats to the east. Climate is mainly wet and maritime tropical, is heavily influenced by the seasonal heavy rains brought by the monsoon (August-September). Its coast runs some 580 km in length and 24% of Kerala is covered with forests. Ayurveda[1], Siddha[2], Unani[3] are the alternative medicine systems that are prevalent. Malayalam is the language spoken by majority of people in the state.

Kerala has a commendable record in terms of the Physical Quality of Life Index (PQLI). Indicators of PQLI like infant mortality (13%), literacy rate (91%), female literacy (86%), and life expectancy at birth for males (69) and females (72), are well above the other states of India. The major reason for this achievement is because of its focus on the service sector.

[1] Ayurveda is the earliest school of medicine known to humans. Charaka, the father of medicine consolidated Ayurveda 2500 years ago. Ayu means Life and Veda means science or knowledge. Ayurveda is a science of life.

[2] The term Siddha means achievements and Siddhas were saintly persons who achieved results in medicine. Eighteen Siddhas were said to have contributed towards the development and this medical system was largely therapeutic in nature.

[3] Unani Medicine is based on the Greece philosophy.

Source: www.images.google.co.in

Health and medical tourism is perceived as one of the fastest growing segments in India. With yoga, meditation, ayurveda (Exhibit II), allopathy, and other systems of medicines, India now offers a unique basket of services to an individual, which is difficult to match by other countries. Kerala is a pioneer in health and medical tourism in India. It has made a concerted effort to promote health tourism along with its unique Ayurveda treatment. Ayurveda is a significant money-earner for Kerala tourism as it has been a key to a substantial increase in the number of visitor arrivals into the state. In order to retain this competitive edge in Ayurveda tourism, the Kerala tourism board and the state government needed to address a lot of challenges like bringing in state-of-the-art quality control standards and standardization in the Ayurvedic treatments given in the state to cope with the demands of the modern times.

Kerala: The Land of Ayurveda

Next to beaches, tourists visited Kerala for Ayurveda, as it had become an integral part of Kerala tourism since mid-1990s. The Ayurvedic segment sectoral study done by Kerala State Industrial Development Corporation Ltd. (KSIDC), during 2003, revealed that the total turnover of Indian Ayurvedic Industry as a whole was of Rs.4000 crores—Kerala's contribution in this accounted to Rs.200 crores. It had over 300 Good Manufacturing Practice (GMP) certified Ayurvedic product manufacturers in 2004. In 2004-05, over 40% of the foreign tourists visited Kerala to experience the healing touch of Ayurveda. The state also had many hotels that offered fine spa facilities for the tourists. Apart from hotel spas, the state had various Ayurveda ashrams that were practicing the Ayurvedic treatments (Exhibit III).

Now, Ayurveda has almost become synonymous with Kerala. The popularity of this traditional medicare has led to mushrooming of a number of Ayurvedic centers across the state. Some of the major Ayurvedic firms in the state are—Pankajakasthuri, The Arya Vaidya Pharmacy, The Vaidyaratnam Oushadasala, Nagarjuna, Sitaram, Sreedhareeyam, SD Pharmacy, Kandamkulathy, Dhanwanthari, Bipha, Sree Sankara, Nupal, Kerala Ayurveda Pharmacy Ltd., and Relax Herbals and Exports. Apart from Kerala, there are also similar ayurveda proponents elsewhere in the country, such as Baidyanath and Dabur in north, Zandu in Mumbai and many other smaller units across India. The large number of Ayurvedic centers has led to employment generation as each unit requires a doctor, four masseurs, and at least seven to nine staff members.

To evaluate the safety and service standards of these Ayurvedic Centers and to classify them accordingly, the state government has come up with a proactive measure of approval in the form of Green Leaf and Olive Leaf. "Green Leaf" is the highest classification awarded to a Ayurvedic center which fulfills all the essential and optional conditions prescribed by the state of Tourism Department. The essential

Exhibit II: Ayurveda – A Holistic Healing Science

Ayurveda, a holistic healing science evolved around 600 BC in India, the origin of which can be traced back to the *Vedas* (*Rig, Yajur, Sama and Atharva*), which are the oldest available classics of the world. *Rigveda and Atharva* (5000 years BC), the earliest documented ancient Indian knowledge, have references on health and diseases. Ayurvedic texts like *Charak Samhita* and *Sushruta Samhita* were documented about 1000 years BC. Ayurveda is a science of life. Life according to it is a combination of senses, mind, body and soul. So it is clear from this definition of life that it is not only limited to body or physical symptoms, but also gives a comprehensive knowledge about spiritual, mental and social health. The treatment mainly comprises of powders, tablets, decoctions, medicated oils, etc., prepared from natural herbs, plants and minerals.

In the United States, Ayurveda is considered Complementary and Alternative Medicine, (CAM)-more specifically, a CAM whole medical system. Many therapies used in Ayurveda are also used on their own as CAM – for example, herbs, massage, and yoga. CAM is a group of diverse medical and healthcare systems, practices, and products that are not currently considered part of conventional medicine. Complementary medicine is used together with conventional medicine. Alternative medicine is practiced in place of conventional medicine. Conventional medicine is medicine as practiced by holders of MD (Medical Doctor) or DO (Doctor of Osteopathy) degrees and by their allied health professionals. Some conventional medical practitioners also practice CAM. Whole medical systems are healing systems and beliefs that have evolved over time in different cultures and parts of the world.

According to Ayurveda, health is the state of balance and disease is the state of imbalance. The aim of this system is to give complete health and not just getting free from physical diseases and stressed on the prevention of body ailments in addition to curing them. Two most important aims of Ayurveda are to maintain the health of healthy people and to cure the diseases of sick people. It is a unique, indispensable branch of medicine—a complete naturalistic system that depends on the diagnosis of body medical humours—*Vata* (resembles the classical element air), *Pitta* (fire) and *Kapha* (water) to achieve the right balance. It helps in understanding each individual at a very subtle personal level and giving a detailed description about diet, daily routine, lifestyle, actions and activities to be followed and believes in the treatment of not just the affected part, but the individual as a whole, making it the natural way to refresh, eliminate all toxic imbalances from the body and thus regain resistance and good health contributing to having a happy, healthy and peaceful society.

Compiled by Priyaa Ravikanth.

conditions include having qualified and sufficient Ayurvedic physicians and personnel to attend on both male and female tourists separately, high quality medicines and health programs, excellent, clean and hygienic equipment, environment, facilities and infrastructure, etc. The optional conditions specify that the center should have high standard architectural and interior features, and extra facilities such as steam bath rooms, meditation/yoga centers, herbal gardens,

Exhibit III: Major Treatments and Rejuvenation Therapy

Some of procedures used in Ayurveda are described below:

Major Treatments

1. **Abhyangam**: It is a highly specialized oil massage. The massage strokes are given according to the disease. Each session lasts for around 45 minutes. It is effective for treating obesity, diabetic gangrene, etc.
2. **Dhanyamla Dhara**: Warm herbal juices are poured on the body rhythmically using a special vessel. Each session lasts for an hour. This procedure is for treating hemiplegia, and paralysis rheumatic complaints.
3. **Dhara**: Treatment for insomnia, vatha dominated diseases and anxiety. Herbal extracts, medicated milk, and medicated butter milk are poured on the forehead for about 45 minutes daily for two to three weeks.
4. **Kativasthi**: For nagging back pains. A small ridge made on the back with herbal paste. Warm medicated oil is allowed to stand within this. This treatment lasts for about an hour.
5. **Kizhi**: Hot pouches containing herbal powder are applied on the body. This procedure is for treating osteoarthritis, arthritis with swelling, spondylitis, sports injuries, etc.
6. **Ksheeradhoomam**: Fomentation with medicated milk. It is used for treating facial paralysis, Bell's palsy, speech disorders and other nervous disorders of the face.
7. **Lepanam**: Medicated herbal paste is applied on the body part to ease inflammation.
8. **Nasyam**: Treating headaches, paralysis, mental disorders, and certain skin diseases. Nasyam is performed by applying herbal juices or medicated oils through the nose. Treatment given daily for a couple of weeks.
9. **Njavarakizhi**: This is a specialized treatment primarily used in Kerala. Njavara is a kind of paddy. A medicinal preparation of Njavara is packed in a cloth bag. The hot cloth bag is then rhythmically applied to various parts of the body. Njavarakizhi makes the body supple, and removes stiffness of joints. It is a treatment for rheumatism and arthritis. Njavarakizhi is even believed to increase appetite by improving digestion. It is also used to correct mental imbalances.
10. **Pizhichil**: Lukewarm herbal oils are rhythmically applied on the body by two to four trained therapists. This procedure lasts for about an hour to an hour and a half. It is usually done for two to three weeks. This treatment is for arthritis, and various nervous disorders.
11. **Sirovasthi**: A cap is fitted on the head and medicated oils poured into it. The treatment lasts for around an hour. Usually done daily for a week. It is used to treat facial paralysis, severe headaches, and other diseases caused primarily due to *vatha*.
12. **Snehapanam**: The patient consumes medicated ghee for a period of 8 to 12 days. The quantity consumed is increased progressively. It is a treatment for curing osteoarthritis, psoriasis, etc.

Contd...

Contd...

13. **Thalam**: Medicated oil is applied on the head for half an hour to 45 minutes. Thalam is done for insomnia, migraine, etc.
14. **Udvarthanam**: Herbal powder massage—Lasts for half an hour to 45 minutes. Usually done daily for two to four weeks. Effective in treatment of hemiplegia, paralysis, obesity and certain rheumatic ailments.
15. **Urovasthi**: Warm medicated oil is allowed to stand over the chest for 45 minutes. Treatment for asthma, and other respiratory ailments.
16. **Vasthi**: Application of herbal oils, herbal extracts through the rectum. Done for 5 to 25 days. Vasthi is good for treating arthritis, paralysis, and chronic constipation.

Rejuvenation Therapy

The Following are the major rejuvenational therapies of Ayurveda:

1. **Rasayana Chikitsa**: Rasayana Chikitsa is given for toning the skin and for strengthening the tissues. The objective is to achieve health and longevity. This treatment improves vitality and mental agility. It tones up the immune systems of the body. This procedure includes herbal body massages, and steam baths in addition to rejuvenative ayurvedic internal medicines.
2. **Kayakalpa Chikitsa**: Human beings always wanted immortality. While that is an impossible dream (at least as of now) Ayurveda provides longevity by retarding the aging process. This therapy includes intake of rasayana, and special diets. It is highly effective, especially for those people who are yet to turn 50.
3. **Sweda Karma**: Medicinal steam bath to eliminate impurities from the body. Herbs are boiled and the steam is passed over the entire body for 10 to 20 minutes daily. This treatment improves the skin tone, and reduces fat.

Compiled by Priyaa Ravikanth.

etc. Only those centers that fulfill the essential conditions are awarded the "Olive Leaf" classification. The state has also designed guidelines for accreditation of Ayurvedic and Panchakarma[3] centers.

Kerala has been significantly contributing to ayurvedic treatment, apart from the many effective local editions and their basic panchakarma techniques (Exhibit IV). Due to unsettled political conditions and several invasions from outside the country, Ayurveda faced neglect in the past centuries. Its growth was limited, its teaching and training were stopped from being spread, and its monopoly in practice was eroded greatly. The rebirth of ayurveda has been mainly due to the

[3] Panchakarma is a classical form of detoxification. It is a group of treatment, five in number.

Exhibit IV: Contributions to Ayurveda
Some of the major contributions of Kerala to Ayurveda: 1. Vishachikitsa (toxicology) 2. Marmachikitsa (a treatment system based on vital points on the body) 3. Gajachikitsa (treatment for elephants) 4. Dhara, Pizhichil, and Njavarakizhi are treatment methods introduced by Kerala practitioners. 5. Marcopolo, the great traveler, notes the physicians and astrologists of Kerala with great reverance.
Source: www.ayurvedic-spa-vacation-in-kerala.com

continuous efforts of the Kerala Government. Almost every home in Kerala has some medicinal plant and people in general are aware about Ayurvedic remedies and its use. Also, Kerala is the place where ayurvedic education has been kept in its classical form, while incorporating rapidly developing modern science. Kerala-trained ayurvedic physicians are in demand not only in India, but all over the world and the style of Ayurveda followed in the state addresses issues which are not resolved by modern medicine.

Kerala's equable climate, natural abundance of forest (with a wealth of herbs and medicinal plants), and the cool monsoon season (June-November) are best suited for Ayurveda's curative and restorative packages.

Tourism Industry in Kerala

Kerala has emerged as a global tourism destination by offering a rich tourism experience keeping by the customs and traditions of the state intact, while at the same time being receptive to new ideas. As early as 1986, Kerala had identified tourism as a potential industry for the state and subsequently all appropriate benefits granted to other industries had been accorded to the tourism sector. These included subsidies, technical guidance, marketing assistance, publicity through government publications, help in availing loans, etc.

Now, Kerala attracts high income tourists in both domestic and international categories. Tourists come mainly for holidaying, sightseeing, medical treatment and relaxation. The top five countries in terms of tourist origin are the United Kingdom, Germany, USA, Sri Lanka, and Maldives. A sizeable number of tourists also come from France, Japan, Arabian Gulf, Italy, Australia, and Switzerland.

Exhibit V: Awards and Recognition Received by Kerala Tourism
1. WTTC selected Kerala as a Partner State.
2. The Das Golden Stadttor award at the ITB Berlin considered to be the travel industry's Oscar.
3. One of the three finalists at the WTTC "Tourism for Tomorrow" awards in the destination category.
4. National Geographic Travel after 2 years of research had chosen Kerala, as one of the 50 must see destinations of a lifetime.
5. Best Performing State Award instituted by *Outlook Traveller* for the year 2000-01.
6. One of the 100 great trips for the 21st Century, by "*Travel and Leisure*"
7. One of the ten hot spots for the millennium, by "*Emirates Inflight Magazine*".
8. One of the ten love nests in India, by "*Cosmopolitan*" .
9. One of the six destinations of the millennium, by "*Khaleej Times*" .
10. In 2004 and 2006, Kerala won three PATA (Pacific Asia Travel Association) Gold Awards*– a. The Thenmala Ecotourism Project in environmental/ecotourism category, b. East Fort Conservation Project in Thiruvananthapuram in the heritage and culture category, c. CD titled "Ayurveda: The mantra of Niramaya" for CD-ROM category.
* *"PATA Awards for Kerala Tourism", Business Line, February 23, 2004.*
Compiled by author.

The private sector has played a critical role in promoting tourism in Kerala while the government's role has changed over the years by becoming more of a facilitator for growth of the industry. The industry's spectacular performance over the past decade has largely been driven by private sector investment and involvement. Kerala is the leader in India's tourism growth and WTTC (World Travel and Tourism Council) has predicted a growth of 11.4% per annum between 2004 and 2013. Experts opined that innovative marketing and target specific promotion are two prime factors that have helped Kerala in sustaining and increasing its tourism growth.

Success of Tourism Industry in Kerala

"The phenomenal growth of Kerala in the tourism sector is reflected by the various awards and recognitions that has come our way"

– K C Venugopal,
Minister for Tourism, Kerala.

The state has emerged as the most acclaimed tourist destination of the country in the recent past. Despite the general backwardness in industrial development, tourism is the only industry flourishing in the state over a number of years. In 2003 the number of foreign and domestic tourists to the state increased by 26.68% and 5.44% respectively compared to 2002 (Table 1), and earnings from tourism recorded an increase of 39.35% in 2003 over the previous year (Table 2). It accommodated 10.70% of the country's total foreign visitors. Tourism contributed 6.29% of the states' GDP[4] and generated employment opportunities for nearly 7 lakh people. In 2004 around 3.6 lakh foreign tourist arrivals were registered, and tourism generated Rs.6,800 crores, of which Rs.1,200 came in by way of foreign exchange and 8 lakh jobs were generated.

Table 1: Tourist Arrival and Resulting Income from 2000 to 2003

Year	No. of Arrivals (Foreign + Domestic)	% of Change Over the PY	Income (Foreign + Domestic)	% of Change Over the PY
2000	52,23,154	2.61	4,000	–
2001	54,48,522	4.31	4,500	12.50
2002	5,80,020	6.47	4,931	9.58
2003	61,65,849	6.29	5,938	20.42

Compiled from Tourist Statistics 2003, Dept. of Tourism, Government of Kerala.

Table 2: Tourist Arrival and Resulting Income from 1999 to 2003

Year	No. of Arrivals Over the PY	% of Change	Income	% of Change Over the PY
1999-2000	12,046	–	1,70,449	–
2000-2001	26,148	117.07	4,45,437	161.33
2001-2002	41,161	57.42	11,30,839	153.87
2002-2003	65,075	58.09	18,06,330	59.73
2003-2004	1,18,404	81.95	40,44,571	123.91

Compiled from Tourist Statistics 2003, Dept. of Tourism, Government of Kerala.

Kerala received the award for the best performing state in tourism continuously from 1998 to 2001[5] and also from 2002 to 2005[6] by "Government of India" for the state's promotional and marketing efforts, infrastructure development,

---

4 *www.keralatourism.org*

5 It did not receive the award for the year 2001-02.

6 *www.keralatourism.org*

performance of state-owned tourism complexes, human resource development, and development of sustainable tourism and tourist arrivals, both domestic and international (Exhibit V).

Marketing and Positioning Strategies

Kerala Tourism Development Corporation (KTDC) established a brand name "*God's Own Country*" for promoting tourism in the state. It has developed a large number of unique tourism products based on its culture and tradition. The traditionally made boats called *Kettuvalloms* that were used as a mode of transportation from remote villages to the port town of Kerala have been converted into luxury houseboats to sail through the backwaters. The other innovative products offered are Ayurveda, Thekkady tiger trail[7], and traditional art forms. The strategy for marketing was to position Kerala as a unique standalone destination targeting up-market tourists seeking peace and difference.

The increase in tourist arrivals was the result of aggressive marketing and promotion of the destination in road shows and travel and trade fairs, as the states' tourism board participated in major international and domestic tourism trade fairs along with the private sector. Kerala did not have to invent new attractions and build expensive tourists attractions. It capitalized on its natural strength and tailored it to suit the tourist requirements. The publicity instruments of the state like pamphlet/brochure, etc., were designed to emphasize its tradition and cultural heritage. Its competitive advantage was its *Ayurveda health rejuvenation package*. The focus on traditional Ayurveda, backwater boat races, performing arts, cuisines, etc., depicted the same. The upside of this strategy was that it had promoted in the process its culture and tradition to the world and carved out a niche and a distinct identity for itself. The elegant mix of herbal cures, spa tourism, beach holidays and wildlife backed by world-class marketing had let Kerala to be voted among the best destinations.

Kerala's USP was the ABC acronym for Ayurveda, Backwaters and Culture and cuisine. There was a demand for stress busting vacations as people preferred to take vacations where their health was also looked after and where they could rejuvenate. Kerala identified this need and to tap the potential, it established

---

[7] Thekkady wildlife sanctuary adventure trekking and camping.

Ayurveda resorts and spas by the beaches and backwaters so that the combination was of a wellness holiday at a location which was naturally endowed.

Kerala tourism highlighted its cool monsoon season (June-November) as the best period for taking Ayurveda treatments. Earlier, the advent of the monsoon had meant a sharp fall in the number of tourists visiting the state. The tourism department worked out promotional schemes to attract tourists to the state during the "off season"[8], especially the monsoon. The schemes were designed to highlight the traditional belief that Ayurveda treatments are most effective when taken during the monsoon. A *monsoon food festival*, a music festival, a theatre festival and *monsoon treks* were some of the events planned.

KTDC along with the Indian Railways reached an agreement to promote the state tourism wherein the Railways were to participate in mobilizing both domestic and foreign tourists from different parts of the country to the state. The promotion campaigns were planned and the interior of the coach designed to present a typical Kerala atmosphere. During the journey, the tourists were served Kerala cuisine. On entering Kerala, the coach was to be detached at a designated station, and from there, KTDC was to take over the tour. The tourists then traveled by road in KTDC coaches. After completing the Kerala tour, they would return to the rail coach which would again be attached to a train to take them back. Railways were also planning to introduce Ayurveda coaches in which the tourists were to experience some of the aspects of Ayurveda like the traditional Ayurveda massages.

Kerala, with its rich tradition of Ayurveda, is highly popular with the German tourists. Tourist arrivals from Germany, the fifth biggest market for Kerala, had been growing at a spectacular rate of 18% between 2004 and 2006. The February 2002 issue of *Geo Saison*, Germany's largest selling travel magazine, featured Kerala and its heritage of Ayurveda. It generated widespread interest at the ITB[9] 2006 and showcased the traditional architecture of the State, which attracted visitors wanting to try out the rejuvenating Ayurvedic massage. According to EK Bharat Bhushan, Principal Secretary, Kerala Tourism, "*We are looking at Germany as a big market for Kerala, especially for our wellness product Ayurveda. A print and TV campaign along with road shows promoting Ayurveda will be launched in Berlin and other major cities in Germany*"[10].

[8] Very heavy rain southwest monsoon period from June to September.

[9] ITB Berlin—A major international tourism trade show and tourism trade fair.

[10] God's Own Country wins over hearts at ITB with "Ayurveda", *www.travelandtourism.mathrubhumi.com*, April 2006.

For virtual marketing, the state used the latest developments in Information Technology. The website of Department of Tourism, Government of Kerala, *www.keralatourism.org,* offered comprehensive information for tourists. Tourism department branded and promoted Ayurveda through Internet, ad campaigns, print brochures, travel marts, coffee-table books and CD-ROMS at various international platforms such as World Travel Mart, London, ITB Germany, etc. It also created short films on Ayurveda for television channels like BBC and CNN. In 2006, the Publication on Ayurveda *The Mantra of Niramaya* secured the PATA (Pacific Asia Travel Association) Gold Award in the Education and Training category. In 2004, it won PATA Gold Award in the CD-ROM category for its CD titled "Ayurveda: The mantra of Niramaya".

Challenges for Kerala Ayurveda

The revival of Ayurveda is visible all over Kerala. However, most practitioners are concentrating on the business side, i.e., cultivation and collection of herbs, large-scale manufacture of medicines, their sale, distribution and export. Units with little expertise in medicine have mushroomed in Kerala to cash in on the growing popularity of the traditional system. They escape the arm of law since there is no regulatory system to examine and prevent adulterations. Kerala massage has become more of a commercial product. Most spas offer guest pampering rather than a complete wellness program, with many packages that are tailor-made to suit the budget and needs of tourists. Almost everything is sold under the Ayurveda umbrella. A growing concern among the experts is whether Ayurveda, which is now used as a tool to promote tourism in such a massive fashion because of the interest shown by the West, will become so expensive that it would go out of the reach of locals? There is no confirmation about formulations in the market—whether they adhere to the 54 textbooks[11] of ayurveda which are listed in the Drug and Cosmetics Act. Most herbal plants are collected from forests, and the forest areas are shrinking alarmingly. Providing constant supply of herbs without affecting the ecology has become a challenge.

Ayurveda was also promoted by the luxury hotels and tourism promoters by offering Ayurvedic packages—a range of Ayurvedic drinks and beverages and food, a massage, some oil treatment, a panchakarma therapy session and a few herbal

---

[11] Classically there are 2,500 formulations, about 2,250 of which are herbal-based, 150 are of mineral origin and 50 of animal origin.

products to take home along with the complimentary towel and dressing gown. Some unauthorized Ayurvedic parlors do not follow the prescribed norms. Many of their treatments are not scientifically designed or do not have trained masseurs; they employ female masseurs to lure clientele. Diet regimen is not strictly followed. Widely differing rates are charged for treatment and patients, and foreigners especially are deceived with the basic principle of Ayurveda getting ignored. Most tourists went back from India thinking that a massage with herbal oil was Ayurvedic treatment. However, the fact is that the massage is just a small part of it. An equally important component of the treatment is the diet and lifestyle of the patient and the herbal supplements prescribed. This can be provided only by a trained Ayurvedic physician, and such commercialization and exploitation only harms this traditional science and poses a serious problem to the future of this holistic system.

Road Ahead

Ayurveda, the ancient Hindu system of medicine that has been lying low for centuries, is set on a revival path by Kerala. Ayurveda clinics are having a boom time. Posh resorts, massage parlors and clinics have sprung up across the state attracting film stars, foreign tourists, politicians, non-resident Indians and even foreign heads of state. Apart from providing an alternative mode of treatment for many, Ayurveda is drawing foreign currency into Kerala.

Kerala has declared 2006 as the year of medical tourism and has planned to promote its traditional Ayurveda extensively. In 2006, Kerala tourism board decided planning to rope in country's popular film stars Amitabh Bachchan[12] and Aishwarya Rai[13] as a part of their campaign to attract international audience. Amitabh Bachchan is planned to be the brand ambassador for Kerala's tourism products and Aishwarya Rai for Ayurveda tourism. Kerala is cashing on the strong brand image it has built over years as a tourism destination and its Ayurveda treatment. Will Kerala be able to overcome all the challenges and maintain a sustainable growth to emerge as an Ayurveda capital of India remains to be seen.

(Priyaa Ravikanth is former Faculty Associate, the Icfai Business School Research Center, Ahmedabad. She can be reached at priyaa.ravikanth@gmail.com).

---

12 Famous Indian actor.

13 Famous Indian actress. She was crowned Miss World in 1994.

20

Apollo Hospitals: Leading the Way to Healthcare Tourism

Sarosh Thadamalla, Ruchi Mankad, Amy Sonpal Patel, Seema Agrawal, Anandan Pillai and Himani Yadav

Medical tourism in the 21st century has become a major earner of foreign exchange for many nations. Many Asian countries like Thailand, Singapore and Malaysia have started depending on medical tourists' revenues especially in the periods after Asian financial crisis. India with its rich pool of medical professionals and well-developed private hospitals could be able to offer high-quality medical care on par with well developed western nations but quite economically. Apollo Group of Hospitals, a leader in the private sector in India has grown multi-fold from a single hospital in 1983 to a leading chain of hospitals and global healthcare provider within a period of two decades. Against this backdrop, the case study details out the status of Apollo Hospitals Group as a leading provider of high quality medicare to the visiting foreign patients and how it equipped to meet the demands of medical tourism. The case study further captures the experiences of a few foreign patients who got treated at Apollo.

"Our mission is to bring healthcare of international standards within the reach of every individual. We are committed to the achievement and maintenance of excellence in education, research and healthcare for the benefit of humanity".[1]

– Apollo Hospitals, India.

In 2003, Terry Salo, aged 54 years, resident of Victoria, British Columbia flew 22 hours to reach Chennai, India for a hip replacement surgery[2] as he was forced to wait for more than a year for free care in his home country under Canada's national health service and the pain had become unbearable. He paid $4,500 for the surgery at Apollo Hospitals Enterprises Ltd (Apollo), besides airfare and other expenses which otherwise would have cost him three times the money for a similar treatment in Europe or in the US.

At Apollo, he was one among the 60,000 foreign patients treated over the past three years. Set up in 1983 as a single hospital, Apollo had grown to 45 hospitals with more than 6,700 beds. With a turnover of over $5420 million in 2004, the Apollo Hospitals Group (Exhibit I) had emerged as one of the single largest Indian hospital chains and a global healthcare provider in Asia. Besides hospitals in the Middle East Asia and Sri Lanka, the group had primary clinics and pharmacies spread across India.

Dr. Pratap C Reddy, Chairman of Apollo Group of Hospitals mentioned, *"Our thrust is to make India the healthcare destination of the world.*[3]*"*

Healthcare Tourism

The trend of seeking medical care in foreign countries began some thousands of years ago. Patients and pilgrims came to ancient Greece from all over the Mediterranean visiting healing God, Asklepios, at Epidaurus. The earliest form of health tourism was, visiting mineral and hot springs in the Bronze Age. By the middle Ages, belief in the curative powers of thermal springs was firmly established. In the late 19th Century, the emerging urban middle class sought the benefits of fresh sea and mountain air as an antidote to the pollution wrought by industrialization. The early 20th century saw the emergence of "health farms" where the emphasis was on fitness and good diet[4].

International patients seeking urgent medical care, in a different country became an attractive industry worldwide by the turn of 21st century. The ease and lower cost of travel catapulted the industry into the limelight. Patients (medical tourists) undertook travel for treatment for varied reasons. A person became a medical tourist when she combined her vacation with plastic or cosmetic surgery. But most sought treatment because of cost advantage or lack of facilities in their country.

Growth and Development in Asia

According to a study in 2000, the size of the Healthcare tourism Industry (Box1) was $40 billion. Growing at 20% per annum, it was expected to reach more than $100 billion by 2004.[5]

Box I: An Overview of the Healthcare Tourism Industry

Country	No. of foreigners treated last year	From	Money earned	Strengths
Thailand	6,00,000	US, UK	$470 m	Cosmetic surgery, Organ transplants, Dental treatment, Joint replacements
Jordan	1,26,000	Middle East	$600 m	Organ transplants, Fertility treatment, Cardiac care
India	1,00,000	Middle East, Bangladesh, UK, Developing countries	N.A	Cardiac care, Joint replacements, Lasik
Malaysia	8,5,000	US, Japan, Developing countries	$40 m	Cosmetic surgery
South Africa	5,0,000	US, UK	N.A	Cosmetic surgery, Lasik, dental treatment
Cuba	N.A	Latin America, US	$25-50 m	Specialist niche treatment: Vitilgo, night blindness, cosmetic surgery

Source: "The Health Travellers", www.businessworldindia.com, 22nd December, 2003.

Medical tourism in Asia emerged when following the Asian financial crisis, hospitals started to seek alternative revenue sources. The industry was growing rapidly and turning out to be an immense business opportunity for many nations. In 2004, five countries in Asia – Thailand, Malaysia, Jordan, Singapore and India attracted over 1.3 million medical travelers and earned over $1 billion in treatment costs alone. (Exhibit II) Thailand was well reputed as a tourist destination and led in the Asia-Pacific region with about 400,000 foreign patients each year.

Major centers for medical tourism in Thailand were Bangkok and Phuket, with six medical facilities in Bangkok having obtained hospital accreditation from the United States. The major attractions were cosmetic surgery and dental treatments. Eye surgery, kidney dialysis and organ transplantation were also among the most common treatments sought by medical vacationers in Thailand. Bangkok's Bumrundgrad hospital had more than 200 surgeons who were board-certified in the United States, and one of Singapore's major hospitals was a branch of the prestigious Johns Hopkins University in Baltimore.

Dubai, a destination known for luxury vacations was scheduled to open the Dubai Healthcare City by 2010. Situated on the Red Sea, this clinic would be the largest international medical center between Europe and Southeast Asia[6]. In 2004, more than 2,50,000 patients visited Singapore. Governments had led the development of this industry in some countries. The Malaysian government successfully exerted its leadership to facilitate and encourage industry development[7].

Healthcare Tourism in India

India is a relative newcomer to medical tourism, is quickly catching up. Indian Healthcare Federation (IHCF), a nodal body in India was working with tour operators and key medical service providers to promote attractive packages for medical tourism. Estimates indicated that the number of foreign patients was growing by 30% each year in India. Unlike many of its competitors in medical tourism, India had the technological sophistication and infrastructure to maintain its market niche. Indian pharmaceutical products met the stringent requirements of the US Food and Drug Administration. Indian doctors were among the best in the world. Escorts Heart Institute and Research Center in Indian cities Delhi and Faridabad, performed nearly 15,000 heart operations every year, and the death rate among patients during surgery was only 0.8%, less than half that of most major hospitals in the United States.

India was among the world's leading countries for biotechnology research. India was also pushing ahead with stem cell research at a level approached only in Britain. Additionally, many Asian airlines offered frequent-flyer miles to ease the cost of returning for follow-up visits.

By 2004, India was a key player in medical tourism with 1,00,000 foreign patients coming in every year and revenues of Rs.1,500 crore. "*We must leverage India's competitive edge, especially its cost advantage. Medical expenses are one-fifth of those in the west. A heart surgery in the US costs $30,000 while it cost $6,000 in India. Bone marrow transplant in the US costs $250,000 while in India it costs around $26,000,*" mentioned Fortis Healthcare chairman & managing director Harpal Singh.

The major players included Apollo Hospitals, Escorts, Max India, Wockhardt, Manipal Pai Group and Fortis Healthcare. Apollo Hospitals was the leader in the healthcare Industry.

Apollo Hospitals Group

In 2005, Apollo Hospitals Group (Apollo), the "*Architect of Healthcare*" of India, was the fourth largest private healthcare group in the world and the largest in Asia. It had won almost every honor in the country and a few overseas too. Apollo had performed over 48,000 heart surgeries with a success rate of 98% and had treated over 10 million patients from 55 countries.

The first corporate hospital was established in Chennai in 1983 by Dr. Pratap C Reddy (Dr. Reddy), Chairman of the Apollo Hospitals Group (Box II). Apollo had set up its first full-fledged, multi-specialty hospital with the latest technology and a large team of dedicated specialists and consultants. Over a period of two decades, the Apollo Group had expanded its reach in areas such as hospitals, clinics, pharmacies, telemedicine, project consultancy and operations management, medical BPO services, education and research (Exhibit III). Apollo laboratories performed clinical trials for Western drug companies, such as Pfizer Inc. and Eli Lilly & Co. Apollo also evaluated X-rays and CT scans for foreign hospitals.

Box II: The Apollo Group	
Apollo Hospitals Enterprise Limited	AHEL Pharmacies Business
Keimed.com Limited	Online Equipment Services Pvt. Ltd
Apollo Health & Lifestyle Limited	Apollo Health Street Limited
Medvarsity Online Limited	Apollo Telemedicine Enterprises Limited
Apollo Hospitals Education and Research Foundation	Family Health Plan Limited
Lifetime WellnessRx International Ltd.	
Source: www.apollohospitalgroup.com	

The core of its business was a fast-growing class of Indians who had the money to forego free treatment at state-owned hospitals. Of India's one billion people, roughly 250 million were considered middle-class. Complete check ups typically cost about US$90 to $180. By 2005 it had established 45 hospitals in India.

Apollo Hospitals introduced Apollo Clinics to provide quality healthcare to more people and in more regions. The objective of the Apollo Clinics was to address the day-to-day healthcare needs of a typical family by providing them with a range of superior quality healthcare services under one roof at affordable prices. Through its subsidiary – Apollo Health and Lifestyle Limited (AHLL)– the Group established the first Apollo Clinic in April 2002 in New Delhi, India. In 2005, there were 29 Apollo Clinics operational in major cities of India.

Every Apollo Clinic had a well-stocked, 24-hour Pharmacy, managed by qualified and well-trained pharmacists. By 2005, Apollo Pharmacies had become the largest chain of pharmacies in India. It had over 200 pharmacies across the country with a turnover of Rs.26.2 million in 2004-2005 and a potential of Rs.32.5 million in the year 2005-2006[8]. Apollo Pharmacies had become synonymous with round-the-clock service, ready availability of all drugs, competitive prices and assured quality.

MedVarsity Online Limited (MOL) (MedVarsity), Apollo's major Web initiative, was incorporated in the year 2000. It was India's first portal dedicated to medical education. MedVarsity was a virtual medical university which provided total access to experts in the field of medicine anywhere in the world. The official website *www.medvarsity.com* was launched in October 2000.

Apollo in collaboration with Indian Space Research Organization (ISRO), started South Asia's first satellite-based telemedicine centers. Telemedicine technology used electronic communication networks for the transmission of data related to the diagnosis and the treatment of medical conditions of patients in remote areas. 'Telehealth' not only covered 'telediagnosis' and 'teletreatment', but it also covered patient and professional health-related education, public health and health administration. In 2005, Apollo was the single largest telemedicine solution provider in South Asia, with over 76 centers in India and abroad. Bill Clinton, former President of the United States, on Apollo's telemedicine initiative, "*I think it is a very wonderful contribution to the healthcare of the people who live in rural villages and I hope that people all over the world will follow your lead, because if they do then the benefits of the hi-tech medicine can go to everyone and not just people who live in big cities*[9]."

Investor interest in India allowed the hospital group to raise money by listing parts of its growing business, including the parent company, on the Bombay Stock Exchange (BSE). In 2004, the groups' overall asset value was over US $50 million. Apollo Hospitals Enterprise Ltd., had successfully raised $65.1 million through the issue of 8.35 million Global Depositary Receipts (GDRs). Each GDR represented one underlying share and was listed on the Luxembourg Stock Exchange. The issue generated demand of about 4 times from investors across US, Asia and Europe. The GDR was priced at $7.8 (Rs.340) per GDR against a closing price of Rs.347.95 per share on the BSE, Mumbai on July 07, 2005.

Apollo opened its first overseas clinic in Dubai in March 1999. By 2005, it had established its hospitals and clinics in Sri Lanka, Bangladesh, Ghana, Nigeria, Qatar, Kuwait, South Africa, Tanzania, Mauritius, Yemen, Oman, Bahrain, Vietnam and Thailand.

During the first three quarters of the fiscal year ended March 31st 2003, Apollo posted net income equivalent to US$ 6.4 million, more than the US$ 6.2 million it earned in the full prior fiscal year. Its revenue totaled about US$ 84 million for the nine months, compared with $75 million during the same nine months of the year before. During the fiscal year 2003, nearly 62% of Apollo's revenue came from its core hospital business, 36% came from pharmacies, and the balance from the newer outsourcing businesses.

Apollo in Healthcare Tourism

Apollo had achieved significant success in attracting foreign patients. It had capitalized on its ability to provide high-quality service at a lower price than competitors charged and with a shorter waiting time. 70% of Apollo's doctors had studied, worked or were trained in institutions and hospitals in the West. Foreign patients accounted for 7 to 9% of Apollo's business, and the company expected their number to grow by 20% a year. The business accounted for 25% of Apollo's total net profit.

Apollo had a separate arm for international patients at its hospitals across India. The services of the International Patient Care offices were designed to make their stay smooth and pleasant. Apollo's International Patient Centers made arrangements for their travel, airport pick-up, coordination for doctor's appointments, accommodation for relatives and attendants, locker facilities for all valuables, provision of cuisine options, provision of interpreters and arrangements with leading resort chains for post-operative recuperation. On the patient's arrival in India, they were greeted at the airport by Apollo staff and escorted to the hospital. They stayed in private rooms with one-on-one nursing care. After recuperation, patients could visit tourism destinations as part of their package. Apollo's Hyderabad hospital, a lush 30-acre complex offered patients a wellness center, private accommodation, and international cuisine. The group had treated 96,000 foreign patients by 2003[10].

Apollo was setting up marketing offices in cosmopolitan cities such as London and Dubai to attract new patients[11]. It was negotiating with oil multinational ARAMCO to offer special packages to its employees. Apollo had even tied up with companies like NIIT and Aptech so that attendants of patients who came for treatment for 2-3 months could take short-term IT courses.

Apollo had its own travel agents, who arranged for sightseeing trips for patients and attendants. It had a library for patients and their attendants and a cyber café, which charged nominal rates. The Apollo Hospital in Chennai had three-bedroom apartment blocks in the city center, where patients and their families could stay for three to four months.

The Apollo hospital in the city of Goa had tied up with a 150 cottage beach resort, where foreign patients rejuvenated, underwent Ayurvedic treatments and meditation therapy after cosmetic surgery.

Experiences at Apollo

Apollo had successfully treated varied international patients; some of whom came looking for superior medical service, some for cost advantage and some for combining treatment with pleasure.

The father of baby Tharushika from Sri Lanka who had got his daughter treated said "*The doctors and nursing staff were wonderful. They took time to listen to and to explain everything to me and my wife about my daughter's heart surgery. We come from a very poor rural area of Sri Lanka and never thought we would ever have to come to Apollo Hospital here in Colombo. The staff took away our fear and put us at ease at once. The fact that this was an international hospital with many patients and we may be just another number was in my mind but the care and attention to detail given to my little daughter was priceless. We deeply appreciate all the help and assistance given to my family, and have already recommended to several families from our village. My little precious daughter is now running and playing all over our house with bright eyes, laughter and smiles.*"[12]

Robert Walter Beeney of US had been unable to walk when he came to Apollo for hip replacement surgery in January 2005. He not only recovered within twenty days from the surgery, but also visited the famous monument Taj Mahal.

Amanda Lockhart from UK had come to Sri Lanka with the idea of having a gastric bypass surgery and to spend a few days enjoying the beaches and the sun. She thus described her experience "*I had only communicated with the doctors and the hospital representative in the UK via e-mail and phone, and decided to take the trip. From the pick-up from the airport to dropping me off at the hotel for my few days of sun and fun, I was actually treated like a queen. We never get this much of care and attention here in UK hospitals. Apollo doctors spent a lot of time explaining to me about my surgery and what I will go through. The hospital staff was very friendly and always wanted to satisfy me with whatever I wanted. The room I stayed in during my hospital stay is better than a 5 star hotel room. The entire hospital was very clean and the staff took pride in keeping it that way. I look forward to reuniting with my newly found friends at the Apollo Hospital, Sri Lanka."*[13]

Another patient, Mr. Thomas Raudaschl from Canada, who had come to Apollo, said after his successful operation "*My hip was going bad after years of use as a mountain guide and the Canadian healthcare system would cover it except you would have to wait 2-3 years to get it done. I wouldn't be able to work, the loss of wages, depression, the pain you have to live with. Among other things there were places in Europe and also the United States. But the price at Apollo in India was a third and the quality of service excellent"*[14]

Competition Landscape

Apollo faced tough competition from various players like Escorts Heart Hospital, Fortis in the domestic markets (Exhibit IV) and Asian institutions such as Bangkok based Bumrungrad Medical Centre, Clifford Hospitals of China, and John Hopkins of Singapore in international markets.

Thailand

Before 1997, many hospitals were built in Thailand with huge investments. Medical tourism was viewed as a viable option, and since then they developed the industry. Bumrungrad Hospital in Bangkok was the first to be accredited by JCIA[15] (an arm of JCAHO[16]) in the Asian region in February, 2002. Thailand provided services like, Cosmetic and reconstructive surgery, Cardiac surgery and post-operative care, dental services, Treatment of bone related ailments and cataracts, Gender re-assignment surgery, Traditional Thai massages, Meditation centers and Pharmacology. The hospitals focused on cost leadership (services were 50-70% cheaper) which led to 3,50,000 patients in 2003.

The Tourism Authority of Thailand (TAT) played a vital role and was responsible for marketing and public relation activities. Thailand had achieved a high degree of coordination between Department of Export Promotion, Ministry of Public Health and Foreign Affairs, Immigration Bureau, TAT, Thai Hotel and Thai Airways International.

Singapore

Singapore delivered high quality services by setting high standards in healthcare. John Hopkins and National University Hospital (two renowned hospitals) were accredited by JCIA in August 2004. Singapore differentiated itself by excellence in medical expertise, efficiency by one-stop centers in key regions and high standards in treatment of illnesses.

The number of international patients who visited Singapore rose to 2,00,000 by 2002. In October 2003, Singapore Tourism Board, Economic Development Board and International Enterprise Singapore announced the launch of 'Singapore Medicine', a multi-agency government initiative aimed at developing Singapore into one of Asia's leading destinations for healthcare services. Under the Singapore Medicine, the island aimed to attract 1 million international patients by 2012 and revenue of US$2billion.

Malaysia

Till January, 2005 Malaysia did not have a hospital accredited by JCIA but 35 hospitals served international patients. They offered services for Recuperation and rehabilitation therapy, Cosmetic surgery, Cardiology, Ophthalmology, Orthopedics, Health screen packages, Curative/Therapeutic services and Dental services.

A National Committee comprising of hospitals, airlines, hotels, travel and tourism agencies was formed in 1998 for the Promotion of Health Tourism. Association of Private Hospitals Malaysia (APHM) uniformly decided the quality of services provided and set the lower and upper limits of prices for health packages. Prices of services were higher than Thailand, yet the quality of services was under question since they lacked any international accreditation.

International patients mainly came from Indonesia, Vietnam, Singapore, and Thailand.

India

India provided quality services such as Organ transplants, Cardio-vascular surgeries, Hip Replacement, In-vitro fertilization and Eye treatment[17]. India enjoyed the advantage of low cost, strong reputation in the advanced healthcare segment and the diversity of tourist destinations available in the country. New ideas were developed to make India more attractive. Niche strategies such as telemedicine were developed.

Americans who were uninsured had to spend a lot of money for treatments. On the other hand, the British had to wait for 2 years on a National Health Service waiting list. These gave India an opportunity to boost its equally qualitative services at almost one-fifth cost. Moreover, cultural diversity, natural beauty and fabulous cuisine attracted them to India. But, Dr. Cherian said[18], most of the patients are from Asia as India does not have the necessary infrastructure to cater to European and US requirements. "Our roads are dirty, water is bad, even internet connectivity—which people from the West consider a must—is not up to their standards, despite all our claims of IT proficiency."

The Indian healthcare industry complained of lack of support from Government. Moreover there was a lack of coordination among various players in industry such as airlines, hotels and hospitals. Absence of uniform pricing policies across the country created doubts in the minds of foreign patients. India confused medical tourism with other aspects of holistic healing like ayurveda, spa, yoga, meditation[19]. India did not provide medical visas to foreigners.

Though Thailand, Hong Kong, Singapore, South Africa provided tough competition to Indian industry, cost of services favored India.

The Road Ahead

According to a study conducted by McKinsey in 2004, medical tourism could help up-market tertiary hospitals gain additional revenues of $1-2 billion by 2012 provided the industry reoriented itself to attract foreign patients[20].

But many analysts feared that, increasing emphasis on medical tourism could have an adverse effect on public healthcare system. The National Human Development Report had pointed out that "There has been a misplaced emphasis on maintenance and strengthening of private healthcare services, at the expense of broadening and deepening of a public healthcare system targeted at controlling the incidence of disease, particularly of communicable diseases, in rural areas"[21].

Many healthcare professionals and experts were of the opinion that healthcare tourism was not a tourism product. A tourism expert mentioned, "I wonder if an ill person or a patient can ever become a tourist. Tourism is not always about money but it definitely is about joy, peace and leisure. Imagine a person whose sole focus is on treatment or better health – would he hop from one place to another exploring and discovering a destination? Those who actually come to the country with health problems concentrate on that aspect alone. So, it might be a gainful proposition for the health care industry but certainly not for the tourism industry"[22].

But despite all these doubts, Apollo was all geared up to take advantage of what seemed like big opportunity. Moving a step further it entered in a partnership with one of the largest healthcare groups of Africa, Hygenia Nigeria to provide medical services to its patients. It had also initiated talks with UK about sub-contracting some of the medical surgeries to Indian hospitals.

Exhibit I: About Apollo (2004)	
Patients	10 million
Total Number of Employees	over 10000
Total Number of Surgeries	2,80,000 major + 5,00,000 minor
Heart Surgeries	48,000 - success rate of 98.5%
Neuro Surgeries	10,538
Total Number of Renal Transplants	over 5000
Total Number of Hospitals	45

Compiled by Icfai Business School Research Centre, Ahmedabad.

Achievements of Apollo Group

- Apollo is registered as a 'Medical Billing Company' in the United States and is connected electronically (for submission) with all major payers including Medicare and Medicaid.
- Apollo has developed IDX (implementation capabilities that enable implementation at a significantly lower cost at the client site, thereby reducing the threshold for physician group practices to adopt the IDX billing.
- Apollo has won the single largest revenue cycle management contract being outsourced to India.
- In Medical coding, Apollo is working with our US clients and is amongst the largest certified medical coding team in India.

Source: www.apollohealthstreet.com

Exhibit II: Treatment Cost ($)

Procedure	US	India	South Africa	Thailand
Facelift	8,000-20,000	10,000-20,000	1,252	2,682
Hip Replacement	17,000	2,500	6,671	N.A.
Open Heart Surgery	150,000	5,000-10,000	13,333	7,500
Eye (Lasik)	3,100	7,000	2,166	730

Procedure Cost (US$)	United States	India
Bone Marrow Transplant	250,000	69,000
Liver Transplant	300,000	59,000
Heart Surgery	30,000	8,000
Orthopedic Surgery	20,000	6,000
Cataract Surgery	2,000	1,250

Source: "The healthcare service market for the international consumer-An analysis of the Philippines," www2.getz.de, January 17th 2005.

Exhibit III: Apollo's Business Model

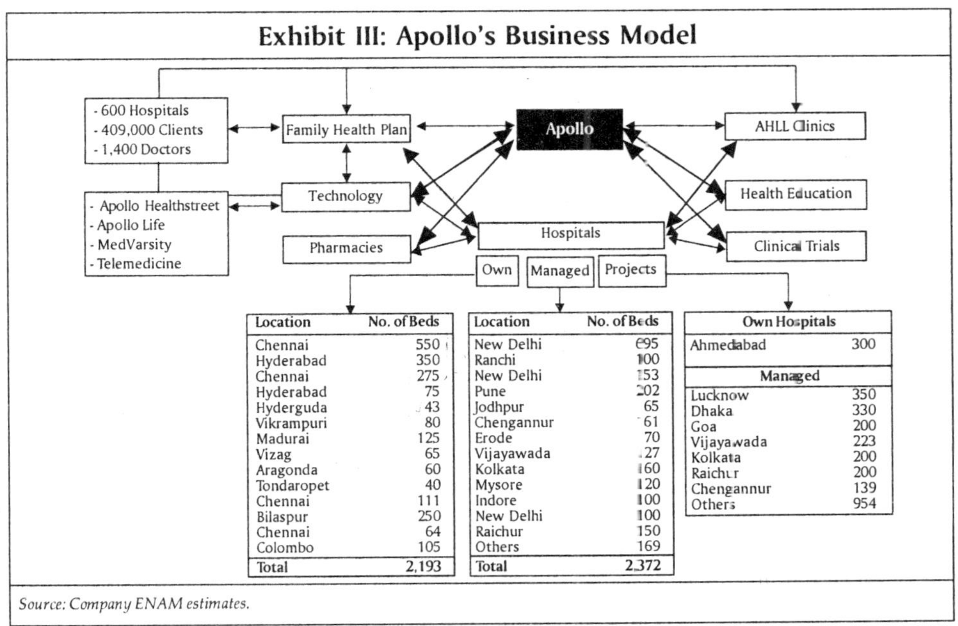

Location	No. of Beds
Chennai	550
Hyderabad	350
Chennai	275
Hyderabad	75
Hyderguda	43
Vikrampuri	80
Madurai	125
Vizag	65
Aragonda	60
Tondaropet	40
Chennai	111
Bilaspur	250
Chennai	64
Colombo	105
Total	**2,193**

Location	No. of Beds
New Delhi	695
Ranchi	100
New Delhi	153
Pune	202
Jodhpur	65
Chengannur	61
Erode	70
Vijayawada	127
Kolkata	160
Mysore	120
Indore	100
New Delhi	100
Raichur	150
Others	169
Total	**2,372**

Own Hospitals	
Ahmedabad	300
Managed	
Lucknow	350
Dhaka	330
Goa	200
Vijayawada	223
Kolkata	200
Raichur	200
Chengannur	139
Others	954

Source: Company ENAM estimates.

Exhibit IV: Apollo's Competitors in India			
Current Status of Private Sector Players			
Corporate Hospitals	**Existing Facilities**	**Future Plans**	**Investment**
Max Healthcare collaboration with Harvard Medical International Inc.	• Primary care clinics and diagnostics day care centers in Delhi	Set up two super speciality hospitals. Coming up in Delhi – Max Devi Hospital	Rs.4.5 bn in the next five years
Apollo Hospitals Enterprises	• 39 hospitals (owned, managed and joint ventures), 10 clinics and 91 pharmacies	Wants to manage 28 more hospitals in two years including some in Muscat, Dhaka, Accra, Riyadh and Abu Dhabi	Rs.300 mn
Escorts Limited	• Escorts Heart Institute, New Delhi; Escorts Hospital and Research Center, Faridabad	Setting up a 155 bed super speciality hospital in Amritsar and other super speciality hospital in Jaipur	Rs.1.3 bn
Wockhardt Limited	• Heart Hospital and Heart Institute, Bangalore • Wockhardt Hospital and Kidney Institute, Kolkata • Health Foundation Kolkata • Health Hospital Mulund, Mumbai	Three new super speciality hospitals in three years	Rs.3 bn
Aditya Birla Group	• Currently runs 15 hospitals	400 bed super speciality hospitals in Pune, Maharashtra	Rs.1 bn
Apollo-Gleneagles Hospital	–	Tertiary care hospital, Kolkata	Rs.60 mn
PD Hinduja National Capital Research Center	• Super speciality hospital in Mumbai	One super speciality hospital and two satellite clinics	Rs.1 bn
Fortis Healthcare	• Operates Fortis Heart Institute in Mohali, near Chandigarh	–	Rs.1.5 bn

Source: Business Today.

Annexure I:

Financial Highlights-Apollo Hospitals Enterprise Ltd

(Figures in Millions)

S.No	Particulars	31-03-2005 (audited)	Year Ended 31-03-2004 (audited)
1.	Net sales income from operations	6550	5374
2.	Other income	71	46
	Total Income	**6621**	**5420**
3.	**Total Expenditure**		
	a. Increase/decrease in stock trade	–	–
	b. Consumption of raw materials	2991	2450
	c. Staff cost	1016	790
	d. Other expenditure	462	339
	e. General administrative expenses	987	740
	f. Selling and distribution expenses	84	103
4.	**Interest**	242	222
5.	**Depreciation**	311	272
6.	Profit (+) loss (-) before tax (1+2-3-4-5)	528	504
7.	**Provision for Taxation**		
	Current	231	132
	Deferred	(27)	86
8.	Profit before minority interest (6-7)	324	286
9.	Minority interest	(32)	2
10.	Share in associates	28	(2)
11.	Profit attributable to group	384	282
12.	Paid-up equity share capital (face value: Rs.10/- per share)	416	395
13.	Basic and diluted EPS for the period	9.45	7.14

Source: Annual Report 2004, Apollo Hospital Enterprises Ltd.

(Sarosh Thadamalla, Ruchi Mankad, Amy Sonpal Patel, Seema Agrawal, Anandan Pillai and Himani Yadav are associated with the Icfai Business School Research Centre, Ahmedabad.)

Endnotes

1 Mission of Apollo Hospitals, India.

2 Solomon, Jay, "A Hospital Empire, Mr. Salo Has 'Real Doubts'," *www.apollohospitals.com*, April 26th 2004.

3 The Rediff Interview with Dr. C Pratap Reddy *www.rediff.com*, September 30. 2003.

4 Kim Ross "Health Tourism : An Overview," *www.hospitalitynet.org*

5 Gowri Shankar Nagarajan "Medical Tourism in India: Strategy for its Development," IIM, Bangalore, 2004.

6 *www.udel.edu*

7 "The Health Travellers," *www.businessworldindia.com*, December 22nd 2003.

8 *www.apollohospitals.com*

9 *www.apollohospitalgroup.com*

10 Prosenjit Datta, Krishnan Gina S. "India: Gearing up for the opportunity," *www.business week.com*, December 22nd, 2003.

11 PricewaterhouseCoopers' Global Best Practices® knowledge base.

12 "International Patient Experiences," *www.apollohospitals.com*

13 Ibid.

14 Op cit. "International Patient Experiences".

15 Joint Commission of International Accreditation (JCIA) is a part of JCAHO.

16 Joint Commission on Accreditation of Healthcare Organizations (JCAHO) was the oldest private, independent, non-profit organization which accredited health care organizations in US.

17 "Medical Tourism in India : Strategy for Its Development," *www.crisilonline.com*

18 Rupa Chinai, Rahul Goswami "Are we ready for medical tourism?," *www.hind.com*, April 17th 2005.

19 "Medical Tourism : The Perfect Cure," *www.expresstravelandtourism.com*, September 25th, 2004

20 "India is a favorite destination with tourists looking for medical care," *www.eians.com*

21 op.cit, "Are we ready for medical tourism?"

22 Jyoti Koul "Medical Tourism: The Perfect Cure," *www.expresstravelandtourism.com*, July 2004.

23 IDX is a leading provider of software, services and technology for healthcare provider organizations.

References

1. Solomon, Jay, "A Hospital Empire, Mr. Salo Has 'Real Doubts'," *www.apollohospitals.com,* April 26th, 2004.
2. Kim Ross "Health Tourism: An Overview," *www.hospitalitynet.org*
3. "The Health Travellers", *www.businessworldindia.com*, 22nd December, 2003.
4. Gowri Shankar Nagarajan "Medical Tourism in India: Strategy for its Development," IIM, Bangalore, 2004.
5. *www.udel.edu*
6. "The Health Travellers," *www.businessworldindia.com*, December 22nd, 2003.
7. *www.apollohospitalgroup.com*
8. Prosenjit Datta, Krishnan Gina S. "India: Gearing up for the opportunity," *www.businessweek.com*, December 22nd, 2003.
9. "Medical Tourism in India : Strategy For its Development," *www.crisilonline.com*
10. Rupa Chinai, Rahul Goswami "Are we ready for medical tourism?," www.hind.com, April 17th, 2005.
11. Jyoti Koul "Medical Tourism : The Perfect Cure," *www.expresstravelandtourism.com*, September 25th, 2004.
12. "India is a favorite destination with tourists looking for medical care," *www.eians.com*
13. "The healthcare service market for the international consumer – An analysis of the Philippines," *www2.getz.de*, January 17th, 2005.
14. *www.businesstoday.com*
15. *www.apollohealthstreet.com*
16. *www.google.com*

21

Community Initiatives in Ecotourism: A Case Study from Sikkim, India

Ecotourism in Sikkim offers an opportunity to improve the livelihoods of its local communities and protect its unique cultural heritage. The Sikkim Biodiversity and Ecotourism Project (SBEP) is a collaborative initiative among Mountain Institute, G B Pant Institute of Himalayan Environment and Development, Travel Agents Association of Sikkim (TAAS), Green Circle (an NGO), Khangchendzonga conservation community (an NGO) and local communities to conserve the biological diversity of key destinations. The inherent objectives of the project include linking enterprise operation with conservation action and merging traditional cultural practices. The project is aimed to work with private sector, government and the local communities in order to build people's skills, interests and knowledge to increase awareness about resource conservation, increase economic returns from ecotourism and positively contribute to the ecotourism policies.

Introduction

The rich natural and cultural heritage of Sikkim has made this small Himalayan state in Northeastern India an attractive destination for international and domestic tourists. With over 90,000 domestic and 6,000 international tourists in 1995, tourism is rapidly becoming an important economic activity for the Sikkimese people. Ecotourism, with its focus on environmentally sound practices and generating widespread economic benefits, offers an opportunity for Sikkim to improve the livelihoods of its mountain communities and protect its unique heritage.

The Sikkim Biodiversity and Ecotourism Project (SBEP) is a collaborative initiative designed to conserve the biological diversity of key destinations. At the heart of the project are participatory approaches that link enterprise operation with conservation action, while merging traditional cultural practices. Working with communities, the private sector and government, the project builds upon people's skills, interests and knowledge to:

- Increase awareness of resource conservation in the communities and private sector;
- Increase economic returns from ecotourism services and enterprises; and
- Contribute to policies that meet ecotourism and conservation goals.

The project is a joint effort of the Mountain Institute and the G B Pant Institute of Himalayan Environment and Development. Project collaborators include the Travel Agents Association of Sikkim (TAAS), Green Circle (a Sikkimese NGO), the Khangchendzonga Conservation Committee (a community NGO) and local communities at key tourism sites.

Project Area

Khangchendzonga National Park and communities in surrounding areas in western Sikkim are the focus of the project. Within the park is Sikkim's major trekking route, the Yuksam-Dzongri Goecha La Trail. The trail offers an exhilarating climb through dense forests and impressive mountain views. The forests and alpine meadows are some of the most biologically diverse in India and contain over 30 species of rhododendrons, 400 species of orchids and many other flowering plants. The park and surrounding areas also contain a large mammal population (over 80) and more than 300 species of birds and butterflies.

The spiritual and physical focus of the area is Khangchendzonga, the world's third highest mountain peak (8548 m) and revered as the protective deity of

Sikkim. At the trail head is Yuksam, Sikkim's first capital. From Yuksam, visitors can take short walks to several archeological ruins and to Dubdi Monastery, Sikkim's oldest monastery. A variety of ethnic groups, including Lepchas (the indigenous people of Sikkim), Bhutias (long-time Tibetan residents) and Nepalis, as well as Tibetan refugees, live in this culturally and historically rich area. The majority of the population pursues traditional agricultural livelihoods, while in recent years some have ventured into tourism activities. Other project sites include Khecheopalri lake, one of Sikkim's most sacred and popular lakes, and Pelling, a settlement near Pemayangtse Monastery.

Project Components

The SBEP focuses its work in three key areas that link conservation with ecotourism enterprises.

1. Increasing community and private sector biodiversity conservation initiatives. Activities include:
   - Community ecotourism plans covering site-enhancement and trail and site maintenance;
   - Natural resource management and monitoring, and conservation education;
   - Supporting fuelwood reduction by trekking operators and local lodges; and
   - Supporting local NGOs working in ecotourism and conservation.
2. Increasing economic returns from community-based and TAAS ecotourism. Activities include:
   - Training in ecotourism services (e.g., for guides, lodge-owners, cooks, porters);
   - Supporting new community ecotourism enterprises (e.g., vegetable growing, indigenous foods, fuelwood-saving equipment and short, guided treks);
   - Developing marketing strategies for community-based ecotourism and TAAS ecotourism activities; and
   - Conducting market research and developing new ecotourism products such as off-season activities and eco-lodge designs.

3. Improving and contributing to policy-making on conservation and ecotourism. The activities include:
    - Scientific and participatory monitoring of project activities and impacts;
    - Applied research on conservation and ecotourism;
    - Sharing of research and monitoring findings among policy-makers, communities and the private sector; and
    - Promoting public-private sector dialogue through workshops, exchanges and policy review.

Innovation figures strongly in the project. Participants are involved in ecotourism planing, training courses and conservation management and utilize participatory learning tools that build upon best practices and the positive attributes of Sikkim's natural and cultural heritage. A combination of appreciative inquiry[1] and modified Participatory Learning and Action (PLA)[2] tools provide the basis for planning, implementing and evaluating community ecotourism activities. Using the same approach, the project is exchanging experience and expertise with mountain peoples and affiliated projects in Nepal and other parts of India.

Community Ecotourism Planning

A critical element of planning and subsequent actions in ecotourism is the focus on appreciative inquiry, a process which finds and builds upon positive attributes and values in local environments and groups of stakeholders. Unlike traditional rural development efforts that incorporate PLA techniques and focus on problem identification and solving, appreciative inquiry asks questions such as:

- What do you value in your community and environment?
- What excites you most about where you live?

---

1 Appreciative Inquiry is an approach to the field of Organizational Development. Useful initial introductions to the approach can be found in *OD Practitioner, 1996, Vol.28*, and in *Cooperrider, D.L., (1990) Positive image, Positive action: The affirmative basis for organizing, in Srivastava, S., Cooperrider, D.L., and Associates, (eds.) Appreciative Management and Leadership. Jossey-Bass, San Francisco.*

2 Participatory Learning and Action attempts to go beyond Participatory Rural Appraisal (PRA) into planning for action and evaluation by participants. For more details, contact International Institute of Environment and Development, Sustainable Agriculture, 3 Endsleigh St. London WC1, UK.

- What is the most positive vision you have of your environment and community in the future?
- What do we need to do to realize a vision of the future?

The focus is on finding the causes of success and motivation rather than failure as the basis for community planning. PLA tools have been modified to help investigate these questions. This includes – trend lines of issues such as waste disposal, wildlife, and forest cover which are projected over 10-20 year horizons; schematic maps are created to foresee future community and natural resources status; mapping of current and potential ecotourism resources; and ranking of ecotourism attributes such as sites and services. A similar approach is adopted during the evaluation of community conservation and ecotourism activities, when the focus is on "What worked well and what needs to be improved"?

This paper outlines the experiences from community ecotourism planning at Yuksam. Yuksam has served as the basis for further planning in other project sites in western Sikkim, and many of the lessons learned have been incorporated into other project activities such as training in ecotourism professions. The case study of Yuksam is interspersed with field notes from the various sessions and comments from participants.

In May 1996, participatory community ecotourism planning was conducted in Yuksam. The team of five project staff and six local residents worked with local community members to gather information and generate site-specific ideas for linking tourism-related activities to conservation efforts. One major problem identified was that tourists were spending a relatively short period of time in the area. Local community members felt that the opportunity for increased income generation lay in extending the stay of visitors to the area. On an initial experimental basis, team members used a framework of appreciative inquiry and modified participatory learning techniques to suit the purposes of ecotourism planning.

All participants were asked to "discover" the elements in their environment and community that represent the best of what they have to offer. Positive attributes identified by villagers were:

- Lots of Greenery;
- Community unity seen in actions to help others;
- Meeting tourists from many different countries;
- Fresh Air;
- Dense Forests; and
- Historical importance of Yuksam, the first capital of Sikkim.

Participants were then asked to "dream" and to think of what the best vision of Yuksam might be in ten years time. Participants were asked, "What would you like to see in Yuksam ten years from now"? Their responses included:

- More forest cover;
- More tourists in Yuksam;
- No litter in Yuksam and along the trails;
- Local conservation groups or NGOs;
- More income from tourism; and
- Yuksam perceived as a "little Switzerland".

The next phase was to use PLA tools to collect some of the information needed to design a plan for achieving the common dream, one that was inclusive of participants' aspirations, and focussed on the issue of increasing income from existing tourists. A preliminary report was prepared by participants and included:

- A listing of environmental and community attributes;
- Ecotourism resource maps;
- Local stories about sites and history;
- Maps and analysis of the availability and use of forest resources; and
- Socio-economic analysis of tourism benefits.

The final step was to identify actions to be taken in the next three to six months that would begin to deliver their vision. Thus, in addition to the report, specific outputs from the planning exercise were agreed to be implemented in the following four to six months. These included:

- Beautification activities (e.g., planting of native tree species and cleanup campaigns);
- Training courses for lodge-operators, naturalist guides; and
- Collection of material to be used for a promotional brochure about Yuksam and its attractions.

In addition to the activities identified, in October 1996, 28 village members organized their own cleanup campaign of the major trekking route, generating a small initial amount of funds for further activities through the recycling of bottles and tins.

In December 1996, a participatory evaluation of activities since the previous May was conducted and a plan developed for 1997 (see Box 1 for details). In addition to the use of PLA tools (such as pair-wise ranking and standard ranking to assess activities) narrated stories of community action in conservation were also documented. Yuksam residents have readily accepted the principle of local contributions to project activities and enthusiastically attended the training courses, as well as showed a keen interest in enterprises such as low-cost vegetable production, community-wide cleanups and afforestation campaigns. Another activity was a lodge-operators' training, where participants developed standard tariffs and menus. Operators now maintain visitor registers and issue receipts to customers.

Box 1: Field Notes from the Evaluation Session

On the first day of the evaluation session about 15 community members worked together to analyze the activities of 1996 and to identify the successes. A list was made which focussed on the activities which were linked to conservation activities. This gave an opportunity for participants to think carefully about linkages. Since the days were quite cold, participants trickled in slowly but were excited to note their own achievements and were taking pride in them. One major outcome was that the community members wanted to develop a Code Of Conduct (COC). They wanted to inform visitors of what their expectations were and wanted them to consider and follow certain codes of conduct. The COC leaflets would be distributed to trekkers, along with the Trekking Hut Permits, so that all visitors would have a copy of the COC before leaving on a trek.

The evaluation was very insightful highlighting areas that the project and the community needed to work on (e.g., dissemination of results, the nature and benefits of participation, and the role of community groups and institutions in ensuring widespread and enthusiastic participation). Local communities were concerned that the benefits of participation in project activities were seen to be fair, and that the community itself should visibly participate in the decision-making process. For example, the villagers decided who should attend study tours and how the rest of community might share in the benefits of visiting other sites (see Box 2 for more details).

Based on the evaluation, local community members and project staff prepared an action plan for 1997. Tools and outputs, such as mapping trekking routes and future maps of the village, were used as the framework for designing and deciding activities. The final plan used more traditional planning tools such as logistical framework, responsibilities, time frames and indicators of success.

Box 2: Field Notes from the Evaluation Session

Ranking of 1996 activities was very interesting as it showed that community initiated activities such as fighting a forest fire received the highest ranking while study tour activities received the lowest ranking. The community felt that study tours did not benefit the entire community. Therefore, it was discussed as to how a study tour could become more meaningful. The community designed criteria as to what sort of a person should go for a study tour and after returning, how their benefits could be shared by all community members. For the next study tour to Nepal, the community took the responsibility of selecting their own representatives to ensure that experiences from the study tour would be shared with the community.

A critical element developed by village participants during the use of the methodology was the commitment to an action plan, demonstrating as the villagers say, "that we should go beyond talk and do something". In the first exercise it was a cleanup of the village by teachers, schoolchildren and other villagers. In the second session, villagers proposed to raise funds for garbage management and visitor education. By March 1996, three signboards and six garbage bins were in place throughout Yuksam. Community-identified activities for 1997 included:

- Garbage management in the village and along the trail;
- Trail repair by local residents;

- Plantation work and management;
- Training for porters, lodge-operators, guides, pack animal operators, trek cooks;
- Conservation education of visitors and residents; and
- Completion of the Yuksam promotional brochure.

Box 3: Field Notes from the Session

The program started with briefing the village community about the brochure and the COC leaflet. A suggestion was made that sign boards should be put up along with printing and distribution of the leaflet. The question of co-financing was also raised at this time and the villagers readily accepted the idea. On the first day, they collected about Rs.700 (US$ 19) towards erecting the sign boards. Later on in the meeting, the community members discussed the responsibilities, time, and the indicators of proposed future activities for 1997. The *Pradhan* (elected leader) and the other members of the community played an active role in this process while the team members facilitated the discussion. The matter of restoring an old palace was proposed by the Khangchendzonga Committee of Copchay settlement. The village *Pradhan* also volunteered to finance a community notice board where all the important village events would be displayed.

Other results of community ecotourism planning in Yuksam included:

- A series of projects and other events to form the Khangchendzonga Conservation Committee (KCC). KCC developed a COC for visitors to follow in the area. Signboards with the code were erected in Yuksam, and visitors now receive a copy of the code at the lodges (see box 4).

Box 4: Field Notes from the Session

The community identified the Sikkim Biodiversity and Ecotourism field office to be used as a Tourist Information Office. It would also be mandatory for visitors to come to this office for pre-departure briefing and to receive copies of the COC. Signboards in English, Nepali and Bengali would be put up where the COC would be highlighted. The police officer in charge of Yuksam and the *Pradhan*, along with the members of the meeting, talked with shopkeepers about proper disposal of the garbage and warned them that strict action would be taken against offenders. The positive reaction of this short campaign was seen immediately that evening after the market closed and the shopkeepers collected all the trash and burned all the paper and plastics. The shopkeepers have been advised to stop using plastic bags and to keep trash bins for proper collection of garbage. A central site for garbage disposal is being identified by the community.

- Yuksam community members participating as resource persons for a community ecotourism planning effort at nearby Kecheopalri Lake.

Lessons Learned and Further Opportunities

While the community planning methodology is in its formative stages, it was found that the following appear to be critical elements in the process.

- A framework of appreciative inquiry needs to be developed which focuses on what is done well, what works among and excites the groups of stakeholders, and what helps participants develop a positive vision of the future. The purpose here is to start identifying the factors that lead to success among stakeholders. Maps, drawings, lists and discussion all serve to develop and represent people's ideas and visions.
- A process of participatory learning about the environment, stakeholders and other groups and communities that informs the design of plans. Several advantages to this process are to:
  - engage a larger section of the population and to develop rapport and trust with local people.
  - provide a training function among local communities in community-based conservation and ecotourism planning.
  - generate data which serves as planning information and a baseline for monitoring. The initial participatory process helps in providing the foundation for subsequent participation.
- Produce documents and information that can be used by the villagers. Local people use them as reference material, guidelines, source of promotional material, and the community assistant regularly refers to it as a workplan and monitoring tool. These reports also serve to document the process and its progress.
- Developing a participatory plan of action. Often the first plan is one that emerges out of the participatory learning session, covering one to six months and always initiated by one joint action and commitment during the learning phase. A larger plan is usually developed after the completion of the first set of activities. Elements of the plan include – what activity, who is responsible, what is the schedule, what is the level of co-financing and

what are the indicators of success. However, this set of steps is not set in stone and can and should be adapted to the needs and interests of the communities. This plan is presented by the participants to the community for discussion and revision.

- Co-financing by participants is an essential part of project activity implementation. Nearly all activities have a local contribution by communities in the form of cash, labor or materials. This helps local people to decide which activities are most wanted and usually ensures to follow through with project activities.
- Community evaluation of action plans on a periodic basis using participatory indicators and methods, followed by modification and further action plans as required.

Conclusions

Local communities have responded to and participated very positively in the process of planning and action for conservation and tourism. Project staff have always been concerned with ensuring that the process avoids being an expert-driven approach. The process used and its elements are as much the efforts of community participants as the efforts of project staff. Local villagers worked with staff to develop the protocol of questions, defining elements and procedures for evaluation.

The approach may have a tendency to lead community members to develop visions that the project simply does not have the mandate to assist with. To avoid unrealistic expectations of the project and its staff, the boundaries of the project are made clear early in the process. This did not hamper the process, nor has it dampened the excitement. On several occasions, staff have helped communities to find other assistance for activities that the project could not support.

In a state such as Sikkim, where the central and state governments have traditionally been the source of development and conservation support, it has been very encouraging to see a ready acceptance of the concept of local contributions to community-identified actions.

The Village *Pradhan* from Yuksam stated:

> *"Unlike other officials, SBEP staff came and demonstrated activities instead of just talking. Our community is more aware of biodiversity and its conservation as a result of project activities".*

Community members have commented that participation in decision-making and planning has been an empowering process. For example, in May, the cleanup of the trekking trail was not identified as an activity to undertake, but by October local villagers felt confident and motivated enough to organize the activity and publish an article about it in the state newspapers.

Similar exercises have been carried out at two other sites, Kecheopalri Lake and Tshoka (a settlement along the major trekking trail). One clear sign of sharing of information and knowledge is that Yuksam residents have participated in these activities, fostering greater interaction and linkages between the various settlements in this important tourism area and developing the skills of local people in community-based ecotourism planning. A similar approach of appreciative inquiry and PLA was used to frame a study tour to Nepal which was undertaken by Yuksam residents. One local farmer who visited Nepal and studied the importance of sanitation was so enthusiastic that he built a toilet on his return.

The possibility of combining the appreciative inquiry framework with participatory learning and action methodologies is an exciting process. Experiences to date, primarily in community-based ecotourism and conservation planning, indicate that there is potential for the combined approach. Ecotourism, with its focus on environmentally sound practices and generating widespread economic incentives to conserve natural and cultural resources, appears to lend itself extremely well to the appreciative framework of valuing the positive attributes of the local environment and communities. What was found is that appreciative inquiry provides the type of visionary framework for planning and action, and the process and results of using modified PLA tools can be both informative and empowering. The greatest opportunity and challenge for all participants (NGOs, semi-government institutions, the commercial private sector, and community leaders and members) will be to ensure that the capacity to design, implement, monitor and thus learn from the process and results continues in ways that are empowering for all concerned.

22

Lullaby @ Varkala's Awakening

Lullaby@Varkala is an initiative of Kerala Travels Interserve Ltd (KTIL), which is aimed to achieve empowerment of local communities along with the development of tourism. "Wealth generated by the tourism working for the benefit of the local communities and which in turn working for the promotion of the tourism" is the driving spirit behind the project. It is a two phase programme, phase I involving provision of milk, vegetables and clothes to the anganwadi going children and phase II involving provision of other basic infrastructure facilities such as own buildings, electricity and furniture to anganwadis apart from promoting ecological conservation, organic farming and promoting awareness about healthy-tourism practices that act as a fillip to the promotion of tourism. The resounding success of this initiative is manifested in the patronage it received from the local communities and many luminaries apart from the achievement of the designated objectives.

Though a cash cow, tourism bears the unlucky tag of being an elitist past time and one that exploits the very resources it utilises. Kerala especially has a history both of attempts to boost the tourist inflow and of local communities up in arms against the perceived abuse of their land.

The only viable way forward then, is to envisage a tourism model that promotes a symbiotic relationship between the tourists and the common man. One where the wealth generated by tourism benefits the local community of the area, which in turn will enable promotion tourism with a smile. This is tourism beyond tomorrow – this is the driving spirit behind Lullaby@Varkala.

An initiative of Kerala Travels Interserve Ltd (KTIL), the project was the brainchild of Managing Director KC Chandrahasan. KTIL has an illustrious history of socially relevant tourism projects – Thekkady Tiger Trail involved the employment of reformed poachers as tour guides and garnered much acclaim both at the national and international levels.

A unique model, perhaps the first of its kind in India, Lullaby@Varkala has two aspects: one, of social empowerment and the other, of tourism. Beginning from the anganwadi children of Varkala, the project seeks to create a society that is self-sufficient, aware and empowered. All this, through the powerful tool of tourism.

Lullaby... of Social Awakening

The social aspect, forming Phase I of the project, began at the most basic level – anganwadi centers. Anganwadis are educational centers for children of the lowest strata of society. They also function as hubs for dispensation of health and hygiene-related information to the mothers. Sadly, many of the 140 anganwadis spread over 87 sq km of Varkala block were in a state of dis-repair as revealed by the first status survey in August 2005. Some did not have basic facilities like water; others were being conducted in cattle sheds for lack of land. A sorry state indeed for centers that shape citizens of tomorrow.

For the upliftment of anganwadis, and the betterment of the tiny tots therein, KTIL mobilized funds and resources. The idea was to supplement the governmental aid.

By October 2005, provision had been made for supply of milk and vegetables to the children. For the logistical management of the project, 'Prochild' a charitable society was formed. Prochild comprises the municipality chairman, the block panchayat president of Varkala, a representative of KTIL, a representative of Health Action by People, a renowned NGO, a member of the Integrated Child

Development Scheme (ICDS), representatives of the Kerala Shastra Sahitya Parishad, other volunteer organizations based in Varkala and most importantly, the people of Varkala themselves.

The proudest moment for the Anganwadi students, their parents and the teachers was when each student received 2 sets of uniforms each. The sense of self-esteem and joy that has fostered in them has to be seen to be believed. Teachers and parents testify that school going has become a joy and a matter of pride for the children.

Around Rs.15 lakh, drawn from KTIL's tourism revenues, went into the implementation of this first phase. This was a success in every sense – number of enrolled students in the anganwadis jumped from 2712 in August to 2968 by the end of October and has exceeded 3,200 by January 2006. In a short while, volunteers came forward from among the local community to fund the supply of milk and vegetables, to donate land to set up anganwadis and so on.

"The project was supposed to provide milk and vegetables on alternate days. But once implemented, sponsors came forward voluntarily to provide milk and vegetables even for the remaining days. The project's success lies in the joint effort of everyone involved," says Mrs. S K Sailaja Kumari, Child Development Project Officer of the ICDS.

The successful and transparent implementation of this phase garnered KTIL the confidence and support of the people of Varkala. Awareness of the project grew by leaps and bounds. Varkala's social revolution was underway.

Lullaby... of Community Empowerment

Through the anganwadi children, the process of reaching out to the community was initiated. Phase II of Lullaby@Varkala involves computerization of anganwadis, provision of electricity, furniture, construction of new anganwadi buildings and so on. This will involve the outlay of over Rs.25 lakh. Phase II was inaugurated at a public function in January that was graced by luminaries including noted poet Mrs. Sugathakumari. Imbibing the true spirit of the project, this noted social activist sang a lullaby on the occasion. The massive turnout of children and parents was testimony to the acceptance of the project.

'A Model to be Copied'

– Mr. E Ayyappan IAS, Director,
Department of Social Welfare, Government of Kerala.

"Kerala has vast tourism potential due to its geographic peculiarities. But the most amazing thing is that people from abroad are coming to Kerala to study about her achievements in filed of education, health, social life, etc. If Kerala could improve her attitude towards tourists and keep tourist destinations clean, then no doubt more tourists would come into the land, said Mr. E Ayyappan IAS, Director, Department of Social Welfare, Government of Kerala. He said that the Lullaby @ Varkala initiated by Kerala Travels Interserve would help in uplifting the people of the locale socially and economically and that inturn would benefit the tourism industry. As part of the project anganwadi students are given a pair of uniform each and they are also given milk and vegetables on alternate days. In north Kerala some panchayaths and voluntary organisations have taken up some of the anganwadi and are distributing food. The project at Varkala is a novel one. In the next phase of the project people of the locality would be directed towards organic farming, manufacture of handicrafts etc. This would help the locale as well as the tourists. More than that, there would be a total change in the attitude of the people of Varkala and a congenial atmosphere for tourism would emerge shortly. This is a model project which could be copied. If other players in the tourism industry come forward just like Kerala Travels Interserve, the tourism industry in the state would get a face lift, he added.

'For a Better Tommorow'

– Padmashree Mrs. Sugathakumari

"I wish all success to the project lullaby@Varkala" says Padmashree Mrs. Sugathakumari, famous Malayalam poet and noted social activist. "Any effort which is taken for the upliftment of children is equally divine as worship. A pleasant smile of these children in a new dress, having good food will bring a sort of pleasure in our mind." She added. She also appreciated all personals behind this initiative and those who implemented the project lullaby@Varkala successfully.

Lullaby @ Varkala, a project for the social empowerment through tourism, is becoming popular at Varkala where it was recently carried out. The new perceptive of this project serves a lot in bringing the common man closer to the concept of tourism and even make them participate in the various activities. Organizers of lullaby@ Varkala say that the project has turned a huge success by the immense participation of the people.

Phase II also takes Lullaby@Varkala into its larger role of social empowerment. This will involve beach-cleaning drives and ecological conservation led by tourism clubs to uplift the image and environment of Varkala. Organic farming by the parents of anganwadi children will also be promoted. Hoteliers in Varkala and Trivandrum have already agreed to purchase the organically produced fruits and vegetables.

Promoting awareness of healthy-tourism practices will also be a key factor. Tourism is one of the area's biggest money-spinners and people have a right to be involved in the process. This awareness, that they have a say in what happens and how it happens, is an important part of the project.

Lullaby@Varkala's next phase is the "Be with us, Sing with us" programme. This will be a platform for tourists to interact with the children of anganwadis and literally even sing with them. Tourists will be screened by the ICDS members, based on assiduously prepared guidelines. Tourists will be exposed to the spiritual, ecological and social aspects of Varkala through local hosting and home stays. Establishing confidence and camaraderie will enable visitors to experience the culture and cuisine of the land first-hand. Based on this, operators can make packages that suit their requirements.

This programme seeks to dispel the myth of foreigner as a foe. It also gives the visitors an opportunity to get a real taste of the country, not the made-to-order 5 star representations of reality. Kerala's real tourism potential lies not in man-made attractions, but in the land and the people. This is the secret of tourism beyond tomorrow.

Lullaby... An Opportunity for Progress

Once this is initiated, the power will truly be in the hands of people. Once tourism is recognized as an opportunity and not an obstacle, the sky is truly the limit. Hoteliers, tour operators, local authorities, panchayat members and the people themselves will become responsive stakeholders in tourism. The project can turn around Varkala's image as a tourist destination, which has taken a beating over the past years. Varkala's ambience and tourist-friendliness will be in the hands of people. Every tourist will also boost the local economy. There will be increased visibility for local handicrafts, greater sales possibility, related job opportunities, merchandising possibilities and much more.

It has been estimated that an average tourist will-either directly or indirectly contribute Rs.600 a day to the upliftment of the local community, who hither to have never been direct beneficiaries of tourism.

In about 2½ years, this process would have enabled project to be self-sufficient and self-reliant. By then, KTIL would have mobilized Rs 2.5 crore towards the project through corporate sponsorship, NRI contributions and other sources. Lullaby@Varkala, as a social-tourism project will have something for everybody – be it a visitor to Varkala, a young anganwadi student, a resident of the area or indeed, the land of Varkala itself.

This Lullaby is a song of awakening that aims to rejuvenate the people of Varkala and hand over the writing of their destiny to themselves. Lullaby@Varkala is a simple and workable model that can be and should be replicated in places having tourism potential. This is the way forward for tourism: involve the lives of people; ensure tourism with a human touch; take tourism beyond tourism.

INDEX

INDEX

T

U

V

W